WEBS OF CORRUPTION

COLUMBIA STUDIES IN TERRORISM
AND IRREGULAR WARFARE

COLUMBIA STUDIES IN TERRORISM
AND IRREGULAR WARFARE

Bruce Hoffman, Series Editor

WEBS OF CORRUPTION

Trafficking and Terrorism in Central Asia

MARIYA Y. OMELICHEVA
LAWRENCE P. MARKOWITZ

Columbia University Press

New York

Columbia University Press
Publishers Since 1893
New York   Chichester, West Sussex
cup.columbia.edu
Copyright © 2019 Columbia University Press
All rights reserved

Library of Congress Cataloging-in-Publication Data

Names: Omelicheva, Mariya Y., author. | Markowitz, Lawrence P., 1970– author.
Title: Webs of corruption : trafficking and terrorism in Central Asia /
    Mariya Y. Omelicheva and Lawrence P. Markowitz.
Description: New York : Columbia University Press, [2019] | Series: Columbia
    studies in terrorism and irregular warfare | Includes bibliographical
    references and index.
Identifiers: LCCN 2018047975 | ISBN 9780231188548 (cloth : alk. paper) |
    ISBN 9780231188555 (pbk. : alk. paper) | ISBN 9780231547918 (e-book)
Subjects: LCSH: Drug traffic—Asia, Central. | Terrorism—Asia, Central.
Classification: LCC HV5840.A783 O44 2019 | DDC 363.3250958—dc23
LC record available at https://lccn.loc.gov/2018047975

Columbia University Press books are printed on permanent and
durable acid-free paper.
Printed in the United States of America

Cover design: Lisa Hamm

CONTENTS

ILLUSTRATIONS AND TABLES

ILLUSTRATIONS

TABLES

PREFACE AND ACKNOWLEDGMENTS

Links between terrorism and organized crime have persisted for some time. The end of the Cold War drastically reduced state sponsorship of terrorist groups, suppressed their major source of funding, and thus is widely believed to have facilitated crime-terror intersections. Since the 1990s, policymakers and security experts around the world have contended that the emergence of a globalized economy has fostered transnational forms of organized criminality. Many concluded that, concomitant with the changes in the revenue sources of terrorist groups, transnationalized criminal activity had effectively flattened the differences between terrorist and criminal organizations. The evolution and spread of the "crime-terror nexus" was designated as a critical and growing threat to international peace and security.

This narrative resonated with us as scholars of political violence, authoritarianism, and security challenges in post-Soviet Eurasia, a large territory spanning the republics of Central Asia, the South Caucasus, and Russia. The struggling economies, unresolved conflicts, porous borders, corruption, and weak law-enforcement characterizing these states have allowed organized crime and politically motivated violence to flourish in the region. These conditions have fed illicit economies in smuggled goods, narcotics, and arms—as well as money laundering and human-trafficking rings—that increasingly spanned interstate borders. In short, Eurasia seemed to epitomize a region where terrorism, organized crime, and trafficking would converge as it had in other parts of the world.

At the same time, we felt that the presumed linkages between terrorism and organized crime were often poorly understood, both in their inherent complexity and in their varying forms across countries. Thus, before conceiving of the book, we formulated a long-term project on the trafficking-terrorism nexus in Eurasia in which we wanted to explore the nature of trafficking-terrorism connections, understand the conditions facilitating the formation of and changes in those connections, and examine the capacity of national and foreign governments and international organizations to prevent, monitor, and dismantle the nexus. We were lucky to receive generous funding from the U.S. Defense Department's Minerva Research Initiative (ONR No0014–15–1-2788 "Trafficking/Terrorism Nexus in Eurasia" under the auspices of the Office of Naval Research) that supported three years of extensive research culminating in the publication of this book.

We chose to focus this book on Central Asia, one of the major drug-trafficking hotspots in the world, which purportedly supports insurgent movements and terrorism. Although the area serves as a major transit point enabling a steady supply of narcotics from growers in Afghanistan to buyers in Russia and Europe, it has seen surprisingly low levels of terrorist violence. By engaging with this puzzle, we wanted to offer a more thorough and measured assessment of trafficking and terrorism in Central Asia and make several important contributions to the comparative study of crime, terrorism, and their intersections. As we sifted through the evidence, the picture emerging countered many commonly held beliefs about trafficking and terrorism.

First, the book challenges assumptions about the presence and prevalence of the crime-terror nexus itself. While we find compelling evidence supporting the existence of a drug trafficking–terrorism nexus in Central Asia, we show how this nexus has not replaced the functioning of criminal organizations driven by considerations of profit and violent groups driven by political motives. The type of intersection that is most common in Central Asia, in fact, is one where drug trafficking and violent groups do not converge, but coexist within the same areas. Thus, we urge against hasty conclusions in any study of the trafficking-terrorism nexus. In particular, crime-related violence has been mistaken for terrorist activity, a conflation that not only aids Central Asian governments' deliberate framing of violent incidents as terrorist acts but also contributes to an overassessment of the gravity of radicalization in the region. As our study of Central Asia demonstrates, the relationships between criminal and political actors within the nexus do not arise automatically or easily. Rather, they require a complex coordination of interests and activities that are more the exception than the rule.

Second, our novel framework for explaining the trafficking-terrorism nexus emphasizes the central role of the state. Specifically, we explain the forms of the nexus (i.e., the specific relationships linking terrorist and criminal activity) as a consequence of the nature of state involvement in the drug trade. State involvement in this lucrative illicit economy varies considerably, and that variation critically determines how profit-driven criminal organizations and politically minded violent groups come together. Whereas most interpretations assume the state affects the nexus, we demonstrate how the state (in its disaggregated forms) is actually part of the nexus itself.

Third, the book questions the simplistic view that drug trafficking amplifies terrorism. As a region transiting a significant portion of the world's opiates, yet experiencing low levels of terrorist violence, Central Asia provides a natural experiment to examine this surprising contrast. We provide a counterintuitive explanatory account showing that drug trafficking actually mitigates terrorist violence. Our analysis finds that, while governments in drug-transit states are drawn into illicit economies in different ways, they typically forge relationships with a range of nonstate violent actors (insurgents, erstwhile regime opponents, transnational groups) in such a way that reduces levels of terrorist activity by redirecting these actors into other spheres and forms of violent resistance.

The book also offers a wealth of new data and findings on violence, crime, and security service apparatuses in the republics of Central Asia, and uses a mix of quantitative, qualitative, and Geographic Information System (GIS) methods to more accurately examine trafficking-terrorism connections on the ground. We would have been unable to complete all this work on our own. The book is the product of exemplary teamwork. We thank a group of dedicated graduate research assistants—Alina Bashirova, Brittnee Carter, John Stanko, Amilee Turner, YaoHui Wang—for helping us with researching the materials for this book. We are particularly thankful to Di Shi, Regina Smith, Dory Tuininga, and Xanthippee Wedel, who provided us with extensive GIS support for this project. We also wish to recognize the many assistants, colleagues, and experts in Central Asia who, though we cannot identify by name, were essential as we conducted the research and sought to interpret emerging patterns along the way. Given the sensitivity of this research, we also elected to preserve their anonymity in the book.

The Institute for Policy & Social Research (ISPR) at the University of Kansas (KU) has been an administrative vehicle that drove this project forward. Mariya is immensely thankful to the IPSR staff—Jena Gunter and Travis Weller—for dedicating their time to the project. The Department of Political Science at KU has offered Mariya a supportive and nurturing environment for the duration of the project. Mariya is particularly thankful to the KU political science chair, Dr. Don Haider-Markel, for recognizing, encouraging, and supporting her work on this book. At Rowan University, the Department of Political Science and Economics—especially its chair, Dr. Natalie Reaves—provided ongoing support and assistance throughout the project. The book has also greatly benefited from ideas and feedback from a number of colleagues along the way, including Alex Cooley, Henry Hale, John Heathershaw, Ed Lemon, Erica Marat, Jim Piazza, and many others. Drafts of portions of the book were previously presented at annual meetings of the Association for the Study of Nationalities, the Central Eurasian Studies Society, the International Studies Association, PONARS Eurasia, and the Minerva Research Initiative—and the authors' gratefully acknowledge the many very useful suggestions they received at each venue. Parts of chapter 4 are based on portions of an article that was previously published as "Disciplined and Undisciplined Repression: Illicit Economies and State Violence in Central Asia's Autocracies" in *Post-Soviet Affairs* (reprinted here with permission from Taylor & Francis). Two anonymous reviewers made substantial contributions that greatly improved the book in its later stages. We also thank Caelyn Cobb and her team at Columbia University Press for guiding the book through revisions into final production.

Writing a book as part of a larger research project not only consumed much of our professional life but inevitably encroached on our time with loved ones as well. In the end, whether or not the authors complete their work depends on patience, collaboration, and understanding from friends and family. Mariya is immensely thankful to her little sons—Vladi and Alek—who enabled the work-family balance by diligently claiming their time with Mom, thus ensuring she's had some fun throughout the many hours of work on this project. And Lawrence thanks his children, Timur (who came up with the book's title) and Laylo, who both have been so wonderfully supportive and patient as he worked on this project.

INTRODUCTION

Money is the lifeblood of any organization, whether its purpose is providing services and selling goods, or conducting a campaign of terror. Terrorist organizations, just like legitimate businesses, need funds to survive. Quick cash is used to pay their armies of recruits, train and equip them, and purchase destructive materials. It is no surprise that the world's deadliest terrorist groups are also its wealthiest. Al-Dawla al-Islamiya al-Iraq and al-Sham (the Islamic State of Iraq and the Levant, ISIS, or Daesh) has been known as the "best-funded terrorist organization" confronted by the United States.[1] To maintain an army several divisions' strong and control an area roughly the size of Belgium, ISIS has raised revenues through the oil trade, sales from illegally confiscated goods, kidnapping for ransom, taxes and extortion, and even bank robberies.[2] Hamas and Hezbollah have benefited from state sponsorship but also their involvement in organized crime. Hamas's primary criminal activities have been counterfeiting and money laundering, while Hezbollah has partaken in the production and trafficking of South American drugs.[3] Boko Haram has taxed the inhabitants of Nigerian villages and engaged in an intensive campaign of kidnappings for ransom, smuggling and trafficking, and looting spoils to fund its operations.[4] Al Qaeda, too, has levied taxes, known locally as *ushr*, on the producers, distributors, and traffickers of Afghanistan's opiates.[5] Both ISIS and Boko Haram are now probable participants in Africa's drug trade.[6] These are but a few examples that illustrate the linkages between terrorist groups and transnational organized crime that have proliferated in many parts of the world. This book critically examines the nature of these links and their effects on terrorist groups, who increasingly turn to illegal means to fund their operations.[7]

One of the most prominent patterns to emerge is the role of drug trafficking as the main facilitator of crime-terror interactions.[8] The drug trade is "a kind of plow," inducing criminal and terrorist groups to cut trafficking routes that can later be converted to smuggling routes for other commodities and people.[9] Representing the most lucrative source of revenue for organized criminal and terrorist groups, the drug trade has risen to the top of the list of illegal money-raising activities of terrorist organizations.[10] According to a 2011 report from the United Nations Office for Drugs and Crime (UNODC), "the largest income for transnational organized crime comes from illicit drugs, which account for some 20 percent (17–25 percent) of all crime proceeds, and about half of transnational organized crime proceeds."[11] As of November 2011, the U.S. Drug Enforcement Administration had linked nineteen of the forty-nine organizations on the State Department's list of Foreign Terrorist Organizations to the global drug trade.[12] Similarly, twenty-nine out of the sixty-three organizations on the 2010 U.S. Justice Department's Consolidated Priority Organization Targets list, which includes key drug trafficking and criminal organizations, possessed links to terrorist groups.[13]

Examples of terrorist groups engaged in drug trafficking abound. The Afghan Taliban, the Islamic Movement of Uzbekistan (IMU), Al Qaeda in the Islamic Maghreb (AQIM) and its Sahel affiliates, and various offshoots of Al Qaeda in Afghanistan and Pakistan are all involved in the trade in opiates. They use drug revenues to pay and recruit foot soldiers, purchase weapons, and bribe public officials.[14] Reportedly, in recent years an estimated 70 percent of Taliban revenues come from its involvement in the opium trade, and the group uses drug profits to pay militants U.S.$200 per month in a country where police salaries average $70 per month.[15] The drug trade in West Africa, for example, has not only deepened institutionalized corruption and had a destabilizing impact on the region but has also increased the reach of violent extremist groups such as Hezbollah and AQIM.[16] In Latin America, groups such as the Fuerzas Armadas Revolucionarias de Colombia (Revolutionary Armed Forces of Colombia, or FARC), the Autodefensas Unidas de Colombia (United Self Defenses of Colombia, or AUC), and the Sendero Luminoso de Peru (Shining Path), among others, continue to fund themselves through the region's drug trade.[17] In Myanmar (formerly Burma), more than twenty-five insurgent armies, financed by their control over the largest opium trade in Southeast Asia, waged decades of low-intensity war against the state.[18]

These interrelated terrorist and criminal milieus are believed to be a critical destabilizing factor in the global security environment and pose a number of threats to individual states.[19] Linkages between terrorist and criminal groups amplify long-standing challenges for "weak" and "fragile" states in Asia, Africa, and the Middle East.[20] Such states now face transnational dimensions of problems—pervasive corruption, rising criminality, and alternative bases of authority—that were traditionally deemed to be within their borders.[21] Criminal and terrorist organizations alike can exploit areas with weak government control, creating zones of disorder that span borders.[22] These illicit activities also provide sources of wealth that are often hidden in offshore accounts and fuel some of the public frustration with corrupt governments that can lead to violent extremism and calls for regime change.[23] In response to some of these problems, a 2014 UN Security Council resolution called upon states to better understand and address the nexus between organized crime and terrorism as a threat to security and development.[24] The convergence of crime and terrorism, though, not only erodes states and increases criminality among terrorist organizations, it also brings a heightened intensity of violence to organized crime groups. Transnational criminal actors have always sought security for their illicit enterprises, but new relationships with terrorist or insurgent organizations provide more opportunities to wage political violence against governments (or support their terrorist counterparts in their stead).[25] Dismantling this shifting kaleidoscope of illicit activities, therefore, poses new challenges and demands costly resources from the international community.

Despite its multifaceted role in contemporary world politics, the nature and scale of the trafficking-terrorism nexus remains poorly understood by much of the academic and policy literature. On one hand, several recent global surveys have uncovered widespread intersections of drug trafficking, organized crime, and terrorism, but their broad scope has made them less successful in specifying the causes of this phenomenon or identifying the dynamics and motivations of the diverse actors that are tucked under categories of "terrorist" and "criminal."[26] This broad application has led some critics to question the analytical utility of the concept of a crime-terror nexus.[27] To the extent that other scholars have focused their analyses, they often emphasize one particular linkage at the expense of others. By asking, for instance, how terrorist groups secure financing,[28] these studies overlook the fact that the dynamics of individual terrorist and criminal groups shift with changes in local environment, available resource flows, state responses, and the broader regional and international situation.[29] On the other hand, several works have focused on key aspects of the nexus within specific countries or regions. However, by selecting a handful of prominent cases where the nexus exists, these area studies tend to exaggerate its occurrence and effect and focus on the specifics of investigated cases, thereby overlooking systematic and comprehensive explanations of the nexus.[30] Underlying this global-regional divide in the literature is the shared, if implicit, assumption that the crime-terror nexus is pervasive, even though the frequency, dynamics, and effects of this intersection remain open questions.

Through a careful analysis of drug trafficking and terrorism, we challenge the assumption that intersections of terrorist and criminal activity are necessarily a prevalent, or even a common, occurrence in the world today, and question the simplistic view that drug trafficking is a driver of the nexus and an amplifier of terrorism. We argue that the nexus is far more varied, fluid, and shaped by socioeconomic, political, and topographic factors as well as the involvement of the state in drug trade. Although the impact of the drug trade on terrorism is small relative to other determinants of terrorist activity, it is, nevertheless, significant and mediated by the extent to which the state, through its security, law enforcement, and border control agencies, controls the drug trade. Using the case of Central Asia, this book bridges the global and regional divide in the crime-terror literature, brings greater theoretical and methodological rigor to the study of the nexus, and adds to a deeper empirical understanding of how trafficking, terrorism, and crime intersect.

THE NEXUS IN CENTRAL ASIA

The five Central Asian republics—Kazakhstan, Kyrgyzstan, Tajikistan, Turkmenistan, and Uzbekistan—contain conditions that would lead us to expect the trafficking-terrorism nexus to thrive. Geographically positioned between the major narcotics-producing territories (Afghanistan and Pakistan) and the large narcotics markets in Russia and Europe, Central Asia is arguably the world's largest drug trafficking hub. Ties between criminals and public officials of the Central Asian republics emerged during the Soviet era, facilitated by the patronage networks prominent throughout the region. By the time of the Soviet Union's disintegration, all Central Asian republics had functioning organized criminal groups and a legacy of corrupt behavior.[31] The widespread economic dislocation and institutional degradation that ensued after the Soviet Union's collapse facilitated the growth of corruption and capture of state institutions by individuals and groups connected to organized crime. As a result, the Central Asian region saw a rapid increase in organized criminal activities throughout the 1990s.

The majority of criminal groups, especially those that emerged in Kyrgyzstan and Kazakhstan, were rather small in size (three to fifteen members), localized, and specialized in the smuggling of consumer goods, theft, human trafficking, extortion, and arms trade. The scope of these criminal groups has broadened over time with the addition of drug trafficking and high-level official involvement in crime, including the drug trade.[32] Porous borders, weak law enforcement, and proximity to Afghanistan turned these republics into a convenient route for drug trafficking. In 2010–2012, about 25–30 percent of drugs produced in Afghanistan (an annual average of 90–120 tons, primarily heroin) were transported through the Central Asian Northern Route.[33] For some states, such as Kyrgyzstan and Tajikistan, drug trafficking has become one of the largest fully functioning income-generating activities, bringing most of the cash into the underdeveloped local economies.[34] In Tajikistan, criminal groups have been fewer and larger in size, with many led by former warlords. During the Tajik civil war (1992–1997), opposition forces relied on revenues from the drug trade to finance their antigovernment military operations. Many of the field commanders stayed connected to the drug trade even upon their assumption of government positions. This facilitated the penetration of the Tajik state by crime, and the rivalry for control over the drug trade between warring factions formed on the basis of regional and local affiliations.

More alarmingly, the civil war in Tajikistan, political instability in Kyrgyzstan, and other outbreaks of sociopolitical disorder are believed to have drawn nascent terrorist and militant groups based in Afghanistan into the region's drug trade.[35] It is now well established that the IMU, a militant

Salafi organization initially created with the goal of overthrowing President Islam Karimov of Uzbekistan, was a leading trafficker of opiates from Afghanistan, especially under the leadership of Juma Namangani.[36] An IMU splinter group—the Islamic Jihad Union (IJU)—operating with Al Qaeda and their affiliates in the Afghanistan-Pakistan border regions has allegedly retained its involvement in the drug trade that supports the militants and their operations. Jamaat Ansarullah is another Al Qaeda and IMU-linked group in northern Afghanistan that has allegedly targeted Tajikistan, while the Al Qaeda affiliate Jund al-Khalifa (Soldiers of the Caliphate) has carried out attacks in Kazakhstan.[37]

The appearance of ISIS contingents in Afghanistan in 2014 and the internal fragmentation of the Taliban following the death of Mullah Omar have drawn more attention to the apparent links between Central Asian insurgency and the region's drug trade. In August 2015, IMU leader Usmon Ghazi issued an oath of allegiance to Daesh, renaming its militants as ISIS fighters from Wilayat Khorasan, a territory spanning Afghanistan, Central Asia, and Pakistan. In northern Afghanistan, most ISIS soldiers are former members of the IMU. There were also four Central Asian militant units fighting in Syria and Iraq. Two of them—Kateebat Imaam Al-Bukhari (KIB) and Kateebat at-Tawhidwal-Jihad (KTJ)—have joined forces with Al Qaeda's Syrian affiliate, Al-Nusra Front. The other two units—Kazakh Jamaat and Tajik Jamaat—fight under Daesh's command.[38] Although ISIS has faced some countervailing pressures in Afghanistan—its indiscriminate brutality and ban on poppy cultivation has turned the locals against ISIS—it has been tapping into the drug trade through taxes on smuggled narcotics. Scores of the militants, despite fighting under the ISIS banner, reportedly continue using and trading drugs. At the same time, the Taliban were able to retake significant portions of Afghanistan's territory (if only for a short time), including the provincial capital of Kunduz and multiple districts in Helmand Province. By 2016, many other Afghan districts with high volumes of drug production fell under Taliban pressure.[39] Central Asia has thus become a site that is widely viewed as a major intersection of drug trafficking and terrorism, and has been dubbed the "'New Silk Road' of Terrorism and Organized Crime."[40]

Yet terrorist violence in Central Asia has been surprisingly limited. Despite the menacing prognoses of the "Silk Road" turning into a "heroin route" and carving out "a path of death and violence" through the volatile region,[41] Central Asian states have seen relatively low levels of terrorism within their national borders, whether measured by the frequency or intensity of terrorist attacks. In fact, out of 112,252 terrorist incidents registered by the Global Terrorism Database between 1994 and 2016 worldwide, only 211 terrorist attacks took place in the five Central Asian republics.[42] This constitutes about 0.19 percent of the global total. As we discuss in the empirical chapters that follow, terrorist attacks in Central Asia have been relatively rare and small scale, and even those sparse incidents of violence have been disputed in terms of the identity of perpetrators, their motives, and links to other actors. Central Asia has never hosted the well-organized and deeply ideological violent Islamist organizations that can be found in other Muslim-majority regions. Moreover, trafficking-terrorism intersections in Central Asia take varied and complex forms, belying the simple depictions of a seamless and unmediated collaboration. In fact, only two of the sixty groups designated as terrorist organizations by the U.S. government have a definite Central Asia connection—the Islamic Movement of Uzbekistan and the Islamic Jihad Union—and these two groups have only sporadically combined drug trafficking and terrorist violence in Central Asia. Most of their attacks, especially since 2001, have been committed in Afghanistan or Pakistan.

The low level of terrorist violence in Central Asia and the varied patterns of the trafficking-terrorism nexus, therefore, present an empirical puzzle. Many of Central Asia's features of underdevelopment—crumbling infrastructure, state repression, remittance economies, organized crime, and widespread corruption—should make the region prone to instability and receptive to the trafficking-terrorism nexus. This is especially so given the high volume of opioids transiting through the region. Yet the nexus does not predominate across Central Asia's republics nor have they seen marked increases in levels of terrorism as crime-terror theories would predict. By engaging with this puzzle, this book takes a more measured assessment of trafficking and terrorism in Central Asia and makes several broad contributions to the comparative study of terrorism.

First, we demonstrate how intersections of drug trafficking and terrorism are mediated by the state, which mitigates the impact of drug trafficking on the frequency and intensity of terrorist attacks. In drug transit states such as those in Central Asia, governments are drawn into lucrative illicit economies and forge complex relationships with a range of violent nonstate actors—including insurgents, erstwhile regime opponents, and transnational groups that might otherwise engage in terrorist violence. These relationships diffuse terrorist activity by redirecting these actors into other spheres and forms of violence (such as center-periphery conflicts, disputes over territorial control, or interethnic violence). Though initially seeming to be counterintuitive, this finding may more convincingly explain how many infrastructurally weak states—that are notoriously corrupt and linked to the global drug trade—have curiously low levels of terrorist violence. A corollary implication is that our study challenges claims by governments in Central Asia and other drug transit states that their counterinsurgency policies and coercive powers should be credited with keeping terrorist violence at low levels.

Second, we challenge conventional thinking about terrorism and crime that assumes the link between a group's objectives and strategy is a permanent one. As evidence from ISIS, Boko Haram, Hezbollah, Abu Sayyaf, and other terrorist groups demonstrates, ideologically driven organizations have become adept at using illicit economic activities for pursuing their political goals and adjusting their ideology for supporting their criminal involvement. At the same time, criminal organizations can imitate terrorist behavior and turn to antigovernment violence for advancing their economic aims.[43] We also recognize and foreground the multifaceted nature of violence that falls under the analytical category of "terrorism." This book unpacks the "terror" side of the crime-terror nexus to illuminate important variation in the nature and motives of the perpetrators of violence and to distinguish between local militants and groups that are loosely connected to transnational jihad.

Third, we question the claim that more foreign security sector assistance (SSA) will help countries address the crime-terror nexus. By tracing out how states become drawn into, and fundamentally shape, the different types of intersections that emerge, our study demonstrates why some state counterterrorist and countertrafficking initiatives "succeed" while others do not. This carries direct implications for foreign military assistance and why its attempts to address the nexus can be so fraught with difficulty. Over the past two decades, the United States, Russia, European Union members, as well as international organizations have provided substantial SSA to Central Asia. This aid includes funding for various infrastructure projects, conducting joint exercises and training programs, and selling or donating arms and equipment. There has been, however, inadequate attention to whether or not the states in the region have strengthened their security capacities. Although our findings support the argument that SSA may further authoritarian political responses and repressive policies that rely on well-funded security and law enforcement agencies,[44] we also find evidence of divergent trajectories that depend on the particular type of trafficking-terrorism nexus in a country. Some countries receiving considerable foreign assistance have developed their coercive capacity to fight the nexus in the short term. However, the collusion of the state in the drug trade can contribute to the development of specific risk factors—eroded governance and accountability, arms/weapon diffusion, widespread abuses of authority, and moral hazard problems that come from dependence on foreign aid—that make the emergence of alliances between drug traffickers and terrorists more likely, posing important long-term vulnerabilities to the nexus.[45] On the other hand, countries receiving less SSA may have limited coercive capabilities and be unable to prevent the emergence of the multifaceted and stable ties between drug trafficking and terrorism in the short term. Yet, when they have pursued political liberalization, these countries institutionalize limits on the risk factors noted above (abuses of authority, diminished accountability, moral hazard problems) leaving them better situated to address the nexus in the long run. The "success" of SSA, therefore, depends on the nature of relationships within a recipient country's political economy of security, especially if those relationships define a trafficking-terrorism nexus.

Lastly, we argue that these issues and the purported ties between insurgency/terrorism and the drug trade are not unique to Central Asia. We contend that similar trafficking-terrorism linkages have appeared in a variety of countries across West Africa, South Asia, and the Middle East in recent years. Our book, with its emphasis on the types of trafficking-terrorism intersections, the need to situate the nexus in local context, and the role of the state and local political economies, speaks to similar patterns in other parts of the world. In the Afghanistan-Pakistan region of South Asia, for example, conditions similar to Central Asia—difficult-to-guard borders, pervasive corruption, and the involvement of the state in illicit economies—have created ample opportunities for terrorist organizations (the Taliban and Haqqani networks, among others) to enter specific nodes within illicit drug trafficking supply chains, facilitating greater cooperation between the criminal and terrorist groups. West Africa represents a more complex mix of diverging ideologies, criminal activities, and modes of intersections. The majority of criminal and terrorist groups are tightly linked to local political economies, enabling some of the region's terrorist organizations to become adept at opportunistically exploiting international illicit flows of drugs crossing their territories. Western Europe has experienced the challenges of integrating substantial numbers of second- and third-generation Muslims and newly admitted immigrants.[46] Against the backdrop of heightened anti-Muslim and anti-immigrant sentiment, the remote radicalization of these populations may be more possible. Some of these perpetrators were already equipped to fund themselves through petty criminal activities, including the drug trade. Although there are marked differences in the local conditions and the nature of the trafficking-terrorism intersections in Europe, Africa, and Asia, our model of the nexus, the different forms it assumes, and the role of the state provides insight into common features of terrorist-trafficking connections and their effects on terrorist violence.

THE ARGUMENT

This book explains the emergence and nature of the trafficking-terrorism nexus as a consequence of certain geospatial and socioeconomic factors and the critical involvement of the state. As we argue, while socioeconomic and geospatial factors do matter in explaining the intersections of organized criminal activity, drug trafficking, and terrorism, it is the state—specifically its varying forms of collusion in the drug trade—that determines the type of trafficking-terrorism nexus. In the context of Central Asia, the state's involvement in drug trafficking has an *integrative* effect on the nexus that reduces levels of terrorist violence. This combination of factors—specific socioeconomic and geospatial conditions coupled with key mechanisms of state involvement—provides the basis of our model explaining the presence and nature of trafficking-terrorism connections and their effects on levels of terrorism.

First, we contend that drug trafficking and terrorism do not overlap randomly but along particular, identifiable patterns. We argue that terrorism is secondary to drug trafficking (i.e., the presence of illicit drug flows can further both terrorism and the trafficking-terrorism nexus) and examine a range of causal factors that make some spaces more hospitable to drug trafficking and terrorist intersections than others. A number of underlying geographic, demographic, and socioeconomic characteristics are examined to determine which make nodal points of trafficking and terrorism more likely to occur. While scholarship on the nexus has identified a number of important causal factors—such as population density, poverty, and access to transportation networks—that make the emergence of the nexus possible, this book more accurately maps out when and where these particular conditions enable the trafficking-terrorism intersections to occur. As such, the idea of "mapping" is used in this book to denote not only a conceptualization of trafficking-terrorism connections but also the visual, qualitative, and statistical analysis of the conditions that enable the nexus to arise. This is an essential first step in the charting of terrorist, criminal, and state roles and interests that help us understand the background conditions that make a nexus in a particular locality possible.

Second, we argue that the forms of the nexus (i.e., the specific relationships linking terrorist and criminal activity) and its effects are a consequence of the nature of state involvement. This book, then, counters trends in the literature that discount the importance of the state in the trafficking-terrorism nexus or treat it as a single and unified entity. Indeed, the majority of cross-national studies on the topic have elaborated on various forms of the nexus itself, but these models tend to elide the causal role of the state. Some excise the state altogether from their accounts, seeing weakened state capacities, corrupt officials, and porous borders as a product, not a cause, of the "unholy alliance" of criminal and militant networks.[47] Others incorporate the state—usually weak or failed states—as the backdrop or context in which the nexus occurs. They may include the state in piecemeal fashion or as an intervening variable, but they often leave it out of their explanatory models.[48] Empirical case studies, though, have repeatedly demonstrated the critical role of the state in bringing together criminal and terrorist actors.[49] There is a need, therefore, to better conceptualize the state as spatially and temporally multiple, not singular, and as the primary means by which the various (and sometimes conflicting) interests are linked. To address this gap in the literature, this book elucidates the diversity of state forms across time and space, especially at the local level. We show how the "state," conceived as a constellation of interests, agencies, and subnational units, has an integrative effect on the trafficking-terrorism nexus, which also helps us understand how a trafficking-terrorism nexus paradoxically generates low levels of violence in Central Asia. In doing so, we further "granulate" the relationship among drug trafficking, terrorism, and violence within the nexus, and consider the role of the state in this landscape.

In our framework, the state has a causal effect on the integration of crime and terrorism while it is also the main agent of response and a recipient of international aid. This is because we treat the state as a polymorphous agent legitimated by the idea of it being a single and unified phenomenon.[50] The polyvalent forms of statehood found in post-Soviet Central Asia and broader Eurasia, such as informal networks, clans, geographic and tribal divides, and local political economies, are frequently treated as features of regimes and evidence of state weakness or failure.[51] Informal political ties, "shadow" and illicit economies, and alternative bases of authority linked to kinship or regional affiliations have complex relationships with the state in Central Asia.[52] Drug trafficking and organized crime, for instance, have multiple and fluid influences on states in the region. On one hand, they promote state corruption in order to lower the risks associated with criminal activity and benefit from the lack of will to address the trafficking-terrorism nexus that typically follows state protection of and collusion in illicit economic activity. On the other hand, these activities—drug trafficking especially—generate enormous rent-seeking opportunities for regimes and can greatly enhance their coercive capabilities. Linkages with drug traffickers and organized criminal actors are also utilized by governments to influence parts of society that lie beyond the reach of their state apparatuses. Even in states where criminal networks undermine governmental social and economic controls, therefore, the state's coercive capacities may be extensive. In short, Central Asia's criminalized states are generally weak, but their coercive capabilities vary greatly.

As state collusion in the drug trade takes different forms, these varying capabilities give rise to different relationships of trafficking and terrorism within the nexus. Specifically, we contend that a state's security capacity shapes the nexus in three ways: by orienting the state's involvement in illicit economies; by altering the central government's political control over local elites; and by structuring the state apparatus's monopoly of violence over terrorist and insurgent activity. The nature of state security capacity—through these causal mechanisms—directly shapes terrorist-trafficking relationships at the local level. As particular states' capacities come to predominate across localities, they come to characterize a broader, macro-political outcome—the type of trafficking-terrorism nexus—at the national level.

Third, we argue that most forms of the trafficking-terrorism nexus tend to reduce levels of terrorist violence due to the deep involvement of the state. Even when underlying conditions favor increased ideological violence, the state's ability to use its coercive apparatus to root out political and religious dissent or co-opt the local and counter-elites by distributing rents among them can suppress levels of terrorist violence. When the state becomes an influential player in the illicit economy, particularly in the business of the drug trade, it squeezes out independent trafficking groups that may ally with the terrorist organizations. Even when the state has limited security capabilities to exercise control over the lucrative business of the drug trade, trafficking organizations may gain more by exploiting state weaknesses rather than allying with transnational terrorist groups. While states' involvement in drug trafficking is complicated and gives rise to varied forms of the nexus across localities, state engagement in these illicit economies generally tends to dampen the frequency and intensity of terrorist attacks.

Before proceeding, a few caveats are needed. While this book provides compelling evidence supporting the presence of a drug-trafficking-terrorism nexus, it cautions that this nexus has not replaced the fact that criminal organizations are driven by considerations of profit and that terrorist groups are driven by political motives. We do not suggest that many of the traditional differences between terrorist and criminal groups have disappeared. Nor do we intend to diminish the importance of studying global terrorism and transnational criminal activity separately, which has provided researchers with considerable analytical utility for understanding and explaining these phenomena (their origins, strategies, organizational structures, as well as state responses). In fact, one cannot begin conceptualizing the drivers of terrorist-criminal convergence without prior knowledge of the discrete sources of terrorism and crime.

Additionally, the book concludes that terrorists are far from being the biggest fish in the drug trafficking pond. Numerous other actors, including members of the political establishment, play an important role in the drug trade. At times, the official charges of the links between drug trafficking and terrorism serve to obscure the role of state actors in allowing organized crime to grow. In fact, in some Central Asian contexts local authorities have reaped greater profit from the drug trade than the terrorist groups. The collusion of the state is at the core of the problem in the region, and given that corruption in the Central Asian republics is longstanding, it is extremely difficult to eradicate. State involvement in the drug trade is also an obstacle to regional cooperation in counternarcotics operations and counterterrorism. The states of the region have never developed a strong regional identity due to the countervailing claims to territory, religious and cultural heritage, and regional leadership. Their involvement in the drug trade further undermines the trust among these states and discourages them from genuine counternarcotics cooperation.[53]

When the intersection of trafficking and terrorism does take place, it more commonly occurs through the "appropriation of activities," whereby terrorist and drug trafficking groups share their tactics and methods, such as the use of drugs by militants or engagement in drug trafficking by terrorist organizations. Far less common are the terrorist and criminal groups' transformations, when a terrorist group's criminal goals supersede its political motivations over time, and vice versa. Short-term transaction-based alliances between terrorist and criminal groups (such as establishing a system of taxation of drug trafficking) are also rare.[54] In fact, the coincidence of drug trafficking and terrorism within the same space may very well be the most common type of trafficking-terrorism nexus characterizing our post–Cold War world. Through our explanatory model outlined in chapter 1, however, we endeavor to demonstrate the conditions under which a trafficking-terrorism nexus will occur, what shapes the varying forms it may assume, and why the nexus may suppress levels of terrorist violence.

A NOTE ON TERRORISM TERMINOLOGY

We recognize the contentious nature of the terms used in the book (such as narco-terrorism, crime-terrorist nexus, etc.) among some policy and academic audiences. Moreover, as specialists on Central Asia, we are acutely aware that many governments may use these terms in politically expedient ways, often placing insurgents, opposition figures, independent political parties, and/or civil society activists under the moniker of "terrorist." These politicized efforts make reliable analysis of terrorism more difficult. Russia, China, and the governments in the region, for instance, have provided considerably higher estimates of the terrorist threat, using a very broad definition of "terrorist group" that includes nonviolent organizations.[55] Some analyses of terrorism in Central Asia have also relied on a manifestly broad approach that fails to differentiate among a wide range of Islamist groups operating in the region.[56] The crime-terror literature has adopted a similar blanket approach to defining terrorist groups by placing localized insurgencies and transnational militant networks under the same umbrella of terrorist organizations.[57] For instance, while Central Asia has become the third-largest point of origin for Salafi jihadist foreign fighters in the ISIS-controlled territories in Syria and Iraq, few of those fighters have returned to the region or sought to connect with groups in Central Asia.[58]

One of our goals in this book is to underscore the complex nature of violence that falls under an analytical rubric of "terrorism." While we use the term "terrorism" throughout the book as an analytical category to assist in gathering and analyzing data on premeditated use of violence for social, political, and ideological goals, it is partly our intention to question its use and application through a systematic analysis of the developments that it is used to describe. Such an approach enables us to place our study in the context of broader scholarship on terrorism and speak to the limitations of the available data sources. It also allows us to assess the complex relationship of the drug trade with a wide range of perpetrators of violence in the region and show patterns in these relationships, despite the existence of disparate actors and motives involved.

In an effort to make a clear distinction between ideologically driven transnational terrorist networks and diverse types of localized violence in Central Asia, our conceptualization of terrorism in the crime-terror nexus, discussed in chapter 1, differentiates between local militant/political groups and transnational jihadist networks. The former groups are geographically bound and embedded in the local social structures and political economies. Their primary goal is to exercise control over the local space within which they operate. The latter category of actors seeks to challenge transnational discourses, institutions, and global relations of power, and to shape government policies through deadly and impactful acts of violence. They exploit the temporary vulnerabilities of localities to stage attacks or procure revenue to support their activities without seeking direct control of every-day practices in those spaces. The majority of violent actors in Central Asia fall under the first category.[59]

METHODS AND EVIDENCE

Focusing on drug trafficking–terrorism connections in Central Asia, this book seeks to answer several broad questions: Why do terrorism and drug trafficking intersect in some areas but not in others? What is the nature of trafficking-terrorism connections? Does the trafficking-terrorism nexus amplify the threat posed by insurgent groups, terrorist organizations, and drug trafficking networks to regional and international security? What explains the limited success of external security sector assistance in developing state responses to these challenges? In addition, it seeks to explicate the low levels of terrorist violence in Central Asia. The book offers answers to these questions, using a unique combination of quantitative, qualitative, and Geographic Information Systems (GIS) methods that enable us to collect, analyze, and visualize data on patterns of trafficking-terrorism interactions in the region.

Specifically, the book employs a carefully structured three-part research design that nests a small-n research design within a large-n one.[60] First, the book applies GIS-enabled tools to map trafficking-terrorism connections and presents a series of maps visualizing locational patterns of the nexus in Central Asia. This enables us to specify where intersections of trafficking and terrorism occur (or do not occur) down to the local level. The advantage of this "mapping" is that it provides a baseline spatial pattern of the nexus that cannot be seen through the study of an individual case. Second, this geospatial data extracted using the GIS, coupled with provincial-level data collected from the states' statistical agencies, allow for new ways of estimating the effects of socioeconomic, political, and geospatial factors as determinants of the trafficking-terrorism nexus in the region. We use two statistical models to identify, cross-sectionally, which of these factors change the probability that a nexus will emerge (and which do not). Taken together, these socioeconomic, political, and geospatial factors paint a clearer picture of what underlying conditions in a given locality give rise to a trafficking-terrorism nexus. Third, we employ process tracing through a set of strategically selected cases in Central Asia to explain how different forms of the nexus emerge. Based on material from a range of sources (including expert interviews conducted by the authors), these cases specify the critical role of the state and the causal paths by which state involvement forges particular relationships between terrorism and trafficking within the nexus. As such, Kazakhstan, Kyrgyzstan, Tajikistan, and Uzbekistan each serve as a "pathway case" that elucidates the causal mechanisms through which state immersion in the drug trade shapes particular forms of the nexus and either increases or diminishes levels of terrorist violence.[61]

We draw on a substantial body of evidence on drug trafficking, terrorism, radicalization, and security policies in Central Asia gathered from extensive field research, interviews, national statistics, and content analysis of policy documents. We also offer one-of-a-kind geo-referenced data on drug trafficking in Central Asia derived from the UNODC Individual Drug Seizure (IDS) reports.[62] The IDS reports are based on a complex questionnaire developed by the UNODC researchers and filled out by the governments. We supplement this source with event data published on a password-protected Drugs Monitoring Platform, a unique project initiated jointly by the Paris Pact Initiative and the Afghan Opiate Trade Project of the UNODC.[63] The information that is published on the Drugs Monitoring Platform comes not only from the governments but also intergovernmental agencies, including those funded by the UNODC and the U.S. government. These two platforms have been used to systematically collect data on individual drug seizures since 2008. The drug seizures data were cross-checked against the UNODC reports on the drug trafficking situation in Central Asia prepared using surveys and field research by the UNODC specialists. All GIS and statistical analyses used for this book were performed on data collected during the period of 2008–2015.

The UNODC individual drug seizure reports and data from the Drug Monitoring Platform were standardized in preparation for merger into a single dataset. Drugs were categorized for easy grouping, and drug volumes were converted to the same unit wherever possible. In order to merge the dataset while checking for duplicate records, a unique joint identifier was created for each record from the drug name, drug amount, and location and date of the drug seizure. Unique records were kept, while matching records were merged or discarded as appropriate. The location text for each drug seizure record was parsed into individual fields based on administrative level, and where additional details regarding location were present in the notes of the original seizure record, that information was manually extracted.

To geocode the drug seizure locations, we used geonames.org, which is compiled from different sources. Geonames were used to create location reference files in SAS, in a similar manner to a traditional address locator in a geographic information system (GIS) for working with maps and geographic information, such as ArcGIS. The SAS code systematically checked the locations that were parsed in the drug seizure data and assigned latitude and longitude from the reference files to the smallest possible geographic unit in the record. The geonames reference file also contained a list of approved alternative names, which were incorporated into the comparison search. After processing by the SAS code, the output was checked for accuracy. Manual matching was able to increase the geocoding match and specificity in many cases. The geocoded results were imported into Arc-GIS for further analysis and cartographic visualization. The drug seizures were aggregated by province and year of seizure, and summary statistics were produced for the province-level analysis.[64]

The data on terrorist events come from the Global Terrorism Database (GTD), a widely used open source database of terrorist incidents maintained by the National Consortium for the Study of Terrorism and Responses to Terrorism (START) at the University of Maryland.[65] The GTD defines "terrorism" as an "intentional act of violence or threat of violence by a non-state actor." In addition, to qualify as a terrorist event, according to the GTD guidelines, an incident must conform to three criteria: (1) The violent act has to be aimed at attaining a political, economic, religious, or social goal; (2) The violent act must include evidence of an intention to coerce, intimidate, or convey some other message to a larger audience (or audiences) other than the immediate victims; and (3) The violent act has to be outside the precepts of International Humanitarian Law. If an incident does not fit one of these criteria, the GTD records a reservation. This means that the GTD analysts doubt that the incident in question is truly terrorism. Thus, the GTD flags incidents of violence that are criminal in nature or are part of a broader insurgency campaign. All examples of violence that we refer to as "terrorist" in the book are those that are recorded as unquestionably terrorist by the GTD. We explicitly note the instances of violence that failed to meet the GTD criteria. Of the thirty-six terrorist incidents recorded by the GTD in Central Asia for the period of our study, only three were highlighted as "questionable." The GTD data include failed attacks, but foiled or failed plots are not recorded. The attack must be attempted for inclusion in the database. Neither does the GTD include attacks in which there was a threat of violence as a means of coercion if no further action was taken. While this is a limitation of the database, the GTD, nevertheless, remains one of the most trusted sources of both domestic and transnational terrorism. All terrorism records are based on reports from open media sources that have been determined as credible.

Lastly, the book employs a set of in-depth country case studies that draws on a series of semistructured interviews with a wide range of security experts—including government officials, NGO staff, security analysts, journalists, and local scholars—that were conducted by the authors in Kyrgyzstan and Tajikistan in 2016 and 2017. Due to the politically sensitive nature of these interviews, we have decided to keep informants' identities anonymous. These interviews assessed three main issues: (1) the nature of the trafficking-terrorism nexus; (2) the role of the state in the nexus; and (3) the effects of the nexus on levels of nonstate organized violence. The cases of Tajikistan and Uzbekistan were also supplemented by interviews conducted in these countries in the mid-2000s.

OVERVIEW OF THE BOOK

The first part of the book "maps" the trafficking-terrorism nexus, conceptually and empirically. Chapter 1 conceptualizes the nexus and presents the causal framework explaining the convergent factors that are expected to drive the trafficking-terrorism intersections. The first section of the chapter articulates a typology of the nexus that stakes out four different types of relationships between terrorism and trafficking: coexistence, operational, alliance, and convergence. These range from relationships in which terrorist and trafficking actors exist independently within a common geographic territory to a relationship in which the two are so interrelated that they morph into a single entity. The second section, using studies of organized crime, political violence, and terrorism, hypothesizes the underlying conditions that explain where and when a nexus will occur. The third section puts forward a general model of the nexus that explains how the specific roles of the state define the type of nexus that emerges.

Chapter 2 examines what preexisting conditions make a trafficking-terrorism nexus more likely to emerge. It begins with an overview of terrorist activity and the drug trafficking situation in Central Asia since independence. It then undertakes a fine-grained study of these activities in specific countries through a series of maps that visualize the spatial and temporal coincidence of trafficking and terrorism. Next, the chapter sets the trafficking-terrorism nexus against the backdrop of socioeconomic and topographic conditions to assess which causal factors contribute to the trafficking-terrorism nexus in Central Asia. GIS-enabled, statistical tests of the causal factors at a subnational (provincial) level are conducted to determine what drives higher incidences of the nexus and particular aspects of the nexus that appear to be more prevalent than others.

The second part of the book explains the emergence of varied forms of the trafficking-terrorism nexus across Central Asia. Specifically, it examines how different state capacities lead to different relationships between terrorist and criminal actors within the trafficking-terrorism nexus. Based on expert interviews, secondary data (including policy documents, government and news reports, and statistics), and existing literature, detailed country case studies in the region explore the empirical implications of our model of the trafficking-terrorism nexus. Through these cases, the book demonstrates how each country's approach to drug trafficking enabled a particular type of state (in)capacity to predominate in particular localities; how that, in turn, defined what type of nexus emerged at the national level in each case; and what type of nonstate violence arose as a result.

Chapter 3 compares the effects of two widely different state approaches to drug trafficking in Uzbekistan and Tajikistan in the 1990s. In the former, a decision to withdraw the state from the drug trade, coupled with opening rent seeking in licit economic spheres, enabled the security apparatus to effectively prevent sustained intersection of trafficking and terrorism in the country. As a result, Uzbekistan has experienced little nonstate violence (including terrorist attacks) at the expense of heavy-handed repression. In the latter, postwar reintegration of warlords (who had already been involved the drug trade) into the governing apparatus subordinated the state to these powerful political actors, allowing the convergence of trafficking, insurgent, and terrorist groups. These developments in Tajikistan have led to increased nonstate (and terrorist) violence in the country, which was only addressed after substantial foreign assistance was injected into the state security institutions. In exemplifying the polar opposites of nexus, Tajikistan and Uzbekistan illustrate the stark differences that state involvement in the drug trade can make in determining a country's trajectory and its vulnerability to organized nonstate violence.

Using the examples of Kazakhstan, Kyrgyzstan, and Tajikistan, chapter 4 traces out two contrasting trajectories of state responses to the trafficking-terrorism nexus. In Kazakhstan and Kyrgyzstan, a perennially underfunded and weak security infrastructure that has accumulated a record of sporadic and ineffectual policing and border control has opened a space for criminal and extremist actors to coordinate their activities. By contrast, Tajikistan has experienced a remarkably rapid development of its security apparatus that has enabled the formation of alliance relationships within the nexus. Despite a destructive civil war in the 1990s, Tajikistan's security institutions by the late 2000s came to possess advanced technical resources, employed extensive monitoring and surveillance capabilities, and reached far into society. These improvements, however, remained tethered to deep-seated corruption, predation, and participation in the drug trade. In what follows, we trace out these two causal pathways through the cases of Kazakhstan, Kyrgyzstan, and Tajikistan.

The conclusion summarizes the findings of the book, situates those findings from Central Asia within a broader comparative frame, and concludes with a discussion of policy recommendations. In particular, it finds that external security sector assistance—from the United States, Russia, or international organizations—generates mixed success in shaping Central Asian states' capacities to address the trafficking-terrorism nexus, partly because of these states' involvement in the drug trade. First, it specifies the causes of the trafficking-terrorism nexus in Central Asia and discusses the importance of particular socioeconomic factors, geospatial patterns, and state involvement as drivers of the nexus in other parts of the world. Second, it recaps the varied state responses to the nexus in Central Asia and uses those trajectories to stake out a range of state responses by other weak states in South Asia, Southern Europe, and the Middle East. Third, it provides policy recommendations on the utility of security sector assistance to weak states: whether technical support for security infrastructure is warranted; whether it should focus narrowly or be applied broadly across state agencies; how to balance short- and long-term challenges; and how to avoid common pitfalls (such as abuses of authority and moral hazard problems).

1

THEORIZING THE
TRAFFICKING-TERRORISM NEXUS

Intersections of criminality, insurgency, and terrorism have shaped the emergence of a vast landscape of violent actors with diverse organizational structures and changing agendas. Over the past thirty years, these intersections have become increasingly complicated and multifaceted. The interface of the state with organized crime and violence has made the nexus even more complex through the participation of public officials, local politicians, and security agents in criminal activities. While advances have been made in understanding the linkages between terrorist and organized criminal organizations, the origins, nature, and consequences of the trafficking-terrorism nexus remain hotly debated. Any attempt to disentangle and explain the relationships between trafficking and terrorism, therefore, must do so by providing a greater conceptual clarity about the phenomena under study, presenting the assumptions that underlie the conceptual links between drug trafficking and terrorism, and articulating the causal narrative about the role of various socioeconomic, geographic, and political factors in shaping the nexus.

In this chapter, we outline our argument in several steps. In the first section, we provide brief history of the concept of the nexus and critically assess the approaches commonly used to explain it. In the next section, we present a reformulation of the nexus, which also describes the range of outcomes in our theoretical framework. The third and fourth sections then turn to outlining the argument of the book. In the third, we draw on the theoretical and empirical literature on transnational terrorism and crime to make several propositions on what factors make the nexus more likely to emerge. In the fourth, we elaborate a general model by which the state produces specific types of the trafficking-terrorism nexus, and we discuss the implications of these types for varying levels of terrorist violence.

CONCEPTUALIZING THE RELATIONSHIP BETWEEN DRUG TRAFFICKING AND TERRORISM

The idea of a "crime-terror" nexus is relatively new. The concept and broader analytic trends emphasizing the convergence of terrorism and transnational organized crime appeared in the 1990s. The etymology of the term, however, can be traced to the earlier idea of "narco-terrorism" coined by the former Peruvian president, Fernando Belaunde Terry, in the 1980s. In its original meaning, "narco-terrorism" was used in reference to the Shining Path's attacks on the Peruvian counternarcotic police. In the 1980s, the concept was extended to the use of terrorist tactics by drug trafficking organizations in Colombia that sought to coerce the government into abandoning its policy of extraditing drug traffickers to the United States. Soon after, U.S. president Ronald Reagan adopted the term "narco-terrorism" to condemn ties between international drug trafficking and terrorism among the USSR's allies.[1] The concept gained currency in the post–Cold War environment, frequently used in reference to the FARC and the Taliban's reliance on revenues from drug trafficking to finance their insurgent activities. Meanwhile, a more comprehensive idea of the "crime-terror" nexus emerged during the 1990s, inspired by the linkages between criminal groups and insurgent actors amid civil war in the Balkans. As it moved from political discourse to academic and policy analysis, the concept of a "crime-terror" nexus focused less on the appropriation of criminal methods by terrorist groups or violent tactics by criminal cartels, and more on direct interactions and alliances forged between criminal and terrorist groups.

The origins and evolution of the "crime-terror" nexus highlight three approaches to studying intersections of terrorism and organized crime. First, an *operational* perspective emphasizes "activity appropriation" and conceives of the "nexus" narrowly, as the use of crime, such as drug trafficking, by a terrorist organization as a source of funding, or the use of violence by a criminal group.[2] Operational analyses document the scope of activity appropriated by one type of organization from another and determine the degree to which the borrowed criminal or terrorist activity helps the group accomplish its goals.[3] Second, an alternative *organizational* perspective focuses on the organizational linkages between groups: how criminal and terrorist organizations use each other's expertise, skills, networks, and institutional structures for mutual advantage. For example, to facilitate safe passage of its cadres through the European states, Al Qaeda collaborated with Italian mafias, which provided safe houses and forged travel documents.[4] An organization analysis often produces a typology of collaboration between terrorist and criminal organizations and how these organizational linkages further progress toward the realization of the groups' goals.[5]

A third approach, a *threat convergence* analysis, integrates these two perspectives and considers both organizational and operational facets of terrorist and criminal groups' interaction. This integrative perspective conceives of the nexus in a broad sense, either as a "continuum" tracing changes in organizational dynamics and the operational nature of terrorism and organized crime over time, or as a "sliding scale" where groups move back and forth over time between ideological and profit motives and different types of intergroup cooperation.[6] Along this continuum, different types of relationships—alliances, tactical uses of terror or criminal activities for operational purposes, and convergence into a single entity displaying characteristics of both groups—may develop between criminal and terrorist organizations.[7] Tamara Makarenko, who pioneered this approach, has placed terrorist and organized crime groups on different ends of a security continuum.[8] Between these two extremes, there is a "gray area" with several variations and combinations of crime-terrorism intersections that can develop over time, including categories such as political criminals (who are closer to the organized crime end) and commercial terrorism (which is closer to the terrorism end). Marakenko's model sought to capture ways in which groups—through the appropriation of each other's activity or an alliance with the criminal/ideological counterpart—can transform into new hybrid types of organizations that no longer fit neatly into existing categories. Some groups were even hypothesized to exemplify a true crime-terror convergence.

As noteworthy as these three approaches are, they suffer from several shortcomings. First, threat convergence perspectives are based on the assumption that changes in the motivations of terrorist and criminal groups lead to terrorist-criminal intersections. The growing demand for sources of funding, for example, will lead a terrorist group to become more involved in criminal activity. This tight cause-effect relationship leaves little room for considering other motivations, for example, increasing group cohesion or rewarding new recruits as motives for the group's engagement in human trafficking,[9] or the independent effects of other variables, such as socioeconomic development or access to markets, contributing to the emergence of the nexus between crime and terrorism.

Second, a corollary effect is that these approaches account poorly for change over time. Specifically, they are ill equipped to explain why some terrorist groups that are engaged in criminal activities undergo changes in their motivation structure, while others appear to sustain long-term involvement in organized crime without an observable impact on the group's primary goals.[10] For example, the growing demand for sources of funding that incentivizes a terrorist group's involvement in crime may alter the terrorist group's motivational structure over time. Once engaged in criminal activities, politically motivated groups may continue to further their original goals, or crime may become an end in itself rather than just a means of financing their activities. Moreover, the tautological logic underpinning these approaches—which infer causes from the range of outcomes posited on the crime-terror scale—raises questions of research design. As Karl Popper long ago identified, even the most elaborate theories, if premised on circular reasoning, lack explanatory power since they cannot be falsified.[11] Consequently, these "continuum"-based typologies are useful heuristic devices for classifying terrorist-criminal intersections, but they do not (on their own) generate propositions that can be empirically tested.

Third, the conventional notion of the crime-terror nexus takes a blanket approach to terrorism and conceals important variations in the nature and motives of the perpetrators of violence. This all-inclusive approach does not distinguish between the multiple and diverse types of localized militancy embedded in local political economy and social structures, on one side, and transnational terrorist networks challenging global discourses and practices, on the other.[12] As a result, it occludes the relationship between criminal and militant groups with the state and society and how their attitudes to space and locality inform the nature of intersections between the drug trade and violent activities.

Finally, in seeking to craft explanatory accounts that reach across a range of cases, these approaches view terrorist-criminal connections as largely unrelated to the central actor in contemporary politics: the modern state. While many of the networks and relationships connect nonstate actors, nearly all of these interactions are enabled (if not controlled by) the states within which these actors operate. Indeed, many of the empirical case studies accompanying these approaches provide ample evidence of varied ways in which states shape the trafficking-terrorism nexus. Local elites often provide political protection for criminal activity (and to insurgents as leverage against an overreaching central government). State officials within corrupt bureaucracies actively pursue positions that enable them to influence, direct, and extort payments from these informal activities. Sweeping arrests, abuses of authority, and ongoing predatory rent-seeking behavior by state security apparatuses frequently exacerbate these terrorist-criminal interactions in unintended ways.

Our framework begins to redress these problems by designing a theory that enables us to estimate the effects of a range of independent variables on the prevalence of the nexus, assess the role of the state in fundamentally shaping the nature of the nexus, and evaluate its implications for levels of terrorist violence. We begin with the premise that terrorism and drug trafficking are both activities and organizations that have the possibility of sharing organizational and operational similarities and are affected by broadly similar opportunities and constraints. Furthermore, we assume that terrorist and drug trafficking groups are pragmatic actors who forge alliances or engage in criminal and political activity when doing so carries the promise of assisting the groups in accomplishing their goals. Crafting a framework to study the terrorism-trafficking nexus, however, is not without its challenges. We consider drug trafficking and terrorism to be patterned spatial and temporal phenomena that can be studied systematically. At the same time, we engage in a more nuanced study of the crime-terror nexus in local contexts by "unpacking" the "crime" and the "terror" sides of the nexus and closely examining the ties of violent groups to the local politics, society, and economy.

Yet violent actors vary across space and time in complicated ways. Some groups are deeply rooted in their local contexts and seek a degree of autonomy from the state. They emerge out of local disputes, subethnic political divisions, or negotiations of power between the center and periphery, and they are embedded in existing social and commercial networks, long-standing social structures, and local political economies. Although they may opportunistically exploit transnational illicit flows or tenuous affiliations with the international terrorist "brands," these localized insurgencies seek to influence the space within which they operate. Transnational militant networks, by contrast, are more loosely connected to territory, typically conducting their operations in pursuit of broader ideological and political objectives.[13] In practice, of course, it is often difficult to untangle local militant or local criminal groups from their transnational networks. Regions such as West Africa are home to a variety of local violent and criminal organizations that simultaneously form tactical alliances with international terrorist movements and seek to advance their standing in local political and economic milieus. Transnational terrorist groups such as Al Qaeda in the Islamic Maghreb, Boko Haram, and Al-Shabaab have taken advantage of regional dynamics to plug in and benefit from pervasive criminal activities, while seeking to concurrently expand their political influence and military and financial power in their respective localities.[14]

Recognizing these blurred boundaries among militant actors, we eschew labeling all groups implicated in violence "terrorist," saving this designation for transnational jihadist networks. Nevertheless, all types of militant actors—local/criminal and transnational—can engage in violence that can be classified as "terrorist."[15] Terrorism refers to the threat or the use of violence by an individual or group for attaining a political or ideological objective through intimidation or incitement of fear in a larger audience beyond the immediate victims.[16] This definition is broad enough to include violent attacks perpetrated by a variety of actors with diverse motivations. First, although terrorist violence is always premeditated, it can be carried out in furtherance of a variety of religious, nationalist, and other ideological goals. Localized insurgencies and militants use violence to impose or reinforce their control of a particular space, including when their dominance is threatened by the central authorities. Second, our conceptual definition of terrorism makes no claims about the nature of victims, allowing the targets of terrorist attacks to be either property or people, including military personnel not engaged in armed combat. Both local militant groups and their transnational networks can target government representatives, security personnel, or ordinary people. Third, according to our definition, terrorist perpetrators are nonstate actors operating outside of state control (although these groups may be sponsored by states or acting in support of states' interests), not groups operating as official state organizations engaged in terrorist-like practices.[17]

FROM COEXISTENCE TO CONVERGENCE: HOW TRAFFICKING AND TERRORISM INTERSECT

Before examining what causes the nexus, it is necessary to specify the ways in which trafficking and terrorism intersect. We begin by defining the trafficking-terrorism nexus broadly as the spatial and temporal coincidence of drug trafficking and terrorism and propose a pyramidal approach to the nexus that allows us to identify four outcomes, or types of intersections, beginning with terrorism and trafficking coexisting separately and then becoming progressively interconnected. As figure 1.1 illustrates, the pyramid that visualizes them is enclosed in a spatial cylinder symbolizing spatial and temporal dimensions as well as the sociopolitical milieu where terrorism and crime can coexist.

At the very elemental level, represented by the base of the pyramid, is coexistence, where incidents of criminal and violent activity occur in the same geographical, temporal, and sociopolitical space but do not significantly overlap. Criminal and terrorist organizations could be operating independently, or there could be a variety of criminal groups, with some criminal networks engaging in acts of violence. We treat this coexistence of terrorism and crime as part of the nexus and an important starting point for understanding the emergence of interactions between these groups and activities. The remaining types of terrorism-trafficking relationships— operational, alliance, and convergence—arise from particular forms of crime that envelope nonstate actors. When there are no lootable resources, like illicit drugs, to traffic and sell, terrorist organizations will not be able to exploit them. Terrorist groups will typically engage in "cash-for-crime" activities if alternative sources of support are unavailable, less profitable, and carry more risk.[18] Likewise, criminal networks will more likely resort to terrorist violence when the government's interference or "uncooperativeness" or competition from rival criminal groups threatens to severely undermine illicit earnings.

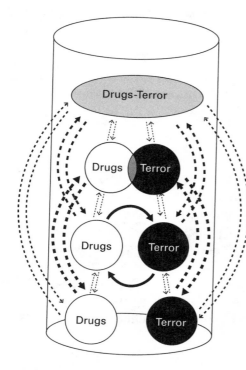

Convergence Relationship
Previously independent criminal and terrorist groups alter their purposes and tactics and morph into a single entity exhibiting characteristics of terrorist and criminal organizations simultaneously.

Alliance Relationship
A terrorist or criminal group forms an alliance of a different nature (ad hoc, short-term, long-term) with their counterpart for ideological, pragmatic, or opportunistic motivations.

Operational Relationship
Drug-trafficking groups use terrorism as an operational tool. Terrorist groups take part in drug trafficking as an operational tool.

Shared Spaces
Terrorist and drug-trafficking groups remain independent, but operate within the same area, utilize similar routes for movement and transportation, and rely on the same networks of corrupt state/local agencies.

FIGURE 1.1 Trafficking-terrorism nexus

An operational relationship is characterized by the appropriation of criminal activities by a terrorist organization or by politically motivated violence by criminal groups. These activities include not only the diversion of a terrorist group into the business of drug trafficking to raise money for financing its activities but also the use of violence by drug trafficking organizations and the radicalization of former criminals that begin applying their criminal skills to terrorist purposes.[19] This relationship may also include the use of drugs by the group's operatives to facilitate the perpetration of violent crime. Saudi Arabian experts, for example, have claimed that there is widespread addiction to drugs among the ISIS militants. These scientists contend that the Islamic State used to get its would-be suicide bombers hooked on drugs before sending them out for the deadly operations.[20]

An alliance relationship is a form of collaboration between terrorist and criminal organizations that entails a material, economic, or skill-based transaction exchange. These ties can be short term and sporadic, but they can also be more durable and multifaceted. The initial limited collaboration may give rise to the creation of long-lasting and wide-ranging associations between terrorism and crime. An alliance relationship may take a form of the terrorist group collaborating with a drug trafficking network to facilitate the movement of drugs from the territory controlled by the terrorist organization and channeling money from the sale of drugs back to the terrorist group. In other instances, a drug trafficking organization may ally with a terrorist group for access to and protection of the drug trafficking routes. Boko Haram, for example, has not only taken part in cocaine trafficking to raise money for its activity; it has also been bankrolled by the traffickers in exchange for support.[21] Al Qaeda affiliates in Afghanistan have partnered up with the New Ansari Exchange, which provided them with hawala-related financial networks—parallel remittance systems outside formal banking operations—for laundering money from drug trafficking operations.[22]

Moreover, alliances can be forged following the "appropriation of activities" or bypassing the "operational relationship," and the latter may result from collaboration between the drug trafficking and terrorist groups. A good example of the movement toward an alliance through an operational relationship is that of the D-Company, an Indian criminal cartel of Muslim militants led by Dawood Ibrahim. A string of violent attacks on India's Muslims in the early 1990s radicalized Ibrahim and his followers, known for their involvement in trafficking in drugs, weapons, and humans. D-Company's radicalization brought it in close contact with Lashkar-e-Tayyiba, a Pakistani terrorist group and an ally of Al Qaeda. This alliance led to the perpetration of a campaign of violence on Indian soil.[23] A different example of an alliance relationship forged without "activity appropriation" is that of Al Qaeda's cells in the Balkan region in the 1990s. Albanian criminal organizations provided logistical support to Al Qaeda for establishing an underground network of its factions in Europe.[24]

The final type of nexus is one defined by a convergence relationship. When the involvement of a terrorist group in criminal activities becomes systematic, or when a relationship between the terrorist and criminal groups is sustained for some time, the possibility emerges that the terrorists become habituated into criminal activities and begin valuing illegal practices to the point of taking on the economic motivation charactering organized criminality. Under these circumstances, their political objectives may remain central to their operational activity, or they may shift away from ideological agendas to profit seeking through the so-called terrorism-crime convergence.[25] This results in a convergence relationship, which may take two forms. In a hybrid structure, the motivations and activities of the terrorist and criminal organizations become so interrelated that these groups morph into a single entity displaying characteristics of both groups simultaneously. Another form of convergence entails the transformation of terrorists into criminals or the morphing of a terrorist group into a mere criminal organization. Many analysts make reference to the transformation of Abu Sayyaf, a radical wing of a separatist Muslim movement in the Philippines, into a criminal gang focused on kidnapping, drug trafficking, and money forging operations.[26] A similar conclusion was applied to the Islamic Movement of Uzbekistan (IMU), which transformed into a drug trafficking ring controlling two-thirds of the Central Asian routes for opiates from Afghanistan.[27] In both cases, Abu Sayyaf and the IMU maintained a veneer of religious goals and continued engaging in a campaign of violence, which makes it difficult to distinguish the new group formation from the previous one. Others argue that Lebanese-based Hezbollah, which began moving small quantities of cocaine from the Tri-Border region in Latin America into fledgling markets in Europe and the Middle East in the early 2000s, has metastasized into a criminal network running the largest and most sophisticated global criminal operations involving drug trafficking, weapons procurement, printing counterfeit Euros, and money laundering schemes moving massive amounts of currency around the world.[28]

The relationship between drug trafficking and terrorism is neither static nor direct. Trafficking and terrorism can transform from one type of a relationship within the nexus to another and back, and the path and time for forming different types of intersection vary. The following section discusses a framework of conditions that are more likely to give rise to the nexus in the first place as well as those that account for the movement to trafficking and terrorism within the nexus.

WHEN AND WHERE WILL A
TRAFFICKING-TERRORISM NEXUS EMERGE?

What, then, causes particular types of the nexus of trafficking and terrorism to emerge in some locations but not in others? Our model advances an explanation of trafficking-terrorism intersections that begins by identifying and evaluating preexisting conditions. Drawing on the existing scholarship on terrorism and transnational crime, this section lays out the range of geospatial and socioeconomic characteristics that increase the probability that the nexus will occur in a given locality. Since many of these features of the local environment have been known to result in increased organized criminal activity and/or terrorism, we propose they may also promote an intersection between these activities. We recognize that there are many competing explanations of terrorism and crime and focus on a sample of the factors discussed previously as contributors to terrorist violence and criminal activity not only in the global context but also in regions and countries exhibiting characteristics similar to those found in Central Asia (for instance, Afghanistan and other states of Eurasia).[29] Before elaborating on these preexisting conditions, however, we first note assumptions underpinning our theoretical framework.

One of the assumptions is that drug trafficking and terrorism—whether as distinct entities or part of the nexus—are spatial phenomena. That is, they are intrinsically connected to some geographical space that they seek to exploit and control and that exhibits certain characteristics making this space attractive to criminal and violent political organizations. Spatial perspectives have become a staple in crime analysis, and geographies of crime is an established area of research examining the sources and effects of crime and its interactions with space and society.[30] The studies of terrorism tend to overlook an important connection between terrorist ideology, strategy, and geography.[31] Although terrorism is distinguished from other types of violence and crime by its motivation and method, terrorists' causes seek to remove people or governments from a certain location, or change political order in some place. Furthermore, it is by situating groups in local context that we can see distinctions among various local militant and transnational terrorist groups. To understand terrorism and crime, as well as the dynamics of individual groups, we need to examine what geography is vital to them: What territory do they use for their operations? What geographical or other spatial obstacles appear in their way? What areas are easy for control and exploitation by these organizations? How do the available resource flows influence the dynamics of groups? The spatial characteristics of crime and terrorism, including their relationship to the state and local communities, are also the key for understanding their nexus. The properties of space that give rise to the distinctive phenomenon of drug trafficking and terrorism are necessary for any type of relationship between them.

Another assumption of the model is that the organizational attributes of groups themselves will impact the nature of the trafficking-terrorism nexus. One of these attributes is the nature of the terrorist groups' leadership. During the periods of a terrorist group's active involvement in crime or criminal-terrorist "hybridization" of the organization, the leadership of the group is less ideological and more profit motivated, or in disarray. Another organizational feature is the structure of a terrorist group. A loose-knit, decentralized structure is more conducive to criminalization of the cells and factions of the terrorist group responsible for raising their own funds for operations.[32] This kind of structure interacts with the nature of the leadership, exacerbating the issue with the lack of a centralized control in the terrorist organization necessary for enforcing its ideological adherence.[33] Lastly, the large terrorist groups that attract young and less ideological members are also more likely to engage in criminal activity. Larger organizations require more funds to survive and carry out their operations.

The studies in conflict and terrorism as well as the literature on organized crime identify a number of properties of space that make some locations "hospitable" to transnational crime, terrorism, and their intersections. One set of explanations focuses on geography as a predictor of terrorism—the size of the territory, the length, remoteness, and topography of its shared borders with other countries, and topographic features of the territory.[34] The mountainous topography of an area that is difficult to monitor and control is attractive to traffickers and smugglers (as long as sufficient infrastructure exists for transporting and selling illicit goods and transmitting proceeds from illegal operations). The difficult-to-govern territories of rough terrain are ideal for terrorist sanctuaries and bases for training new operatives of terrorist groups.[35] In Africa's Sahel and Sahara regions, for example, a combination of the territorial expanse and difficult terrain, coupled with tribal conflicts and porous borders, has permeated large swaths of territories in Algeria, Libya, Mali, Mauritania, and other states with criminal and terrorist activities.[36] In Latin America, the Amazon region, large and impenetrable, has offered sanctuary for narco-guerrillas hiding their massive bases, training camps, plantations, and laboratories in the jungle.[37]

In addition, rugged terrain offers a perfect position for executing attacks on government infrastructure and military personnel. Mountainous terrain can add a strategic advantage to terrorist and criminal groups, enabling them to funnel people and smuggled goods through narrow passable areas.[38] During a ten-year civil war in Colombia (1948–1958), the paramilitary forces of the Colombian Conservative Party and the Colombian Liberal Party took advantage of the country's central highlands to negate the Communist government's logistical and technological advantages.[39] Our expectation, therefore, is that the trafficking-terrorism nexus is more likely to emerge in geographically remote and/or mountainous locations.

A second explanation suggests that borderlands are prone to crime and vulnerable to insurgency and terrorism. Long common borders with areas that experience organized criminal activities, conflict, and terrorism offer opportunities for crime, violence, and terrorism to spill over into the contiguous territories. Human displacement is an inevitable consequence of conflict, which may also cause an influx of refugees across borders. Refugee camps offer an advantageous location for easy recruitment of members to criminal and terrorist groups.[40] Further, any location providing access to two or more countries tends to diminish accountability and increase the likelihood of corruption at the border, particularly where the border divides identity groups with common languages and cultures.[41] Border zones offer both terrorist and criminal groups obvious advantages, if for different reasons. Distinguishing between "political" and "commercial" insurgencies in Latin America, a 2004 Naval War College report states, "The border offers a safe place to the political insurgent and easier access to communications, weapons, provisions transport, and banks. For the commercial insurgency, the frontier creates a fluid, trade-friendly environment."[42]

Different levels of development between neighboring states can also be conducive to smuggling.[43] In the Afghanistan-Pakistan region of South Asia, as well as in western and north-central Africa, porous borders impaired by corruption and a weak rule of law have provided ample opportunities for both criminal and terrorist groups to carry out their activities.

The increased volume of international trade may compel the governments to ease border controls and decrease regulations. As some governments respond to these demands from economic groups by removing regulations, they shift pressure to other states to respond in kind to remain competitive in the international market. The combination of increased trade and travel, and decreased oversight, fosters transnational organized crime and other illicit cross-border activities.[44] Subsequently, the establishment of free trade zones facilitates the movement of licit and illicit goods and people between the difficult-to-govern borderlands and cities. Therefore, we expect the trafficking-terrorism nexus more likely emerges in locations at or near international borders.

Proximity to the capital and major urban cities may also influence terrorist and criminal activity. Terrorist organizations will find a range of "soft" and "high-value" targets, which, if struck with a campaign of terror, promise to spread fear in the population and draw public attention to the group's cause.[45] For criminal groups, urban centers are the "hubs" for an array of business transactions and operational nodes used in repackaging and further transportation of illicit goods. We surmise, therefore, that locations that are close to state capitals and urban centers are more likely to experience the trafficking-terrorism nexus.

Among the socioeconomic indicators of crime and terrorism, the literature has pointed to the potential effects of various demographic characteristics of the population (including its size, density, and urban versus rural makeup).[46] Both the global analysis of terrorism and individual country case studies alike have found that states with large and concentrated populations experience higher levels of terrorist activity.[47] This is attributed to several features of populous areas. They are, for instance, more difficult to police. They also provide a greater pool of potential recruits and a larger audience for the terrorist "spectacle."[48] Criminal groups also benefit from the higher demand for their illicit services and goods in addition to the large pool of new members. We expect, then, that the trafficking-terrorism nexus is more likely to occur in populous areas.

Another expectation is that territories with higher levels of socioeconomic disparity, poverty, and illiteracy will experience more terrorist and criminal activity. Socioeconomic inequality, injustice, and unmet expectations can push individuals toward taking drastic action (e.g., joining an insurgency or committing a crime), in part due to a lack of opportunity and in part as an attempt to alter the sources of their discontent.[49] Although some studies have shown no direct relationship between poverty, unemployment, and terrorist activity,[50] the intersection of terrorism and trafficking brings new financial benefits to economically and socially marginalized groups, including unemployed youths who expect social mobility or who face structural impediments to social mobility, such as ethnic discrimination. Furthermore, the relationship between socioeconomic disparity and crime and terrorism is stronger against the backdrop of rising immigration into the communities. Within Europe, for example, the large influx of migrants poorly integrated into European societies has contributed to the rise of right-wing extremism and widespread feelings of discontent and alienation among the immigrant population. These anti-immigrant and anti-Muslim sentiments, in turn, have increased the susceptibility of these individuals to crime and also radicalization as a solution to their dissatisfaction. ISIS and other Salafi jihadist groups have taken advantage of the discontent and vulnerability of these individuals to indoctrinate and incentivize them for carrying out their attacks abroad.[51] Consequently, we expect to find the trafficking-terrorism nexus in locations with higher rates of unemployment, poverty, and immigration as well as in locations with low levels of educational opportunities.

By testing these expectations, we can better grasp whether or not these geographic and socioeconomic properties of space constitute nodal points where trafficking and terrorism are more likely to occur. Indeed, we contend that these broad-based geospatial and socioeconomic conditions constrain and define individuals' strategies and choices that make their pursuit of a nexus more or less likely, regardless of their ideological, political, or economic motives. If, for example, our hypotheses above are confirmed, then we would expect to see particular criminal and terrorist groups—those that are cohabitating in regions that are poor, remote, near an international border, densely populated, and/or ethnically diverse—to have higher motivations to establish linkages with each other that constitute a trafficking-terrorism nexus. Such conditions might lead terrorists to seek more funding or criminal groups to desire more disruption through terrorist violence. Those motivations, however, are insufficient to account for what type of nexus—coexistence, operational, alliance, convergence—might emerge. Indeed, while they help map out where the nexus is likely to occur, these motives are simply too broad to explain how terrorism and trafficking activities actually intersect. In short, the geospatial and socioeconomic factors influencing these terrorist and criminal organizations do not explain their movement *within* the nexus. Nor do they explicate the causal mechanisms transforming these diffuse motivations into specific incentives and strategies. To understand how and why certain groups are receptive to various forms of the nexus between terrorist and criminal actors, we focus on the complex relationships within each type of nexus, paying particular attention to the involvement of the state.

WHAT TYPE OF NEXUS WILL TAKE SHAPE?

It is our contention that specific relationships between drug trafficking and terrorism within the nexus cannot be understood without considering the role of the state. Indeed, we postulate that the nature and degree of state involvement in the drug trade is the critical driver of the type of trafficking-terrorism nexus that emerges. While state involvement in illicit economies—especially its collusion in the drug trade—tends to ratchet up trafficking-terrorist intersections, we find the state is more likely to influence the nature of rather than the number of intersections. Depending on the state's approach to (or, more likely, engagement in) drug trafficking, different forms of the nexus emerge in specific localities. As a particular form of the nexus, such as operational or alliance relationships, proliferates across localities, it comes to predominate in a country. This, in turn, influences the frequency and intensity of terrorist attacks. In fact, in three of the four types of nexus we outline below, the collusion of the state in the drug trade tends to temper terrorist violence. In this section, we specify which agencies of the state influence the trafficking-terrorism connections, present our typology of state capacities, and outline the causal paths by which those capacities shape the forms of the nexus and affect levels of terrorist violence.

A number of observers have recognized the involvement of state officials in the global drug trade as well as their connections to intersecting spheres of trafficking and terrorism. As Vanda Felbab-Brown, a senior fellow at the Brookings Institution, has quipped, "The best way of being a drug trafficker is to work for the ministry of counter narcotics."[52] Corrupt government officials in Latin American countries such as Colombia and Venezuela have cooperated with FARC, which controls the majority of the world's illicit cocaine cultivation and production.[53] State authorities across Southeast Asia and Northwest Africa (Afghanistan, Pakistan, Turkey, Mali, Nigeria, and Liberia, among others) have been found to be deeply immersed in the drug trade. These same authorities have been particularly keen to point out the growing threat of the nexus of drug trafficking and terrorism. In all drug-producing countries, there is a comprehensive body of evidence implicating the highest levels, including some heads of state, in corruption or collusion with the drug producing and trafficking industry.[54] In the academic literature, too, the collusion of state in organized crime has been recently identified as an indispensable element in the crime-conflict and state-crime nexus.[55]

While the state is central to any analysis of the nexus, its role is quite varied. It is, for instance, not necessarily the weakest states that host powerful criminal organizations and terrorist groups. Conventional wisdom holds that collapsed states like Somalia are the safe "havens" for terrorist organizations. Weak and failed states have also been presumed to provide unique criminal opportunities for groups involved in the procurement and trafficking of drugs, weapons, humans, and other illicit commodities.[56] In fact, weak states—from Tajikistan to Mali—have never materialized as safe havens for transnational terrorist organizations. Research has shown that terrorist groups find weak but functioning states, like Kenya or Pakistan, more attractive as long-term bases for their operations.[57] The states that are ranked at the top of the Fragile States Index (2006, 2011) are not the same as those hosting large numbers of terrorist organizations.[58] Further, terrorist groups can emerge from and operate within countries with strong, stable, and varied systems of government.[59] Patterns of transnational criminal activity are also imperfectly correlated with state failure and weakness because criminal organizations need some business infrastructure, modern telecommunications, and transportation infrastructure to thrive. Alternatively, criminal groups can be deterred by the complete contraction of state and lawlessness afforded by state failure. By contrast, institutional weakness and even state failure can be devoid of such organizations despite the complex symbiotic relationship that can develop between criminals, politicians, and insurgents.[60] This is not to say that criminal and terrorist groups do not benefit from a diminished capacity or willingness of the state to crack down on criminality or contain terror.[61] As we demonstrate in the pages that follow, some degree of institutional degradation or governing difficulties in a particular location often provides an enabling environment for terrorism and organized crime.

Moreover, our analysis of the state and its role in fostering drug trafficking–terrorism intersections approaches the state as spatially and temporally multiple and polyvalent. The state is present in various territories within its borders, and its "face" in these districts and provinces as well as its relations with the local forms of authority are rarely uniform. We recognize, for instance, that different forms of the nexus may emerge across localities, only constituting a macropolitical outcome when they predominate across the country. Likewise, the state manifests itself through the performance of various functions tasked to different branches of state bureaucracy as well as security and military institutions, which themselves exhibit spatial variations and changes over time. For the purpose of our analysis, we focus on three sets of state offices: (1) national government offices (presidential apparatus, military, law enforcement, counterterrorism, intelligence); (2) provincial/district governor and law enforcement offices; and (3) offices of border protection. In each of these offices, multiple influences—regime type, the nature of a country's central leadership, technical resources, institutional capabilities, and so on—combine to affect how the state can carry out the functions aimed at combating drug trafficking, terrorism, and their intersections, while concurrently exerting a causal effect on their integration.

With this conception of the state in mind, we propose a typology of state capacity to prevent and respond to the trafficking-terrorism nexus based on two dimensions: capabilities of state institutions and willingness to utilize these capabilities. The first dimension of state capacity addresses the question, "Is the state *able* to address challenges of drug trafficking and terrorism?" This encompasses the robustness of the structure of coercive institutions established to monitor, prevent, and respond to trafficking and terrorism, and the technical, analytical, financial, and human resources available for these purposes. These aspects of state capability are themselves shaped by the institutional design of the state security apparatus, resource structure, relationship between the central and regional authorities, and the levels and conditions of foreign military assistance.[62]

The second dimension looks into whether the state is *willing* to address drug trafficking and terrorism. The willingness dimension entails putting formal policies and strategies into action, the application of technical/financial/human resources, and outcomes of policy implementation. These aspects of state willingness are themselves shaped by regime type and associated abuses of power and state corruption, including the nature and degree of state collusion in drug trade, which have been major obstacles to countering organized crime, terrorism, and their nexus in Eurasia.[63]

These two dimensions of state capacity are broadly consistent with the observed but undertheorized differences in states' ability to respond to organized crime and terrorist violence. Among other things, experts have noted the need to differentiate between a government's wiliness and ability to deliver peace and security to the people. Somalia, Syria, Afghanistan, Sudan, and Haiti are all among the top ten most fragile states, according to the Fragile States Index of 2016.[64] They, however, face substantially different challenges, ranging from the total lack of state authority to illegitimate government, and from postconflict and postdisaster recovery to ongoing civil strife. State capabilities and political will are also comparable to the commonly used dimensions of state "authority" and "legitimacy." A decrease in state legitimacy and authority often leads to an increase in transnational organized crime and increased opportunities for the crime-terror interaction.

From these two dimensions of state capabilities and willingness to deploy them, we conceptualize four ideal types of state capacity. States with high levels of both dimensions possess *hegemonic state capacity* (when state offices are able to effectively translate all available institutional, technical, financial, and human capabilities into preventing, monitoring, and dismantling drug trafficking and terrorism networks). States with low capabilities but high levels of willingness to root out the problems of crime and terrorism possess *degraded state capacity* (when the state attempts but only partially succeeds in preventing, monitoring, and dismantling the terrorism and trafficking networks). States with high capabilities but low levels of political will to clamp down on criminal and terrorist activity possess *predatory state capacity* (when government offices are used to protect and serve private and criminal interests, and government capabilities are used for rent-seeking and resource-extraction purposes). States with low levels of both dimensions possess *captured state capacity* (when states lacking effective institutions cease to exercise any influence over the interests and activities of trafficking and terrorism networks, which in turn challenge the authority of the state itself). These state capacity types are summarized in table 1.1. It is important to reinforce that these types of state capacity are ideal types. State capabilities and political will are not simply either/or conditions. Rather, they are a matter of degree, as states and territories within states may fall along the two continua in terms of their relative security capabilities and degree of political commitment to addressing the trafficking-terrorism challenge.

We maintain that variation in state capacity along these dimensions accounts for the types of trafficking and terrorism intersections within the nexus as well as levels of terrorist violence that result. Where there is both capacity and will to clamp down on drug trafficking and terrorism, their nexus is unlikely to thrive in any form—a relationship in which the state combats insurgents and diminishes terrorist violence. Where there is will but no capacity, the relationship between drug trafficking and terrorism will predominantly appear in the operational form—a relationship in which opportunities for criminality increase, dampening terrorist violence. Where there is capacity but no will, both operational and alliance ties between drug trafficking and terrorism will proliferate—a relationship in which potential terrorist actors are absorbed into networks of state predation, diminishing levels of terrorist violence. Lastly, where there is neither capacity nor will, we can expect to find cases of trafficking-terrorism convergence—a relationship in which criminal and terrorist violence increase through the breakdown of state authority.

The drug trade has a considerable corrupting power over the state administration, with long-term repercussions for the functioning and legitimacy of the state. In drug transit states, leaders often attempt to shape the drug

TABLE 1.1 Typology of State Capacities

	High willingness	Low willingness
High capability	Hegemonic state capacity	Predatory state capacity
Low capability	Degraded state capacity	Captured state capacity

trade within their borders to eliminate competitors, reorient trade routes away from regime opponents, and concentrate their control over the flow of rents. As with any lootable resource, the challenge these regimes confront, however, lies in controlling an industry that has very low barriers to entry. Any organized group with access to contacts abroad can traffic heroin or opium through transit states without having to develop the infrastructure needed to grow, extract or refine the crops.[65] While potentially lucrative, therefore, regimes must use cooptation to extend control over traffickers. Much depends on whether these bargains absorb traffickers directly into the government, exclude them, or control them through intermediaries. Critical to understanding what type of nexus arises, then, are the different "revenue bargains" between governments and traffickers that enable the former to claim drug rents in some cases and the latter in others.[66] This differential control over drug trafficking, then, determines a drug transit state's coercive capacity and its subsequent levels of terrorist violence.

When central leadership colludes in the drug trade by consolidating its control over the drug trafficking rents, it becomes dependent on the security apparatus to maintain that control. The regime, then, will be motivated to invest in the state security structures, which become highly predatory as security officials get drawn into the drug trade. Control over the drug trade enables an operational relationship between drug trafficking and terrorism by decreasing the costs and risks associated with criminal activity. It also contributes to the formation of alliances between trafficking and terrorism through the selected cooptation of local elites and sowing disaffection and opposition to the regime in others. When the criminalized government has weak security institutions, it may be captured by criminal interests, triggering a proliferation of trafficking and terrorist activity that will transmute into the hybrid criminal-terrorist forms. Conversely, when a state evinces the will to fight drug trafficking and terrorism (due to the meager opportunities for gains from drug trafficking rents, the presence of other sources of revenue, or pressing security concerns), it will establish hegemonic capacities that prevent the intersection of trafficking and terrorism. We will explain these relationships between state capacity, the type of the nexus, and subsequent levels of terrorist violence in greater detail (see also table 1.2).

TABLE 1.2 How State Involvement Shapes the Trafficking-Terrorism Nexus

Critical variable: Type of state capacity	Causal mechanisms: State involvement in terrorism and trafficking	Outcome: Predicted relationship within nexus (and level of terrorist violence)
Hegemonic	Officials combat criminal/ drug networks Central government has consistent control over local elites Government commands a monopoly of violence	Coexistence (terrorist violence diminished)
Degraded	Officials permit criminal/ drug networks Central government has intermittent control over local elites Government able to employ only limited repression to retain its monopoly of violence	Operational (terrorist violence diminished)
Predatory	Officials involved in criminal/ drug networks Central government has control over local elites only through cooptation and conflict Government employs extensive repression and predation to retain its monopoly of violence	Operational and alliance (terrorist violence diminished)
Captured	Officials overtaken by criminal/ drug networks Central government has no control over local elites Government has no monopoly of violence	Convergence (terrorist violence increased)

HEGEMONIC CAPACITY: THE SEPARATE COEXISTENCE OF DRUG TRAFFICKING AND TERRORISM

No state is completely free of organized crime or immune to the threat of political violence. Geographic features of the territory, such as remoteness or mountainous terrain, and its demographic features, such as high levels of urbanization, can pose challenges to the effective control and policing of the territory. Furthermore, other "push-pull" factors unrelated to the government's security capacity and political will, such as the high demand for illicit goods and services, may fuel organized crime. However, countries with robust law enforcement and intelligence institutions and political resolve to fight crime will experience less drug trafficking. Comprehensive counterterrorism policies are necessary for fracturing the alliances of global and local terrorist groups, denying them access to the sources of funding, and hardening the targets attractive to terrorists. Low-level corruption may cause a breach in the state's security capability to prevent and respond to trafficking operations, but it hardly constitutes a threat to state security. In the end, the occurrence of the drug-trafficking-terrorism nexus in states with hegemonic capacity is defined by the separate coexistence of trafficking and terrorism. Certain forms of criminal activity may take place in these states, but they tend to be on a lesser scale than in states characterized by degraded, predatory, and captured capacity. Consequently, the state's ability to keep trafficking and terrorist networks separate will enable it to preserve a monopoly of the legitimate use of violence and diminish the frequency and intensity of terrorist attacks.

DEGRADED CAPACITY: PREDOMINANTLY OPERATIONAL RELATIONSHIPS BETWEEN DRUG TRAFFICKING AND TERRORISM

States with weak security capabilities attract "thriving drug trades" and remove obstacles to violence.[67] Diminished coercive capabilities are a key factor enabling criminals and terrorism to productively engage in the drug trade.[68] It is understandingly so. Trafficking and terrorist groups have been adept at exploiting the loopholes in state security, such as the lack of trained staff and equipment at national border checkpoints, deficient mechanisms of inspection and monitoring of transport, and the lack of security at public places and airports. The weak intelligence capabilities to investigate and prosecute organized crime lower the costs for establishing and running an elaborate drug trafficking infrastructure. The low capacity of intelligence and threat analysis to detect terrorist threats offers a window of opportunity for terrorist groups to set up their local cells and carry out mobilization and recruitment campaigns. Stand-offs between regional and central governments as well as government factionalism will also result in poor coordination, low implementation, and interagency strife, affecting state capacity to effectively fight terrorism and crime. All in all, drug trafficking and terrorist groups can leverage voids characterizing the degraded state capacity to further their operations.

There is also comparative evidence that a state's lack of security capabilities and the promise of impunity will encourage criminal organizations to pursue lucrative sources of revenues in illicit economic spheres (such as drug trafficking).[69] In addition to providing cash in support of the terrorist groups' operations, drug trafficking may facilitate terrorist activity indirectly by reducing the effectiveness of counternarcotics and counterterrorism measures.[70] The rise in the drug trade places increased demand on state security capabilities, taking resources away from other law enforcement and counterterrorism measures. This, in turn, reduces the barriers for terrorist activity. If the state reallocates its limited resources to national security, drug trafficking may increase, furthering terrorism directly as "crime-for-cash." In addition, degraded security capabilities translate into intermittent control over disparate local elites, enabling them to engage in, protect, and profit from drug trafficking in their regions. Some may also provide passage, refuge, and assistance to disaffected groups that joined insurgent or terrorist networks. Among the public, moreover, ineffective uses of repression, such as sweeping arrests or repression of particular ethnic and religious groups, may foster resentment and distrust of the regime. We hypothesize that degraded state capacity leads to predominantly operational relationships within the drug trafficking–terrorism nexus. While pockets of autonomy from the state open the door to potential terrorists' violent opposition to the state or their vulnerability to extremist groups, we expect that the advantages in operational relationships will tilt toward drug traffickers; as a result criminal violence will predominate over terrorist violence in these cases.

PREDATORY STATE CAPACITY: OPERATIONAL AND ALLIANCE RELATIONSHIPS BETWEEN DRUG TRAFFICKING AND TERRORISM

States that fall in this category possess moderate to high security capabilities, often due to substantial foreign assistance. Yet the highly corrupt nature of the state apparatus makes the state an important factor in the drug trade. Although corruption exists in states with degraded capacity, it concentrates at the level of security cadres and officials in junior administrative positions who become involved in crime mainly due to economic destitution. In states with predatory capacity, administrative and security institutions become corrupt to the point of their active participation and facilitation of organized crime, rather than simply allowing it to occur. In short, the government's preoccupation with rent seeking, including taxing the drug trade and amassing personal wealth through other forms of corruption and crime, turns the rest of society into prey.

Under these conditions, state involvement in drug trafficking and terrorism can facilitate their intersection in several ways. First, the state, through its corrupt security institutions, can provide protection for organized crime and trafficking that enables the proliferation of illegal funding and training activities central to the operational relationship between terrorism and drug trafficking. For instance, the protection and complicity of some government representatives with organized crime has allowed for the functioning of a series of trafficking routes in West and North Africa, turning it into a hub for terrorists and traffickers and serving the needs of illicit markets and violent groups around the globe.[71] Second, by using control over drug trafficking spheres as instruments of cooptation and control of local elites that foster fluid relationships of collusion with, disaffection from, and opposition to regimes, predatory capacity can contribute to the formation of alliances between terrorism and drug trafficking. The cooptation of local ethnic elites, many of whom benefited from control of the drug trafficking routes running through their territories, has been a cornerstone of Russia's policy in the tumultuous North Caucasus.[72] Third, by fostering the rise of violent and predatory law enforcement and security institutions that exacerbate dissent, strengthen the appeal of radicalization, and push certain populations toward extremism, states with predatory capacity are likely to facilitate both operational relationships and alliances between terrorist and criminal organizations. We further conclude that these relationships absorb potential terrorist activity into larger pyramids of drug trafficking under national and regional elites, thereby diminishing levels of terrorist violence.

CAPTURED STATE CAPACITY: TRAFFICKING-TERRORISM CONVERGENCE

In states with predatory capacity, trafficking-terrorist intersections are facilitated by criminalized political and security elites with sufficient coercive capacity for controlling the states. The criminalized government has an upper hand in its relations with organized crime. In states with captured capacity, characterized by weak critical administrative, judicial, law enforcement, and security institutions, criminal organizations gain control over state institutions or "obtain preferential treatment from public servants through extortion."[73] The wholesale state capture by organized crime, termed "narcostatization," when drug trafficking penetrates state institutions, is extremely rare. Some of the examples include nonsystemic rogue states like Afghanistan in the 1990s, Colombia in the 1980s, or North Korea.[74] It is more common for politicians who are reluctant to cede control over states but too weak to resist to set up informal power-sharing mechanisms with the leadership of organized crime. In these instances, the government is dependent on criminal networks and institutions.

These criminal-political alliances are constantly changing and dynamic as a consequence of competition for resources and political control. Competing political-criminal interests fighting each other further fragment a state with low capabilities to exercise effective control over its entire territory. The conflict of interest may occur vertically between the political-criminal factions within the state along religious, ethnic, or ideological lines, or horizontally between the central and regional state apparatuses. Under these conditions, state involvement in drug trafficking and terrorism can facilitate their intersection in several ways. First, state officials become overtaken and subsumed by organized crime and trafficking groups, which enables the explosive proliferation of a wide range of terrorism and drug trafficking activities that morph into a single web of activity. Second, the state's loss of control over local elites leads those elites to become immersed in the fully intersecting spheres of terrorism and trafficking. Third, the state's loss of a monopoly of violence entails the fragmentation of its state security agencies, many of which separate from the state and join terrorist and criminal organizations. Indeed, state involvement in the relationship between crime and terrorism is so extensive as to be a triadic one (of state-crime-terrorism). In this context of a breakdown of state authority, the convergence of terrorist and criminal activity and its fusion with coercive agents of the state escalates terrorist violence.

In Central Asia, the social bases of organized crime are not transnational criminal networks spanning multiple countries and regions but local social groupings based on regional and kin ties.[75] Given the complex mosaic of the Central Asian state borders, these affiliations may span state boundaries or subnational divisions. The primary relationship of organized criminal groupings in Central Asia has been with these local institutions of formal and informal authority rather than transnational militant movements. Borne out of historically contingent competition for resources and power at the local level as well as in relations with the state, some of these local militant/political groups have challenged the state monopoly on the use of violence. The relationship of state capacity and the trafficking-terrorism nexus described above mostly characterizes the patterns of relations between the local criminal and militant/political groups among themselves and with the state, although some of these groups have held tenuous connections to transnational terrorist movements. Because these criminal and militant groups have competed among themselves but also with the state for social, moral, and political authority as well as control over the legal and illicit markets in their territories, they have resorted to sporadic, small-scale, and calibrated violence in the Central Asian region.

Even when underlying conditions favor increased violence, the particular ways in which a state becomes involved, for example, by co-opting the local elites and using its coercive apparatus to liquidate the defiant militant/political groups, has had a powerful dampening effect on the frequency and intensity of terrorist violence in the region. When a state has predatory capacity characterized by consolidated state control over the drug trade, independent trafficking groups have limited ability to ally with the terrorist or militant movements, which are suppressed by the state, including through the penetration of society by security institutions. With a degraded state capacity, trafficking groups have a greater incentive to exploit state weaknesses rather than engage with transnational jihadist movements. The state in Central Asia has played the role of the "quintessential protection racket with the advantage of legitimacy" struggling with other groups to achieve monopoly over the means of violence and control over economic activities. And, in this process of contention over control of resources and power, transnational jihadist movements have played a marginal role.[76]

CONCLUSION

This chapter outlined a two-stage argument in which combinations of the specific geospatial and socioeconomic conditions coupled with key mechanisms of state capacity provide the basis of our model explaining the presence and nature of trafficking-terrorism connections. In the pages that follow, this book explores the empirical implications of this model. The following chapter, through a mixed-method analysis (including GIS-enabled and statistical methods), estimates the effects of underlying conditions in a locality, determining where and when a terrorism-trafficking nexus is likely to emerge. Later chapters, employing controlled case study comparisons of selected Central Asian countries, explain how variation in the type of state capacity leads to particular relationships between criminal and terrorist groups within the nexus.

2

MAPPING HOW TRAFFICKING AND
TERRORISM INTERSECT

C entral Asia has been the chief conduit for Afghan opium and heroin bound for markets in Europe and Russia. The UNODC estimates that about one kilo in four of heroin produced in Afghanistan (an annual average of 90–120 tons) travels through the region.[1] Most
of these drugs are transported through the so-called Northern Route, which
originates in the northern provinces of Afghanistan and runs through a
number of pathways that cross the territories of Tajikistan, Kyrgyzstan,
Uzbekistan, and Kazakhstan, before ending up in Russian and European
markets. Turkmenistan, historically more insular, is less connected to the
Northern Route. Most of the heroin and opium traverses the Turkmen territory along an alternative "Balkan route" on to Iran and Turkey before
arriving in southeastern Europe. In addition to the problem of drug trafficking, Central Asian governments have had concerns about the spillover
of insurgency from Afghanistan, which has been mired in civil conflict for
over three decades. Since the toppling of the Taliban government, which
ruled Afghanistan from 1996 until 2001, the fledgling government authority in Kabul has been fighting a deeply entrenched insurgency. Political
weakness of the central government in Afghanistan has been exploited by
transnational terrorist and criminal networks, which have found sanctuary in multiple Afghan provinces. While they provided logistical and material assistance to fighters fleeing Tajikistan's civil war and occasional support to opposition-figures-turned-insurgents, these networks have left
surprisingly few traces in Central Asia.

These two broad trends—the rise of a massive cross-border drug trade and the development of Afghanistan as a global hub of insurgency and international terrorism—have become increasingly interwoven. It has been assumed that Central Asian states' experiences with drug trafficking and proximity to transnational terrorism hubs in Afghanistan would lead them into trafficking-terrorism connections much like their southwestern neighbor. Despite these expectations, the nexus of drug trafficking and terrorism in Central Asia has been only tenuously linked to the trafficking-terrorism intersections in Afghanistan. It remains unclear, whether these trends have led to a proliferation of trafficking-terrorist connections across Central Asia, and when and where such connections occurred.

Any analysis of the drug trafficking-terrorism connections in Central Asia, then, must begin with an effort to delineate these activities, identify the specific locations where terrorist and trafficking activities coincide, and examine the conditions that make these locations attractive to the nexus. This chapter accomplishes these goals. Through brief case studies and a quantitative analysis, we examine terrorism and trafficking across Central Asia and identify the core features of locations where the nexus has been more likely to emerge. The remainder of the chapter consists of six sections. In the first, we set out the recent historical context that led up to the emergence of trafficking and terrorism in Central Asia. In the following four sections, we focus our analysis on drug trafficking and terrorism in Tajikistan, Kyrgyzstan, Kazakhstan, and Uzbekistan, respectively, presenting a series of maps visualizing the spatial and temporal coincidence of trafficking and terrorist activity in these states. The last section provides an analysis, using a series of GIS-enabled and statistical tests, of geographic and socioeconomic conditions enabling the intersections of trafficking and terrorism. We then briefly conclude.

THE ROOTS OF THE MODERN-DAY
NEXUS IN CENTRAL ASIA

The trade of opiates through Central Asia took off in the early 1990s. Before their independence in 1991, the Central Asian republics were cordoned off from Afghanistan, but the Soviet-Afghan war that lasted from

December 1979 through February 1989 opened the region to various influences, including the drug trade. Initially conducted in small quantities predominantly by Afghan war veterans, trafficking in opiates and heroin
from Afghanistan through Central Asia was quickly taken over by criminal groups, who saw large profit margins, few obstacles, and relatively low
risk in engaging in the drug trade.[2] The economic turmoil accompanying
these states' transitions to independence, plummeting living standards, and
weaknesses of political regimes were among the main facilitators of organized crime in Central Asia, including trafficking in opiates. The Central
Asian criminal groups have been involved in a variety of illicit activities:
contraband, human trafficking, extortion, production and trade in marijuana, and looting of natural resources. The region's proximity to Afghanistan, however, has played the largest factor in the development of drug
trafficking in these states, with criminal organizations, criminalized government officials, and militant groups adding drug trade to the portfolio of their illicit activities.[3] Three of Central Asia's southern states—
Tajikistan, Turkmenistan, and Uzbekistan—share a collective border of
about 2,300 kilometers (1,430 miles) with Afghanistan.

Afghanistan became a top opiate-producing state in the late 1980s as a
result of two developments. Iran, Turkey, and Pakistan, the three main
sources of opium production in the 1970s and the early 1980s, began enforcing bans or stricter drug control laws, prompting a shift in the production
of heroin to Southwest Asia. Concurrently, the conflict in Afghanistan
transformed from a resistance to the Soviet Union to a civil war between
the various mujahideen groups.[4] The Reagan administration and the
Pakistani government provided financial support for the anti-Soviet resistance, but even the best-funded groups became gradually involved in
opium production in one way or another.[5] The abrupt interruption in external funding for the mujahideen groups that followed the U.S. departure
from Afghanistan compelled the various factions vying for power in Kabul
to rely even more on the drug trade for financing their operations.[6] Some
groups of fighters "taxed" the opium production and trade in the territory
under their control, while others became actively involved in the drug
trade through the establishment and control of heroin production facilities and the trafficking of opiates.

In the late 1980s to the early 1990s, these developments promoted a flour-
ishing drug trade that became the major source of money for Afghanistan's

violent nonstate actors. The rise of the Taliban to power in Kabul in 1996 did little to curb the production and trafficking of drugs in Afghanistan. The Taliban managed to reconcile an apparent disconnect between their Islamic ideology and the drug trade by issuing an Islamic injunction that allowed the farmers grow opium, because it was supposed to be consumed by "kars" [unbelievers] in the West, but they imposed a strict ban on the growing of hashish that could be consumed by Afghans and Muslims.[7] By proscribing the consumption, but not the production and trade, of opiates, the Taliban allowed for doubling the poppy harvest between 1996 and 1999.[8] When the Taliban government placed a ban on and applied a concerted effort to eradicate heroin production in 2000–2001, the production of opiates surged in the northern areas controlled by the anti-Taliban Northern Alliance. Thus, the Taliban have been connected to the growth of opium, and, to a lesser degree, the production of heroin and trafficking of drugs.[9] To benefit from the latter, the Taliban entered into various agreements with criminal and insurgent groups, who paid rents on their profits from drug trafficking activities in exchange for immunity from the Taliban government.

Other mujahideen factions that merged in the anti-Taliban Northern Alliance and later made up a considerable portion of the interim government in Kabul have also been directly involved in controlling and benefiting from the production of opium.[10] Although the Northern Alliance broke into different political factions following the establishment of the Karzai administration, its different members leveraged their way into the government. As a result, high-ranking officials in the Defense and Interior Ministries of Afghanistan responsible for counternarcotics initiatives, heads of various Afghani provinces, and members of the former president's family were allegedly tied to the drug trade.[11] The presence of warlords with links to drug trafficking in the current Afghani government necessarily complicates any effort to reduce drug production and trade in the region.

The steady supply of drugs from Afghanistan and the presence of various groups interested in selling or transporting drugs to markets in Russia and Europe have contributed to the emergence of a very complex, decentralized, and fluid drug trafficking milieu in Central Asia involving diverse actors seeking to benefit from the drug trade. The majority of these actors are small- and mid-size criminal groups engaged in the local production and distribution of cannabis and synthetic drugs, and less so in the distribution of opiates purchased from Afghan traders. Driven by profit motives and enabled by kinship, language, and clan ties, these criminal organizations are considered "the middlemen in the regional drug trade."[12] This pattern largely characterizes criminal groups operating in and around the drug trafficking hubs in Kyrgyzstan (Batken, Bishkek, Issyk-Kul, Jalal- abad, Osh, and Talas) and Kazakhstan (Shymkent, Aktau, Almaty, Atyrau, Shymkent, and others). The ethnic composition of these organizations is rather eclectic, with the Chechen and Kurdish groups in both Kyrgyz- stan and Kazakhstan engaged in smuggling heroin and opium across Central Asian borders, while the Tajik, Uzbek, and Kyrgyz criminal groups are responsible for smuggling drugs from Afghanistan to Central Asian states. Roma groups sell drugs in the intrastate markets.[13]

The larger criminal groups capable of trafficking sizable volumes of opi- ates exercise considerable control over the drug trade in Central Asia. They are similar to the Afghan drug syndicates in that they are firmly rooted in the region's politics, economics, and social situation. Whether as a result of the entry of criminal bosses into the local and national governments or due to intimidation and extortion of public officials by criminal groups, these drug trafficking networks have developed intimate ties with the Cen- tral Asian state power structures. As a result, they bring together crimi- nals and public officials from government, defense, and law enforcement agencies, sometimes from more than one state. In Tajikistan, for example, the drug market has been loosely divided among several clan-based groups whose areas of operation coincide roughly with the country's provinces. The members of each group control the drug trafficking routes and are highly influential in the governance of their respective regions and, in some cases, governance at the national level.[14] While profiting from the drug trade remains the key motivation of criminal groups, this goal may be connected to control over the political and geographical space that is utilized for the drug trade. Subsequently, these criminal groups or their individual mem- bers may develop political motivations and resort to violence for political ends.[15]

Terrorists and insurgents are another group that has been linked to the drug trade in Central Asia. Although these actors are a distant second to the local criminal organizations in terms of their level of control over the drug trafficking milieu and the volume of drugs trafficked through the region, they have been in the limelight regionally and globally because of their perceived capacity to destabilize Central Asia. Until the U.S.-led military operation in Afghanistan, the Islamic Movement of Uzbekistan (IMU) was deemed the main terrorist group and a major element of the trafficking-terrorism nexus in Central Asia. With its roots in the conservative Salafi movements in Uzbekistan's Ferghana Valley of 1989–1991, the IMU was formally created in 1998 following the cessation of the civil war in Tajikistan, where the IMU fought alongside the United Tajik Opposition. The following year, it was implicated in a series of bomb explosions in Uzbekistan's capital and a violent incursion into Kyrgyzstan through Tajikistan with a declared intent to infiltrate Uzbekistan, topple the secular government of President Karimov, and create an Islamic state spanning Central Asia. The IMU repeated its incursions in 2000 and was placed on the U.S. Department of State's list of "Designated Foreign Terrorist Organizations."[16]

It is now well established that the IMU's raids in 1999 and 2000 were driven less by political goals and more by the desire to secure the route that the IMU militants used for the transportation of drugs.[17] From a military and strategic standpoint, these operations were too small to create an Islamic caliphate but also large enough in terms of manpower, weapons support, and logistics to defeat the crumbling Kyrgyz military and allow the IMU to infiltrate Uzbekistan. The choice of locations targeted by the militants, the timing of the attack (between one of the highest yields of Afghan opium in June and the closure of the mountain passes in September), and the implications of the Kyrgyz "drug barons" in facilitating these attacks all suggest that the IMU was motivated by a criminal agenda linked to the drug trade.[18] At first glance, the IMU was well placed to control a share of the drug trafficking market in Central Asia. It was connected to the Taliban and Al Qaeda and had ties to the Tajik government (through former warlords) and Kyrgyz drug mafia. Juma Namangani—the head of the IMU at the time—was a leader with dubious theological foundations, extensive military experience, and a background in the drug trade.[19]

The U.S.-led military efforts in Afghanistan, however, decapitated and fragmented the IMU, removing it as a proponent of the nexus in Central Asia. The group tried to revitalize its activities under different leadership that sought to rebrand the movement. Comprising mostly non-Uzbek fighters, the IMU distanced itself from both Uzbekistan and Central Asia and operates now primarily along the Afghanistan-Pakistan border.[20] Its splinter group, the Islamic Jihad Union (IJU), either claimed responsibility for or was imputed in a handful of additional terrorist attacks in Central Asia. Some experts maintain that the now-deceased senior leader of the Al Qaeda movement, Abu Laith-al-Libi, and a liaison between Al Qaeda and the IMU was behind the first suicide bombing in Central Asia carried out by the IJU in April 2004.[21] Until recently, there has been no confirmed evidence of the IJU's involvement in drug trafficking.

TAJIKISTAN

A DRUG TRAFFICKING HUB IN CENTRAL ASIA

Tajikistan has been the drug gateway to Central Asia. On average, more than two-thirds of Northern Route opiates have been annually trafficked through this state. Tajikistan's 810-mile border with Afghanistan has been the most vulnerable in Central Asia in terms of topography, climate, and security. It is remote, marked by the Panj River, which changes its course throughout the year, and difficult to access. There are five official border crossings between Tajikistan and Afghanistan,[22] with the majority of trade volumes coming through the "Friendship Bridge" connecting the border town Shir Khan Bandar in Kunduz Province of Afghanistan and the town of Panji Poyon in Tajikistan. Financed by the U.S. Army Corps of Engineers and inaugurated in 2007, the Tajikistan-Afghanistan bridge is equipped with drive-through scanners and customs offices at both ends. According to the UNODC, however, the high volume of construction materials, particularly cement, transported over the bridge makes the detection of drugs particularly challenging.[23] It is noteworthy that the Kumsangir District of the Khatlon Province on the Tajikistan side of the bridge has not reported drug seizures.

The improved customs controls and border security at the border crossings has not interrupted the flow of Northern Route opiates to Tajikistan. Some traffickers choose to bypass border crossings all together and carry smaller but frequent shipments of opiates using illegal crossings. Furthermore, deep-seated corruption and the presence of well-organized criminal networks with ties to the local and central governments in Tajikistan facilitate the flow of drugs. An added challenge is that northern Afghanistan provinces bordering Tajikistan have been the sites of opium poppy cultivation or transit points for opium trafficking. Afghanistan's Badakhshan Province, sharing a long border with Tajikistan's Gorno-Badakhshan Autonomous Oblast (GBAO), for example, has been a location for opium production and the central point for drug trafficking networks in the regional drug trade. Although the Takhar and Kunduz Provinces of Afghanistan, which border Tajikistan's Khatlon Province, have been poppy free, they too have served as transit points for heroin and opium trafficking from the southern and western provinces of Afghanistan (see figure 2.1). These are also the areas where Afghanistan's government authority has been weak or has been challenged by the Taliban and other militant formations. Subsequently, Khatlon has accounted for 20–40 percent of heroin and opium seized in Tajikistan.

GBAO saw a surge in the trafficking of drugs in the mid-1990s, during the Tajik civil war, when the region found itself on the side of the United Tajik Opposition. As part of a power-sharing agreement signed at the end of the war, GBAO initially retained its own police, military, and tax system, but has been unable to pull its sparse population out of poverty. The province is home to minority Pamiri ethnic groups, including the Ismailis, who are Shia Muslims. In Afghanistan, Ismailis make up the majority of the population in the districts bordering Ismaili villages in GBAO. The ethno-religious and linguistic ties facilitate the drug flow across the border, while weak law enforcement makes detection of drug trafficking virtually impossible. The climate and topography also make government surveillance and control of licit and illicit trade in this territory very difficult. This explains a relatively small, if still steady, traffic of drugs in GBAO.[24]

Once across the Tajik-Afghan border, drug trafficking continues further on to Kyrgyzstan, but some shipments are consolidated and repackaged in Dushanbe or Sughd. This is supported by seizure data, which demonstrate that considerable seizures of heroin and opium are now made in the capital of Tajikistan, Dushanbe, and further downstream, rather than at the border. From Dushanbe, drug shipments can be trafficked into the Batken and Osh regions of Kyrgyzstan through Sughd (mostly through the cities of Kudjand and Isfara), or to Uzbekistan. Khujand (Sughd) also serves as a transit point to Uzbekistan.[25]

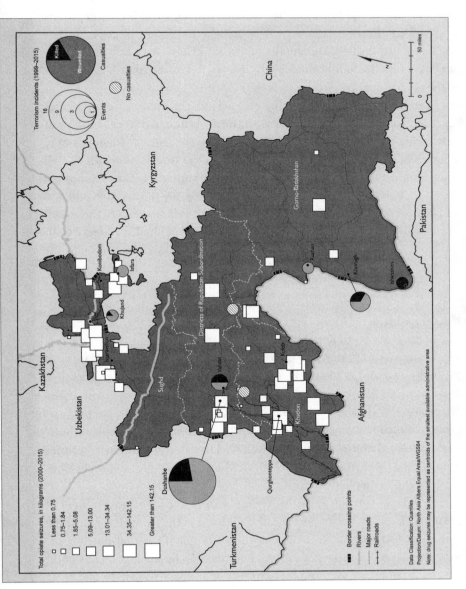

FIGURE 2.1 Map of terrorism and opiate seizures in Tajikistan, 2008–2015

Source: United Nations Office on Drugs and Crime (UNODC); National Consortium for the Study of Terrorism and Responses to Terrorism (START), Global Terrorism Database, 2018, https://www.start.umd.edu/gtd

TERRORISM AND INSURGENCY IN TAJIKISTAN

Terrorist violence in Tajikistan has been interlinked with the country's low-intensity conflicts in its eastern regions, where the central government's reach remains limited. During the 1990s, Tajikistan was a hub of nonstate violent actors (including those with links to terrorist groups), largely due to the bloody civil conflict and postwar skirmishes with remnants of fighters from the civil war era. During this period, the Dushanbe authorities regarded Islamists who fought against the governmental forces in the war as its principal security threat and challenge to the regime. The 1990s were a period of increased terrorist violence, which was interwoven with its civil war. The postwar government, led by long-standing president Emomali Rahmon, however, has succeeded in eliminating the most viable political and Islamic opponents, and there have been relatively few terrorist attacks.[26] The data, however, offer little support to the stream of jihadist violence spilling from Afghanistan into Tajikistan and Central Asia. According to the Global Terrorism Database (GTD), Tajikistan experienced a total of eleven terrorist incidents between 2008 and 2015, with one incident that took place in Isfara (Sughd) in 2009 designated as criminal, rather than terrorist, violence. Five incidents took place in GBAO, three in Dushanbe, two in Sughd, one in the Districts of Republican Subordination (DRS), and none in Khatlon, bordering Afghanistan's provinces Takhar and Kunduz with some of the highest volume of insurgent activity. A total of twenty people were killed and forty-four injured (including one in the "questionable" incident) in the attacks on the Tajik government, military, and police targets. No terrorist group claimed responsibility for these attacks, although the Tajik authorities impugned the previously unknown Jamaat Ansarullah, a splinter group of the IMU, in suicide bombings at the regional police station in Khujand, Sughd, in September 2010.

Since the U.S. troop surge in Afghanistan in 2009, the government of Emomali Rahmon began portraying Tajikistan as the frontline against the spillover of Afghanistan's insurgency and a target of international terrorism. Tajikistan's intelligence reports and remarks by public officials point out the existence of overlapping networks of Taliban, Al Qaeda, and IMU militants linked up with other Pakistan-based terrorist groups who are seeking to subvert Tajikistan and other states of Central Asia. In particular, Tajikistan's government sees the string of clashes between its forces and former opposition fighters that occurred in 2010–2011 as evidence of an ongoing terrorist threat. These incidents included the August 2010 escape of twenty-five prisoners from the high-security detention center in Dushanbe run by the State Committee for National Security, the September 2010 militants' ambush of the government security forces that killed twenty-five soldiers and wounded eleven others, and a series of clashes between the Tajik military and alleged militants that occurred over the course of a counterterrorism operation in the spring of 2011. The government reported that it detained 196 militants in 2011 (an increase from 38 in 2010). Tajikistan's Drug Control Agency announced that it arrested several traffickers who turned out to be the IMU members, thus suggesting a possibility of the nexus between drug trafficking and terrorism in Tajikistan.[27]

KYRGYZSTAN

THE "KYRGYZSTAN CORRIDOR" FOR DRUG TRADE

Among the five Central Asian republics, Kyrgyzstan has the longest experience with the cultivation and trafficking of drugs. The Soviet Union produced about 80 percent of the legal supply of opium in the Issyk Kul region of Kyrgyzstan, parts of which were trafficked to other parts of the USSR and China.[28] Opium poppies were also grown in the south of Kyrgyzstan, and the city of Osh was once dubbed "the Bogota of the East."[29] The Soviets banned all opium cultivation in 1974, and Kyrgyzstan is not considered a drug producer at present. Instead, it has been used as a transit territory for Afghan opioids bound for Russia and Europe through the so-called Kyrgyzstan corridor.

Nearly all intercepted Afghan opiates enter Kyrgyzstan from its southern Osh, Jalal-Abad, and Batken regions. Osh and Batken Provinces share a 603-mile-long border with Tajikistan, only about a half of which has been delimited (see figure 2.2).[30] The presence of enclaves in the tumultuous Ferghana Valley shared between Kyrgyzstan, Tajikistan, and Uzbekistan presents a major challenge to effective border control. The two largest exclaves are the Tajikistani enclave of Vorukh and the Uzbekistani exclave of Sokh, both located in Batken.[31] In 1999 and 2000, the IMU used these enclaves as bases for staging raids into Kyrgyzstan and storing Afghan opiates for further transit. Kyrgyzstani police and security officers are not allowed to operate within the enclaves, which do not follow the law of the territory they are located in. This law enforcement vacuum makes these territories perfect locations for smuggling and trafficking activities.[32]

The Osh region, Osh City,[33] and Batken Province have become the sites of major interceptions of large drug shipments in Kyrgyzstan. The two most prominent routes used for transporting drugs to these provinces run through the poorly controlled Osh-Khorogh Highway and the Khujand Road to Batken. Some sections of the border between Tajikistan's Khujand Province and Kyrgyzstan's Batken Province have neither border markings nor border control, making this area particularly vulnerable to drug trafficking.[34] Attempts to open and secure drug routes from Khujand to Batken were reported in the late 1990s. According to several academic accounts, powerful Kyrgyz and Uzbek criminal groups in Osh had ties with former members of the United Tajik Opposition (UTO) in Tajikistan (who had maintained close relations with the IMU). Reportedly, former civil war warlords who received posts in the postwar government of President Rahmon provided unofficial protection to the IMU, allowing it to establish control over the drug routes in the north of Tajikistan and the south of Kyrgyzstan.[35]

Various drug trafficking routes forming the "Kyrgyz corridor" connect in an Osh City area used for consolidation and repackaging of opiates, as evidenced in the large quantity of drug seizures in the city. Some drugs move onward to Kazakhstan, while others are transported to Bishkek. From the capital, drugs blend into a large trade flow traveling to Kazakhstan and Russia by private cars, train, and air. Bishkek City and the Chuy region are also main areas where drugs are circulated and sold for local consumption. Primitive heroin-producing laboratories were reported as operating in Chuy in 2007–2008.[36] However, no production facilities have been discovered in recent years in the region.

Since Uzbekistan shut its border with Kyrgyzstan following the 2010 interethnic clashes in Osh and Jalal-Abad, only a small volume of drugs has been smuggled from that direction. Kyrgyzstan also shares a 533-mile border and two border crossings with China, but there have been no reports of overland drug trafficking through the Chinese border. For a number of years, China, Kyrgyzstan, and Uzbekistan have been in negotiations about constructing a railway linking Kashgar City in China with Uzbekistan's

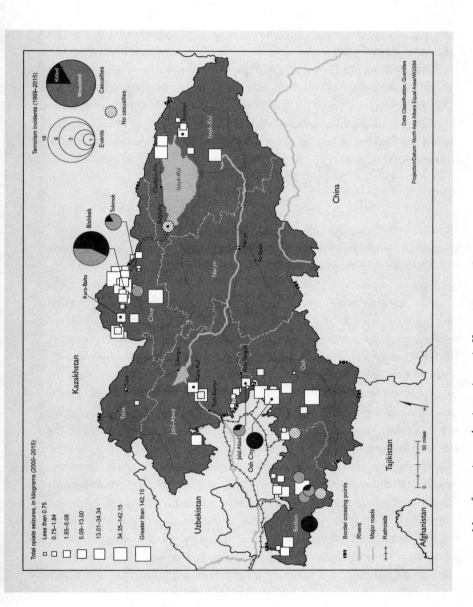

FIGURE 2.2 Map of terrorism and opiate seizures in Kyrgyzstan, 2008–2015

Note: Drug seizures may be represented as centroids of the smallest available administrative area

Source: UNODC; START, Global Terrorism Database

Andijan, through the Arpa Valley and the town of Kara-Suu in Kyrgyzstan. If and when this regional rail line becomes fully operational, the amount of drug trafficking by rail through Kyrgyzstan to China may increase unless commensurate security upgrades are undertaken at these border crossings. The Chuy Valley and the Issyk-Kul region of Kyrgyzstan are the primary cultivation areas for hashish and marijuana. Cannabis produced locally is used for domestic and regional consumption rather than international distribution. Local criminal groups holding considerable sway in local affairs control the market of "light" drugs in Kyrgyzstan, but they exercise little influence in the context of a broader drug market.[37]

TERRORISM IN KYRGYZSTAN

Most of the terrorist violence in Kyrgyzstan has consisted of small-scale attacks, benefiting from an influential criminal underworld and a disruptive rotation of political elites. According to the GTD, a total of twenty-eight terrorist incidents have occurred in Kyrgyzstan since 1991, including six that took place between 2009 and 2015. Of twenty-two incidents that occurred between 1995 and 2008, four were designated as "questionably" terrorist. A total of nine people were killed and twenty injured in twenty-eight incidents. With the exception of the IMU, which took responsibility for the 1999 raids, no other group claimed responsibility for the attacks. Approximately half of the GTD-registered terrorist attacks took place in the capital of Kyrgyzstan, Bishkek, while 38 percent of the incidents occurred in the southern Batken, Osh, and Jalal-Abad Provinces (see figure 2.2).

Since its independence in 1991, Kyrgyzstan has seen its share of domestic security concerns. Political instability in the neighboring republics only exacerbated these security problems. Caught amid the post–civil war infighting in Tajikistan, the purported Islamist insurgency in Uzbekistan, and the Taliban's resistance in Afghanistan, Kyrgyzstan has also been a target of incursions by militant organizations. The largest raids were those conducted in August 1999, when IMU fighters crossed into Kyrgyzstan, taking a number of hostages, including foreign citizens. On several occasions in 1999 and 2000, the crumbling Kyrgyz military clashed with armed fighters seeking to cross into Kyrgyzstan. After these raids, the Kyrgyz government declared international terrorism a threat to Kyrgyzstan's national security. This official narrative continues to this day.[38] In the 2000s, the

Kyrgyz authorities blamed the IMU and the East Turkistan Liberation Organization (ETLO)[39] for terrorist violence.

In 2011, the Kyrgyz authorities announced the creation of a new home-grown Shia group—Jayash al-Mahdi (JM)—that was believed to have carried out bombings and attempted bombings from December 2010 to January 2011. JM's activity came to a halt in January 2011 when the Kyrgyz security forces killed its alleged leader and captured more than a dozen of its operatives. Some of the purported members of this group received lengthy jail sentences in a controversial trial that concluded in 2013.[40] Another series of incidents that has been used to support the official "terrorist narrative" includes a July 2015 shoot-out in Bishkek between the Kyrgyz security forces and the alleged members of an ISIS cell. This was followed by a spectacular escape of the "JM and ISIS terrorists" from a maximum-security prison in Bishkek in October 2011 and the ensuing two-week counterterrorism operation to apprehend them. While the recaptured Islamists were waiting for a trial on charges of terrorism and breaking out of prison to join ISIS in Syria, another group of assailants attacked a police station in Bishkek in November 2015, killing one officer. The authorities attributed the attack to Islamists and responded with another security operation in December, in which they killed two alleged terrorist suspects responsible for the murder of a police officer.

Many analysts have convincingly argued that Kyrgyzstan's government has deliberately exaggerated the threat of terrorism to curry political and security favor from the United States and Russia, to placate its more powerful neighbors, and to benefit domestically from exploiting the terrorist narrative. The official claims of growing religious radicalization have been based on shallow, circumstantial, and fabricated evidence.[41] And many question the nature and sources of the reported violence, believing it often intersects with criminal activity and the drug trade.

KAZAKHSTAN

A TRANSIT COUNTRY FOR AFGHAN OPIOIDS

Kazakhstan's position astride key trafficking routes to Russia and Europe from Afghanistan makes it a strategically situated transit country for the region's heroin and opium trade. According to UNODC estimates, between fifty and fifty-five metric tons of heroin were trafficked through Kazakhstan annually in the 2000s.[42] Although all of Kazakhstan's provinces report the presence of a drug trade, the main drug trafficking activity concentrates along the 3,955-kilometer (2,460-mile) border with Kazakhstan's Central Asian neighbors—Kyrgyzstan, Uzbekistan, and Turkmenistan—and on the long 7,644-kilometer (4,750-mile) border with Russia (see figure 2.3). Small amounts of heroin have also been trafficked by rail from Kazakhstan into the westernmost Chinese province, Xinjiang.

Most of the opioids reach Kazakhstan from Kyrgyzstan through a series of routes that start in Osh and Bishkek in Kyrgyzstan and proceed alongside the well-developed rail and road networks into Kazakhstan's southern cities of Shymkent and Almaty, and then on to the border cities of Aqtobe in West Kazakhstan, Koshketau and Petropavlovsk in North Kazakhstan, and Ust-Kamenogorsk in East Kazakhstan. With its sizable Uzbek population and proximity to Uzbekistan's capital, Tashkent, Shymkent has become the key entry point for opioids into Kazakhstan. Considerably fewer heroin and opium shipments cross the remote 413-kilometer (257-mile) border of Turkmenistan with Kazakhstan.[43]

Kazakhstan also cultivates and produces hashish and marijuana. The heartland of cannabis in Kazakhstan is the Chuy Valley, which straddles Kazakhstan and Kyrgyzstan. It is estimated that between 350,000 and 400,000 hectares of mostly wild cannabis grow yearly in southern Kazakhstan (in the Jambyl region of Kazakstash, with smaller territories cultivating cannabis in the Almaty, Kyzyl-Orda, and South Kazakhstan Provinces).[44] Cannabis produced locally is used for domestic and regional consumption, rather than international distribution.[45] Opium poppies also grow naturally and intermittently in parts of Kazakhstan, but no heroin-producing laboratories have been reported in the country.[46]

The fact that Kazakhstan has large swaths of open land has hampered the centralization and monopolization of the drug trafficking market by large criminal syndicates. This landscape of steppes and semi-deserts with rare natural obstacles has also been conducive to the development of transboundary transportation networks. The Russia-Kazakhstan border, the lengthiest continuous border in the world, is crossed by sixteen railways, six highways, thirty-six paved roads, and dozens of unpaved roads. Since 2011 this border has not been equipped with customs points, due to the

Custom Union agreement between the two countries and Belarus. This contactivity across such vast terrain has been beneficial to the drug trade, and rail and road networks have become popular means of drug trafficking.[47]

Even though Kazakhstan's borders with Uzbekistan and China have been marked with the best-equipped and staffed border checkpoints in the region, the sheer size of the country and the volume of trade from Uzbekistan and Kyrgyzstan have been too high to allow for the diligent checking of all cargo. One of the most popular methods of concealment of drugs is within shipments of fruits and vegetables or in packed lots of industrial goods directed to Russia.[48] These challenges partly explain the relatively low volumes of drug seizures in Kazakhstan, despite the fact that it is the last country crossed by Afghan opioids before the drugs enter their destination markets in Russia. Furthermore, even when there have been drops in opium production in northern Afghanistan—which ought to push traffickers toward the Balkan route or the southern route through Pakistan—the ease of trafficking through Kazakhstan has continued to pull traffickers to the northern route.[49]

THE LATE ADVENT OF TERRORISM

Terrorist attacks in Kazakhstan occurred relatively late compared to its Central Asian counterparts. In the 1990s, the Kazakh government exhibited confidence in the republic's invulnerability to Islamist threats. Public authorities contended that their country provided a poor soil for religious radicalization. Indeed, prior to 2011 only eleven terrorist incidents were registered in Kazakhstan by the GTD. One attack that took place in September 2000, when two police officers were shot dead in Almaty, was attributed to the Uighur Liberation Organization.[50] Currently known as the East Turkistan Libertarian Organization, the group advocates for an independent "Turkistan" and separatism from China. Similar to other terrorist attacks, this shooting was minor in terms of lethality but had a bigger symbolic impact that was strengthened by the broadening discourse of Islamist danger and the global "war on terrorism." Over the 2000s, the Kazakh government had grown increasingly wary of the republic's burgeoning religious sector, with government and security services pointing to certain conditions, such as the republic's proximity to hotbeds of instability, as conducive to terrorist violence.[51] This concern was also due to the increased involvement of Kazakhs in militant and terrorist activity in other states, particularly in the North Caucasus of Russia, Kyrgyzstan, and Tajikistan.[52] Salafism, an ultraconservative Islamist ideology, came to Kazakhstan by way of the North Caucasus and took hold mostly in the Atyrau, Mangghustau, and Aqtobe regions in western and central Kazakhstan. These are territories with historic ties to Russia's North Caucasus: in 1994, Soviet leader Joseph Stalin ordered the deportation of the whole Vainakh population (Chechen and Ingush) to Central Asia. Kazakhstan is a home to sizable Chechen and Ingush diasporas. Yet the 2000s remained largely without major terrorist violence despite the rise in the activities of Hizb ut-Tahrir al-Islam and a number of other Salafi groups in Kazakhstan, such as Jamaat Takfir, in the country's western region.[53]

In 2011, however, Kazakhstan's reputation for stability was shattered by a series of terrorist incidents. A spate of violence began with a suicide bombing at the National Security Committee in May 2011 in Kazakhstan's western town of Aqtobe, later designated as the first mafia suicide attack in the country. The same year in July, security forces carried out an offensive on suspected Islamists that left thirteen dead in western Kazakhstan. Atyrau became the site of two explosions in late October for which a new militant group, Jund al-Khalifa (Soldiers of Caliphate, or JaK), claimed responsibility. And, in November, a suspected Islamist bomber identified as Maksat Kariyev shot and killed nine people before self-detonating in Taraz. Eight more terrorist incidents of a lesser magnitude took place in different parts of Kazakhstan in 2012 and 2013, targeting government representatives, police, and journalists. No group took responsibility for those attacks.

The Kazakh authorities laid blame for two explosions in Atyrau and shootings in Taraz on Islamists. However, the links of assailants to global jihadist movement were tenuous, at best. The first mention of JaK appeared between 2008 and 2011, with some experts claiming that the group was an offshoot of the IMU operating in the Afghanistan-Pakistan border region. JaK's Kazakh wing, known as Zahir Baibars Battalion, was also established around that time by nine Kazakh mercenaries who became affiliated with JaK in 2011. The same year, JaK released a video in which its members threatened the Kazakh government with retaliation if it failed to retract a law

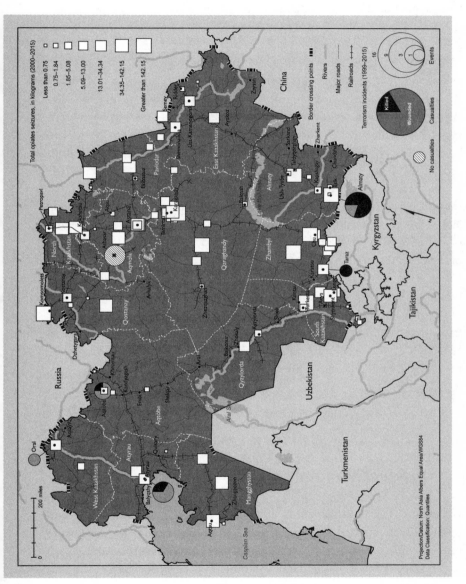

FIGURE 2.3 Map of terrorism and opiate seizures in Kazakhstan, 2008–2015

Note: Drug seizures may be represented as centroids of the smallest available administrative area

Source: UNODC; START, Global Terrorism Database

banning women from wearing the veil. In 2012, JaK published two more videos of attacks against International Security Assistance Force (ISAF) troops in Khost Province, Afghanistan.[54] It also claimed responsibility for the 2012 Toulouse shooting attributed to Mohamed Merah, a French citizen, who was killed in a shootout by French police.[55]

Several details of the Atyrau bombings raise suspicions about the official narrative imputing the orchestration of these attacks to JaK. First, the suicide bomber and his accomplices were in their early and mid-twenties at the time of the attack. It is, therefore, unlikely that they received training or had built their jihadist reputations as JaK's foot fighters in order to be placed in charge of its underground cell in Kazakhstan. Second, both attacks involved primitive improvised explosive devices, one of which detonated prematurely, killing the assailant, while the second one caused neither property damage nor human casualties. This suggests that the group lacked the kind of training and preparation that would have been expected of a jihadist cell with transnational links. Third, these attacks (as with most of the other terrorist incidents) targeted Kazakhstan's security and government institutions rather than highly populous spaces that would have increased their lethality. This, too, is largely inconsistent with the pattern of terrorist attacks masterminded by transnational jihadist groups. A more likely explanation is that the assailants veiled their actions in the shroud of the JaK's ideology to raise the prominence of the attacks, which were prompted by religious motivations with a more local focus.

UZBEKISTAN

THWARTING THE DRUG TRAFFICKING FLOWS

Uzbekistan is a significant transit country for Afghanistan's heroin and opium. Given its small, well-guarded border with Afghanistan, Uzbekistan receives most of its opioids from Tajikistan. Marked by the Amu Darya River, Uzbekistan's 137-kilometer (85-mile) border with Afghanistan was shut completely in 1998 to prevent the spillover of war from Afghanistan, prompting the construction of one of the world's most heavily guarded border barriers. The border includes a barbed-wire fence, an electrified barbed-wire fence, watchtowers with radio communications, and heavily equipped border patrol soldiers. The main border crossing is located at the Afghanistan-Uzbekistan Friendship Bridge, which connects the two countries by rail and road. As one of the main trade partners of Afghanistan, Uzbekistan sees sizable daily turnover of cargo carried by vehicles and trains. This increase in the turnover of cross-border goods has not been met with concurrent proportionate improvements in antismuggling capacity, especially on the Afghanistan side. Loopholes and breaches in customs security systems have allowed for the trafficking of drugs across the official border crossing, as evidenced by drug seizures in Termez (see figure 2.3). However, the volume of drug trafficking across this border has been considerably smaller than across Uzbekistan's border with Tajikistan. Ethnic identities in Afghanistan's drug producing provinces also promote trade via Tajikistan. Uzbeks are a minority in the provincial districts on the Afghan side that are dominated by ethnic Turkmen. Uzbek is the mother tongue for just over 10 percent of the population in these districts. Indeed, the majority of drug traffickers operating in this region are Turkmen and Pashtuns with nominal ties to the ethnic Uzbeks on Uzbekistan's side.[56] Uzbeks, by contrast, constitute one of the largest ethnic groups in the population of Takhar Province, bordering Tajikistan, serving as the key conduit for drug trafficking from Afghanistan.

Given strict border controls on the Uzbekistan-Afghanistan border, traffickers prefer to smuggle small quantities of heroin across illegal crossing points, or make their way into Uzbekistan through the Tajikistan border that offers more opportunities to enter undetected via thousands of miles of open desert and rugged mountains. The length of the border (1,333 kilometers), the ongoing issues with border delimitation and demarcation,[57] and presence of family and kin-ties in the communities straddling the border facilitate the illicit transborder activities, including the drug trade. The border, however, is also relatively well monitored, notwithstanding official corruption at the border crossings, and Uzbekistan and Tajikistan have had a mutual visa regime since 1999. Uzbekistan has built barbed-wire fences on parts of its border with Tajikistan and placed minefields with no warning signs on others. These measures, however, have not deterred the residents of villages on the Tajik side or traffickers. There are occasional armed confrontations between the traffickers and Uzbekistan's border guards as well as detentions and harsh prison punishments for border transgressors.

The Uzbekistan-Turkmenistan border, however, has seen smaller heroin and opium flows into Uzbekistan. Despite the benefits of proximity, infrastructure, and topography, the two countries have a very small trade turnover, which makes it more difficult for traffickers to exploit the trade flows compared to other border crossings. Turkmenistan's late president Saparmurat Niyazov ordered the construction of the barbed-wire fence on the border in 2004, and Uzbekistan's authorities have kept a close eye on its border with Turkmenistan given that Turkmenistan's border with Afghanistan has had lax security measures. Like its neighbors, Kazakhstan and Kyrgyzstan, Uzbekistan has a long history of cannabis use. Cannabis grows wild throughout the county and is also cultivated, although the total area with cannabis plants is tiny compared to that in Kazakhstan. Since the local harvest of cannabis is insufficient for export, it remains mostly in Uzbekistan. The country has also had poppy fields, but an aggressive poppy eradication campaign rooted out domestic opium production and also affected cannabis cultivation.[58]

THE FLEETING TERRORIST THREAT

After a series of relatively large attacks in the late 1990s to early 2000s, terrorism in Uzbekistan has steadily diminished. During glasnost in the late 1980s, independent political and religious movements questioning President Islam Karimov's legitimacy emerged, with many seeking to overthrow the secular government of Uzbekistan. The three provinces of Uzbekistan's Ferghana Valley that had reportedly been home to a network of underground mosques and clandestine religious circles during the Soviet era provided fertile ground for the emergence of religious activism. Partly shaped by Karimov's heavy use of coercion, several movements formed Islamist factions. Among these were Adolat's militant wing, Islom Lashkarlari, and members of another Islamist group, Tawba, which engaged in violent activities against secular authorities in Namangan, prompting a further crackdown by the Karimov government. The leaders of these groups ultimately fled to Tajikistan to take part in the Tajik civil war and later formed the core of the IMU. Founded in 1998, the movement's initial goal was to topple the Karimov government and replace it with an Islamic state under sharia. In the 2000s, the IMU broadened its agenda to the creation of a regionwide caliphate and reinvented itself as a key player in the global jihadist movement and an ally of Al Qaeda and the Taliban.[59]

The largest terrorist attack in Uzbekistan occurred in February 1999, when six car bombs exploded outside government buildings in the downtown of Tashkent, killing 16 people and injuring more than 120 others. The authorities claimed that the bombings were an assassination attempt targeting President Karimov and contended that the IMU orchestrated the blasts.[60] Having settled in Afghanistan, the IMU reached its peak in 2000 with approximately two thousand well-armed foot soldiers in Afghanistan (often participating in the Taliban and Al Qaeda's offensives), but was severely weakened in the combat with the U.S.-led allied forces in 2001. The following year, a splinter group—the Islamic Jihad Group (IJG), which subsequently renamed itself the Islamic Jihad Union (IJU)—peeled off of the IMU with the stated goal of continuing attacks against the Karimov regime.[61] The IJG assailants set off a series of bombs in June 2004 targeting the Israeli and U.S. Embassies and the Prosecutor General's Office in Tashkent. The U.S. State Department listed the IJG a Specially Designated Global Terrorist Organization in 2005.[62]

Only three small-scale terrorist incidents have taken place in Uzbekistan in subsequent years, including two suicide bombings in the Andijan Province that killed two police officers and wounded six persons. Responsibility for both attacks was claimed by the Islamic Jihad Union (IJU).[63] The most recent attack took place in September 2015 in Tashkent, where an assailant threw two incendiary devices at the U.S. Embassy. No casualties were reported for this attack, and no group claimed responsibility for the incident. A pattern of bombings targeting police in Andijan was markedly different from the IJU plots in Germany, where the targets of the attack included Ramstein Air Base and Frankfurt International Airport, which hosted U.S. military personnel and civilians.[64] The attacks took place at a time when both the IJU and IMU were assailed by Pakistani and Afghani forces coordinating an offensive with German-led ISAF operations in Afghanistan. Although the targeting of the IJU that led to the group's movement across the tribal belt area could have sparked attacks in Uzbekistan (and Tajikistan), it is also possible that the threatened movement claimed

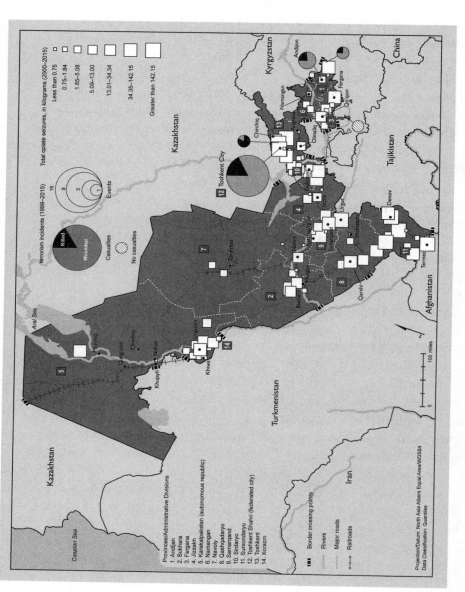

FIGURE 2.4 Map of terrorism and opiate seizures in Uzbekistan, 2008–2015

Note: Drug seizures may be represented as centroids of the smallest available administrative area

Source: UNODC; START, Global Terrorism Database

responsibility for attacks motivated by localized grievances to give credence to its strength and relevance in the region.

SOCIOECONOMIC AND TOPOGRAPHIC DETERMINANTS OF THE NEXUS

Having surveyed where and when patterns of trafficking and terrorism have emerged in each of the Central Asian republics, in this section we examine more rigorously the conditions that enabled those intersections to occur. As the maps of trafficking and terrorist intersections demonstrate, there is a considerable spatial overlap between drug trafficking and terrorism activity in Central Asia. Moreover, this overlap is neither random nor spread evenly across the region but occurs in particular locations—often in the so-called difficult-to-govern territories. Drawing on the comparative study of the crime-terror nexus, as well as the literature on terrorism, we identified a set of geographic and socioeconomic conditions that pose challenges to governing particular locations.

In some cases, the difficulty with effective control and law enforcement has been due to the size of the territory, its remoteness from the capital, and terrain. Proximity to the border with Afghanistan, contested areas along the shared borders with other countries, and the challenging topography of the borders have also facilitated the trafficking-terrorism intersections. These observations are consistent with our expectations about the relationship of the nexus to the geographically remote and mountainous locations, and proximity of international borders. The overview of trafficking and terrorism also highlighted a number of socioeconomic properties of the locations where these activities are more likely to occur. For example, it appears that some of the territories with a history of trafficking and terrorism have been beleaguered by inadequate living standards, including the quality and availability of employment, poverty, wealth disparity, and low income. Both populous and sparsely populated areas in Central Asia have seen drug trafficking and terrorism.

We performed two sets of empirical tests examining the impact of various socioeconomic and geographic conditions on the trafficking-terrorism connections. First, using the province-level data from Kazakhstan,

Kyrgyzstan, and Tajikistan,[65] we examined the impact of socioeconomic status, youth unemployment, education, population, crime, migration, and gender ratio on the likelihood of trafficking and terrorism intersections. Second, we used the GIS to extract various time-invariant geographic attributes of the terrorist locations and performed statistical tests of the relationship between these features of the terrain and terrorism, controlling for drug seizures.

PROVINCIAL-LEVEL TESTS OF SOCIAL AND ECONOMIC DETERMINANTS OF THE NEXUS

To measure the nexus, which refers to the spatial and temporal coincidence of trafficking and terrorism, we created a binary variable, with "1" denoting those province-years where both trafficking and terrorist incidents occurred and with "0" denoting otherwise. Trafficking has been measured by the total volume of drug seizures of opiates (heroin and opium) and cannabis (cannabis resin and cannabis herb) reported in the Drugs Monitoring Platform of the UNODC.[66] The totals in kilograms were aggregated over the administrative divisions in Kazakhstan, Kyrgyzstan, and Tajikistan for each year of the analysis (2009–2015). Terrorism has been measured by the counts of unambiguous terrorist incidents reported in the GTD (see table 2.1).

Several predictor variables used in the study include infant mortality rate (which has been used as a crude measure of the socioeconomic levels in the community),[67] registered crime, gender ratio, percentage of unemployment among youth, and education (as measured by the number of students enrolled in professional programs as a percentage of the total population in a province). For the purpose of the analysis, we created an interaction term using percentage of unemployed youth and numbers of students enrolled in professional education. Our expectation is that the crime-terror nexus is more likely to occur in those provinces with a larger number of young people enrolled in programs of professional education and unemployed.

Low living standards compel destitute people to migrate internally (from rural to urban areas) or to seek jobs overseas. This internal migration, in turn, puts additional social and economic pressure on the territories

TABLE 2.1 Variables Used in the Study of Socioeconomic Predictors of the Nexus

Variable	Empirical indicators and measurements
Trafficking-terrorism nexus	Binary measure: "1" = province-year that experienced both trafficking and terrorism; "0" = otherwise
	Terrorism: Total number of terrorist incidents that occurred in a province during the year
	Drug trafficking: total volume of opiates and cannabis seized per province per year (in kilograms)
Socioeconomic status	Infant mortality rate (infant deaths per 1,000 born alive)
Population	Total population (both genders)
Unemployment	Youth (15–28 years old) unemployed (%)
Education	Total number of students enrolled in professional education programs (public) as a percentage of total population in the province
Net migration	The difference between inflows and outflows of migrant population
Crime	Total number of all registered crimes in a province per year
Public service employment	Total number of people employed in public administration, education, and health services divided by population
Gender ratio	Total number of men divided by the total number of women

accepting the migrants. Therefore, we incorporated the net migration variable into our model of the nexus. In addition, we included a crude measure of services performed for the population, which is measured by the total number of employees in public administration, education, and health services (adjusted for population). The province-level socioeconomic data come from online and print publications of the Central Asian republics' statistical agencies.[68] All of the factors used to model the trafficking-terrorism nexus in this study have been identified as precipitants of terrorist and criminal activity in Central Asia and predictors of terrorism in cross-national empirical analyses.[69]

The complete results of our logistical regression appear in appendix 1. Among the predictors, the infant mortality rate, youth education-unemployment interactive term, public service employment, gender ratio, and crime returned statistically significant coefficients. The findings suggest that socioeconomic development, measured by the infant mortality rate, is negatively associated with the terrorism-trafficking nexus, holding other factors constant.[70] On the one hand, this finding contradicts the expectation that lower levels of socioeconomic development are drivers of the nexus. But this expectation views the nexus as separate from the state. As we demonstrate in the cases that follow, the trafficking-terrorism nexus is a complex set of political, economic, and security relationships that often emerge in areas where power and wealth are concentrated. This finding suggests, therefore, that those areas in Central Asia exhibiting higher levels of socioeconomic development are more susceptible to the emergence of the trafficking-terrorism nexus.

The interaction term (youth unemployment conditional on professional education) is positively related to the nexus, holding other factors constant. This means that the nexus is more prevalent in provinces with a higher number of students enrolled in professional education programs and also experiencing higher levels of youth unemployment. This finding is consistent with qualitative analysis of the nexus both in Central Asia and comparatively. The literature on the nexus has noted that territories with larger youth populations are more conducive to drug trafficking and terrorist activity, especially if young people lack opportunities for self-actualization and employment. In Central Asia, the governments (and some observers) have alleged that radicalization has become particularly prevalent among unemployed youth.[71] We tentatively conclude, therefore, that the nexus is more likely to emerge in localities with higher percentages of youth who lack employment and other opportunities.

A gender imbalance favoring the male population in a province is also associated with a greater likelihood of the nexus, which is consistent with comparative studies' evidence of greater male participation in these activities. As domestic and international migration bring higher proportions of men to their home localities or labor destinations, we expect gender to be a more significant causal variable in the future. In addition, we find that the greater per capita number of employees in public administration, education, and health services decreases the likelihood of the trafficking-terrorism nexus. This fits the Central Asia context, where state intervention in the economy remains a legacy of Soviet-era state socialism. As many political economic studies of the region have shown, state employment provides a low, but consistent, income that also affords opportunities to generate informal income payments.[72] It follows that higher rates of public service employment reduce peoples' need to engage in drug trafficking and other forms of illicit and/or criminal activity.

The crime variable returned a statistically significant but negative coefficient, indicating that provinces with higher volumes of registered crimes are less likely to experience the drug trafficking–terrorism nexus. The registered crime data can denote the capacity of law enforcement agencies to identify crime. Therefore, while this finding is counterintuitive at first glance, it can be interpreted to mean that the provinces where law enforcement agencies have greater capacity to gather criminal data are less likely to experience the trafficking-terrorism nexus, and vice versa. Other findings suggest that there is no direct relationship between population, net migration, and the nexus: terrorist-trafficking connections can emerge in both populous and sparsely populated areas of Central Asia and in areas with varying levels of migration flows.[73]

DRUG TRAFFICKING AS A DETERMINANT OF TERRORISM IN CENTRAL ASIA

Our survey of the trafficking-terrorism nexus in the brief case studies above also revealed a number of instances where drug trafficking provided an impetus for the criminal groups' engagement in violent attacks. To test for the possibility that drug trafficking is a predictor of terrorist activity and to examine the impact of time-invariant geographic factors on terrorism, we conducted a GIS-based spatial analysis and statistical regressions of terrorist fatalities in the five Central Asian republics. We identified the thirty-four incidents registered as terrorist attacks in the Global Terrorism Database that occurred across Central Asia between 2008 and 2016. Using the geo-coordinates of each of the incidents, we identified an area within

200 kilometers of the terrorist attacks and created 200-kilometer buffers around each incident using ArcGIS. To measure drug trafficking activity, we calculated the total volume of all drugs seized (in kilograms), the total volume of opium seized (in kilograms), and the total volume of cannabis seized (in kilograms) within the 200-kilometer buffer of the terrorist incident and one year before the time of the attack.

We also identified a number of geographic and socioeconomic predictors using the Peace Research Institute Oslo (PRIO)-GRID dataset.[74] The PRIO-GRID dataset is a grid structure that was designed to assist in the compilation and analysis of spatial data within a time-consistent framework. It consists of quadratic grid cells that jointly cover all terrestrial areas of the world. Each 0.5 × 0.5 decimal-degree grid cell roughly corresponding to 55 × 44 kilometers (a 3,025-square-kilometer area) contains cell-specific information on socioeconomic conditions, physical conditions, and other information collected from multiple third-party sources.

The initial list of geographic predictors included forestland coverage, agriculture land coverage, mountainous area coverage, urban land coverage, petroleum locations, average travel time to the nearest urban center, and the distance to the nearest contiguous country. The socioeconomic predictors included average infant mortality rate, total population, and gross cell product. The geographic and socioeconomic values associated with each terrorist attack were extracted from the PRIO grid cells falling inside the 200-kilometer buffer area of each terrorist attack location. The geographic predictors were averaged for all the cells within the buffer, while total population and gross cell product were added up for the total values within the buffer. The values for all predictor variables were collected for the most proximate years to the date of a terrorist attack.

We used a stepwise regression method based on Akaike Information Criterion (AIC) to select variables that contributed to the observed pattern of terrorist activity. The stepwise procedure begins with a constant initial model, then adds or removes variables that can pass a criterion to determine a final model. As a result of the stepwise regression, we selected the following variables for the model of terrorism (measured by the total number of casualties caused by the terrorist incident): forestland coverage, urban land coverage, average travel time to the nearest urban center, distance to the nearest contiguous country, and infant mortality rate (see table 2.2). The

TABLE 2.2 Variables Used in the Tests of the Relationship Between Drug Trafficking and Terrorism

Variable	Empirical indicators and measurements	Original data source used in PRIO-GRID
Terrorism	Total number of people killed in all terrorist incidents that occurred in a province during the year	
Drug trafficking	1. Total volume of opiates (heroin and opium) seized in a province during the year (in kilograms). 2. Total volume of all drugs (heroin, opium, cannabis resin, cannabis herb) seized in a province during the year (in kilograms).	
Forestland coverage	Measures the coverage of forest areas in each cell	Sophie Bontemps, Pierre Defourny, and Eric Van Bogaert, *Globecover 2009: Products Description and Validation Report* (European Space Agency, 2009).
Infant mortality rate	Gives the average infant mortality rate within the grid cell	Adam Storeygard, Deborah Balk, Marc Levy, and Glenn Deane, "The Global Distribution of Infant Mortality: A Subnational Spatial View," *Population, Space and Place* 14, no. 3 (2008): 209–229.
Travel time	An estimate of the travel time to the nearest major city (gives the average travel time within each cell)	Hirotsugu Uchida and Andrew Nelson, "Agglomeration Index: Towards a New Measure of Urban Concentration," *World Bank's World Development Report 2009* (Washington, D.C.: World Bank, 2009).

(continued)

TABLE 2.2   Variables Used in the Tests of the Relationship Between
Drug Trafficking and Terrorism (*continued*)

Variable	Empirical indicators and measurements	Original data source used in PRIO-GRID
Urban land coverage	The percentage of the cell covered by urban area	Prasanth Meiyappan and Atul K. Jain, "Three Distinct Global Estimates of Historical Land-cover Change and Land-use Conversions for Over 200 Years," *Frontiers of Earth Science* 6, no. 2 (2012): 122–139.
Distance to border	The spherical distance in kilometers from the cell centroid to the border of the nearest land-contiguous neighboring country	Nils B. Weidmann, Doreen Kuse, and Kristian Skrede Gleditsch, "The Geography of the International System: The CShapes Dataset," *International Interactions* 36, no. 1 (2010): 86–106.
Gross cell product	Gross cell product, measured in $U.S. using purchasing-power parity.	William D. Nordhaus, "Geography and Macroeconomics: New Data and New Findings," *Proceedings of the National Academy of Sciences of the United States of America* 103, no. 10 (2006): 3510–3517.

results of a poisson regression with robust standard errors are reported in appendix 2.[75]

Overall, the results suggest that increased intensity of violence (i.e., where attacks have higher casualties) tends to occur in urban areas, in proximity to cities and borders with land-contiguous states, where drug trafficking is more prevalent. We address each of these in turn. First, and most importantly, we find that the total volumes of opiate and cannabis seizures in the areas surrounding the incidents of terrorism are strong predictors of terrorist activity. For each kilogram of opium seized within the 200-kilometer buffer zone of the terrorist attack and one year prior, the rate of causalities from terrorism can be expected to grow by a factor of 0.001 (or 0.1%); an increase in 10 kilos of opium seizures is expected to increase the rate of causalities from terrorist incidents by 1 percent; and an increase in 100 kilos in opium seizures is associated with a 10 percent increase in the rate of casualties from terrorist activity, holding other factors constant. Substantive interpretations of the impact of the cannabis seizures are similar. These results suggest that drug trafficking activity is a strong predictor of the intensity of terrorist activity.

The greater the average travel times from the location to a nearest urban center, the fewer terrorism causalities this location is expected to have. This suggests that rural, less accessible, areas in Central Asia experience fewer terrorist casualties, whereas localities in proximity of cities are more likely to experience terrorism. These findings are further supported with results from the coefficients on the other geographic factors tested in the models, namely, forestland coverage and urban land coverage. The greater the forestland coverage of the area, the fewer terrorist causalities this area is expected to have, whereas territories with a higher percentage of urban areas are associated with higher numbers of casualties from terrorist incidents, holding other factors constant.

Another geographical variable tested in the model was distance to nearest contiguous country. The areas located farther away from international land borders have fewer casualties from terrorist attacks. Conversely, localities in proximity to international borders with land-contiguous states are more likely to experience high-intensity terrorist incidents. This finding can be seen visually on the maps of the trafficking-terrorism nexus in each of the Central Asian republics.

One socioeconomic variable tested in the regression was average infant mortality rate. The findings show that higher average infant mortality rates are associated with higher numbers of casualties from terrorist incidents. While we found earlier that higher levels of socioeconomic development (as measured by infant mortality rate) make the trafficking-terrorism nexus more likely to emerge, those findings come from the province-level analysis. At a smaller scale, low levels of socioeconomic development are associated with terrorist incidents with more human casualties. Only a study of variation within provinces—at the neighborhood and village level—would unpack and explain these two countervailing patterns; unfortunately, this remained beyond the scope of our study.

CONCLUSION

In this chapter, we have shown that the intersections between drug trafficking and terrorism in Central Asia have not been random occurrences but manifest clear patterns as to where and when they emerge. A range of pre-existing conditions of the area has shaped the trafficking-terrorism patterns in important ways. While we examined a number of specific conditions relating to territory, population, and socioeconomic variables, we found that higher levels of socioeconomic development, a larger percentage of males in the population, and a larger percentage of unemployed youth were more likely to produce the temporal and spatial overlap of terrorism and trafficking in Central Asia, while higher rates of service persons employed in public offices, health administration, and education reduce the likelihood of the emergence of the nexus. Importantly, our qualitative and quantitative tests confirm our proposition that drug trafficking is an important predictor of terrorist activity in Central Asian states. Accessibility of the location and its level of urbanization also matter in that they raise the rate of casualties associated with terrorism.

Through a quantitative analysis and brief case studies, therefore, we have explored the broad contours of terrorism and trafficking in Central Asia, specified their points of intersection, and identified the conditions that predict both the frequency of a terrorism-trafficking nexus and the intensity of terrorist violence within the nexus. While this analysis provided evidence of how certain preexisting conditions make a nexus more or less likely to emerge, and more or less violent, it does not explain the different relationships between terrorist and criminal activity within the nexus. For that, we now explore the role of the state through in-depth case study analyses.

3

CONVERGENCE AND COEXISTENCE

Divergent Paths of Tajikistan and Uzbekistan

Uzbekistan is a lot like the fictional Corleone family in The Godfather book series, which had decided to get out of the [sic] criminal enterprises (racketeering, loan sharking, etc.) after it made sufficient amounts of wealth, and enter into legitimate economic businesses. The Rahmon leadership, though, has not come to the same conclusion.

—FORMER SECURITY SERVICES OFFICIAL, DUSHANBE, APRIL 2017

For a government in a drug transit state, the political decision to remove itself from or remain involved in drug trafficking can be a particularly fateful one. As the mafia analogy above suggests, some governments in Central Asia had determined that remaining involved in this illicit economy was dangerous and damaging to their state apparatus, while other countries remained tied to a rewarding, yet myopic calculus of exploiting their access to lucrative drug rents even as it led to the criminalization of their state.[1] In what follows, we demonstrate that this decision carries long-term implications for a country—for the development of its coercive institutions, the type of relationship that evolves within the nexus between criminal and militant actors and activities, and the forms of organized violence that emerge.

This chapter examines the processes by which minimal state involvement in drug trafficking can effectively combat the intersection of criminal and extremist worlds, while states' full immersion in the drug trade integrates these networks into a single entity. It pursues a comparison of two post-Soviet drug transit states, Tajikistan (in the 1990s) and Uzbekistan, whose state capabilities and patterns of the trafficking-terrorism nexus take starkly different paths. After a brief yet destructive civil war, Tajikistan's amnesty and reintegration process greatly advantaged—for several years—former militants and opposition leaders, who used their influence within coercive and political offices to immerse the state in the drug trade, integrate subnational and transnational linkages, and foster the convergence of criminal and terrorist networks. Consequently, Tajikistan experienced significantly higher rates of terrorist violence during its early post-Soviet years. By contrast, Uzbekistan's early investments in its coercive institutions enabled the state to remove itself from the drug trade and establish hegemonic state capacities to dismantle and prevent interconnections between criminal and extremist groups. This has led to far lower levels of terrorist violence. As such, these two drug transit states illustrate two polar opposite types of the trafficking-terrorism nexus—defined by coexistence (no relationship) on one hand and full convergence on the other—that have shaped different patterns of terrorist violence.

By shining a light on these diverging patterns of state development, this chapter makes several contributions to our study of the nexus of trafficking and terrorism. First, it stakes out two causal paths by which differential state involvement in drug trafficking greatly affects the emerging patterns of terrorist violence. In one path, a state's full immersion in the drug trade subordinates its security offices to the national and regional political elites involved in this illicit economy and keeps those offices dependent on the rents the drug trade generates. The extensive involvement of the state in drug trafficking, therefore, leads to captured state capacities and inserts the state as the mechanism by which criminal and terrorist networks and activities are integrated. In another path, the state's withdrawal from the drug trade (except for providing limited protection of certain transit operations) enables the government to develop a coercive apparatus that remains largely separate from and not dependent upon drug rents. This advances security offices' capabilities to address criminal and extremist activity, empowers them vis-à-vis regional political elites (especially in dealing with these security issues), and diminishes their susceptibility to predation from the drug trade. As a result, the political decision to withdraw from drug trafficking involvement promotes hegemonic state capacities that empower the state to effectively separate criminal and terrorist networks.

Second, this chapter explains why some drug transit countries are vulnerable to higher levels of terrorist violence than others. While drug trafficking is positively associated with higher frequency and intensity of terrorist violence, and certain socioeconomic and geo-spatial conditions tend to promote that violence, here we outline how the role of the state can either constrain or exacerbate those causal processes. Where the state removes itself from drug trafficking economies, its political development and investments in the security apparatus reduce levels of nonstate violence perpetrated by both criminal and extremist actors, even if the regime, itself, becomes marred in repression against secular and religious opponents. Where the state immerses itself in the drug trade, it generates higher rates of nonstate violence and enables—for relatively short periods of time—significantly increased terrorist violence as well.

Third, the chapter applies these varying trajectories to Tajikistan and Uzbekistan, offering a window into the political economy underpinning these countries' (in)security in their first decade of independence. Tajikistan's civil war greatly fragmented its security apparatus, destroyed many foundations of its economy, and left its population traumatized by a conflict that had led to fifty thousand deaths and over a million people displaced. For much of the 1990s, its postwar government remained internally divided, with the central government's ministries (as well as Tajikistan's provinces) run as the personal fiefdoms of powerful political figures who operated independent of a figurehead president. The ministerial appointees of the central government often competed with the local formal and informal authorities for control of the regions. Under these conditions, these figures ran Tajikistan's provinces yet operated in a vortex of organized criminal activity, drug trafficking, and corruption that occasionally integrated members of militant groups with ties to terrorist organizations. By contrast, Uzbekistan emerged from the collapse of the Soviet Union intact, embarking on a program of state building in the 1990s designed to rein in regional power centers and construct a large and robust coercive apparatus. While its immersion in other economic sectors fostered patterns of coercive rent seeking,[2] the regime removed its newly empowered security apparatus from the drug trade and applied extensive repression against any organized actors—criminal or extremist—operating independently of the state. Through the examples of Tajikistan and Uzbekistan that follow, we elaborate on these trajectories, showing how the state's deep-seated involvement in or withdrawal from drug trafficking produces captured or hegemonic state capacities that give rise to different types of the terrorism-trafficking nexus. In the concluding section, we explain why each generates particular levels of terrorist violence in Central Asia.

TAJIKISTAN IN THE 1990S: A PATH TO CONVERGENCE

Following its civil war, Tajikistan's central government struggled to reestablish control over many parts of the country. While Tajikistan was no longer mired in intrastate conflict and disorder, it was not fully consolidated around a single political authority. The country had emerged as an internally divided, fractious state, in which control over resources and distribution of patronage to ruling elites remained the primary means used by the regime to establish central government influence over its regions. Initially, the formula for stabilizing and ruling Tajikistan entailed ceding control over key institutions to former commanders and prominent politicians and nominally absorbing smaller militia forces into various ministries of the national government.[3] The Rasht Valley area emerged as a stronghold of opposition forces during and after Tajikistan's civil war. Some of this opposition stemmed from former commanders, who found themselves increasingly excluded from state office. Other forms of opposition arose from the region's embittered population, particularly its male youth, who were experiencing social discontent and limited economic opportunity. With the latter potentially receptive to calls to arms against the regime, some leaders in the region sought more concessions from the center.[4] As we demonstrate in chapter 4, the regime would later pursue a method of rule that gradually shifted from cooptation to coercion in dealing with opposing elites. During the wartorn 1990s, however, the regime confronted recurring threats of insurgency, competition for power within its ruling circles, and unruly commanders running its security apparatus. As a result, cooptation was necessary for regime survival, based on a revenue bargain in which national government leaders were openly engaged in the country's drug trade.

THE POLITICS OF OPEN DRUG TRAFFICKING

As the fledgling Rahmon government appointed former commanders from progovernment and opposition forces to establish its nominal control over the rest of the country, many of these leaders had already become involved in the drug trade. According to a witness and former member of the United Tajik Opposition (UTO), a fatwa issued by the Islamist religious leadership permitted the fighters to smoke hemp and partake in the trafficking of drugs. Subsequently, the majority of field commanders and fighters engaged in the drug trade with Afghan smugglers.[5] Foremost among them was Yaqub Salimov, Tajikistan's first postwar minister of the interior. As head of the national police force, Salimov allegedly controlled much of the drug trade in the early 1990s (reportedly utilizing trains and military airplanes to transport drugs to Russia). Another progovernment commander, Gaffor Mirzoev, was believed to run an extensive drug trafficking operation while commanding Tajikistan's elite Presidential Guard (and later as the head of the Drug Control Agency). Some observers speculate that opposition commanders, who had neither Uzbekistani nor Russian support, had turned to drug trafficking to finance their war efforts. During and after the war, Mirzo Ziyoev, military chief of the UTO, was believed to be deeply engaged in heroin smuggling. Likewise, an opposition leader during the war, Habib Sanginov, who had risen to be deputy minister of the interior in the postwar government, was reportedly killed in a drug operation gone awry. As one in-depth analysis has concluded, these examples of central political figures are not merely a few "bad apples" but represented an emerging "narco-state" in which high-ranking government officials used their positions to conduct a majority of the country's drug trade.[6]

In fact, these warlords-turned-officials were often directly engaged in the drug trade and other illicit activities, in contrast to the regime's more careful use of intermediaries after the 2000s, such as officials in the military or border control officers.[7] The profits of unrestrained drug trafficking, moreover, fueled the large patronage networks and patrimony of these senior officials, who commanded the support of lower-level officials, regional politicians, and local strongmen who controlled key resources in their *jamoats* (rural municipalities). In many cases, these patronage networks enabled government officials to straddle licit and illicit economic spheres. For instance, Nemat Azizov, Ziyoev's nephew, was a local commander during the civil war and then headed Tavildara District's Ministry of Emergency Situations after the war. Yet he was also a longtime leader of the district's economy, having been a state farm director during the Soviet period and the region's largest landowner after the war. At the same time, he was alleged to have used his political protection and influence to become heavily involved in the drug trade in his region.[8] In short, the open drug trafficking that had emerged during the civil war continued well after the cessation of hostilities, funding the massive patronage relations that extended from senior government officials (who were largely former commanders) down to the local level (where they and their proxies ran localities as personal fiefdoms). This fusion of political and economic influence critically enabled these actors to control territory essential to the drug trade.

CAPTURED STATE CAPACITY

State failure and civil war in Tajikistan had eviscerated the capacity of its security apparatus, leaving it internally divided, demoralized, and subordinated to a wide range of regional and national political figures. Law enforcement and judicial offices had been specifically targeted with assassination, kidnapping, and open attacks during the war, particularly in early stages of state breakdown (in early 1992) as different sides sought to acquire weapons and munitions, seize these institutions and their positions of authority, and mobilize the local police forces. As the breakdown of state authority unfolded across localities, Tajikistan's security apparatus became highly politicized, permeated by cleavages in society and deeply divided. Moreover, the civil war subordinated civil authorities (including regional and local security offices) to the private militias that constituted factions of the progovernment Popular Front of Tajikistan or their counterpart, the UTO. Based on locality, family ties, and other subnational identities, these independent armies were often organized around the personal fealty of warlordlike figures.[9]

As militia formations were integrated into the state's law enforcement and security institutions, cycles of competition and violence frequently broke out between and within pro-government and opposition militias. Between 1992 and 1994, especially, urban violence surged among militia captains who were vying for spoils and position in government. Amid seemingly anarchic conditions, this "time of troubles" and the ongoing competition for political posts (and the access to rents they provided) left Tajikistan's police and security units highly militarized and closely linked to organized crime.[10] These positions were generally the means by which former commanders could translate their control over independent militias into new rent-seeking opportunities.[11] This left their regiments-turned-police vulnerable to absorption into the country's thriving drug trade.

Indeed, the 1997 UN-brokered peace agreement had integrated entire units of the remaining six thousand fighters into local police and security organs. In districts where the UTO commanded a strong presence (Kofarnihan, Khorogh, Vanch, Rasht, Komsomolobod, Tajikobod, and Lenin), its formations donned police uniforms and took an oath of allegiance to the state. Another two thousand fighters under UTO commander Ziyoev joined the newly formed Ministry of Emergency Situations (of which Ziyoev was minister). Part of Ziyoev's domain included a critical drug trafficking transit point, the Panj District in southern Tajikistan. Where progovernment forces predominated (in Hatlon Province, and districts of Hissar, Tursunzade, and Shahrinau), they were similarly absorbed into local law enforcement.[12] Wary of the allegiance of these local forces, the Rahmon government invested little in postwar security institutions, leaving them underfunded, untrained, and lacking prestige. Still dependent on the personal loyalty of their former commanders (now government officials), the forces in areas of the drug trade became readily available instruments for elites to control territory, command drug transit routes, and collect rents.

A CONVERGENCE RELATIONSHIP

Throughout the 1990s and into the early 2000s, Tajikistan's captured capacity facilitated the convergence of crime and terrorism. Having been weakened by civil war, staffed by reintegrated former militants, and utilized by opposing political factions to exercise power, the state apparatus quickly became immersed in the drug trade. In particular, key political figures served as the points of convergence, overseeing networks that linked a diverse set of actors that included drug traffickers, criminal groups, remnants of civil war militias with ties to transnational terrorist organizations, and subsets of Tajikistan's security apparatus. Several features of this convergence relationship within the terrorism-trafficking nexus become readily apparent as we investigate developments in Tajikistan.

First, the state's pervasive involvement in the drug trade became the key driver for the convergence of crime and terrorism. Second, the instances of crime-terror convergence, although widespread, were relatively short lived, occurring at certain phases over the 1990s; otherwise the intersection of criminal and terrorist networks in Tajikistan more closely manifested alliance or operational relationships. As this case suggests, actual convergence relationships—in which militants' engagement in criminal activity or alliances with criminal groups lead them to morph into a single entity— are fleeting. As we show through the examples of the Islamic Movement of Uzbekistan (IMU) and Rizvon Sadirov's group, such a relationship was visible at particular moments in the Tajikistan of the late 1990s and early 2000s and lasted only as long as militant and criminal actors had the capacity to subordinate the state apparatus to their ends. Third, convergence relationships are exceedingly rare. There are very few groups in Central Asia, other than the IMU, that can be classified as terrorist groups and that manifest this particular combination of criminal and terrorist features. Fourth, the full absorption of extremist groups into the criminal spheres of key government and security elites (drug trafficking and organized crime) is most likely to occur when those extremists target common enemies, especially those in other countries. Taken together, these features point to the difficulty in establishing and institutionalizing convergence relationships within the trafficking-terrorism nexus, which make them rare, short-lived, and dependent on specific conditions.

The IMU originated from a small group's opposition to the secular government of Uzbekistan in Namangan City in eastern Uzbekistan in 1990.[13] After being driven from Uzbekistan in March 1992, elements of the group, led by former Soviet paratrooper Juma Namangani, established themselves in the Tavildara Valley of Tajikistan and aligned with and fought alongside the UTO for the remainder of the war. The IMU belatedly and reluctantly acceded to the 1997 peace agreement that ended Tajikistan's civil war and spent the following five years oscillating between bases of operations in northern Afghanistan and Tajikistan, which were strengthened by the Uzbek recruits. During this period, the military formations that preceded the IMU continued their involvement in the drug trade, and the organization grew to become extensively involved in the opiate transport business under the leadership of Namangani.[14] By leveraging its involvement in the drug trade, and strategically locating its camps along trafficking routes, the IMU established ties to both the Taliban in Afghanistan and traffickers in Tajikistan (with some, like Ziyoev, holding key positions in the Tajik government). In short, the IMU was well situated to take advantage of its cross-border contacts with Taliban suppliers: its camps and operations were located in the same mountain passes used to transport opiates, and it had good relations with former UTO comrades-in-arms (who were now commanding border posts, police units, and regional governments).[15] While these relationships interweaving criminal and terrorist networks were relatively short lived, they proved useful in organizing the IMU's 1999 and 2000 incursions into Kyrgyzstan.

Although the IMU's 1999 and 2000 attacks in Kyrgyzstan seemed to be designed to sow political instability, this objective was possibly shared by those involved in the drug trade. As one observer noted, drug traffickers benefit when the government's attention is diverted due to unrest, making it relatively easy to operate "outside the law" during a crisis.[16] Namangani's former comrades in Tajikistan's government, many of whom were involved in drug trafficking at the time, moved quickly to assist the IMU (even organizing Namangani and other militants' transportation to Afghanistan).[17] Under Namangani, this faction of the IMU had become habituated to criminal activities and reportedly began pursuing drug trafficking as an end in itself, even as it continued its role as one of the region's transnational terrorist organizations. At the same time, the IMU, with a track record that included participation in Tajikistan's civil conflict (from 1992 to 1997), armed incursions into Kyrgyzstan (1999 and 2000) and the Sarkhan-Darya region of Uzbekistan (2000), and several suicide bombings in Uzbekistan in 2004,[18] was at the center of one of the most sustained episodes of terrorist violence in Central Asia.

In Tajikistan, 44 terrorist incidents registered by the Global Terrorism Database took place between June 1997 (when the peace agreement was signed) and the end of 2001. More than 70 people were killed and over 130 were injured in these terrorist incidents. In comparison, the following decade (2002–2016) saw only 14 terrorist attacks that took lives of 22 people. While the perpetrators of the majority of these attacks are unknown and the IMU did not claim responsibility for any act of terrorism in Tajikistan committed in the aftermath of civil war, much of that violence had to do with the struggle over power-sharing arrangements, in which the IMU played a significant role. The leadership of the IMU and the broader Islamist and secular opposition to the governing regime competed for influence over the illicit economy and for political and moral authority in the territories where they sought to establish control. Some of this violence was committed by former UTO fighters connected to the IMU. The Tajik leadership, fearful of the renewal of fighting on its territory, accommodated many of the IMU's demands. Through former UTO leaders appointed to ministerial posts, the Rahmon government assisted in the transportation of the IMU's detachments into the areas controlled by the Tajik opposition and ensured safe passage of IMU militants (with their families, but also weapons and drugs) through the territory of Tajikistan to Afghanistan.[19] Other terrorist incidents were instigated by exclusion of the former warlords from the new power arrangements. The following example of the Sadirov brothers exemplifies this trend.

Bakhrom and Rizvon Sadirov were regarded to be among the most dangerous men in Tajikistan. Both fought with the Islamist opposition in Tajikistan's civil war but swapped sides following disagreements with the Islamist leadership, purportedly over their gross brutality, among other things. The brothers joined the presidential guard in 1996 but quickly alienated the Tajik government by kidnapping seventeen people, including UN personnel, foreign aid workers, and journalists, in early 1997. The government struck a deal with the warlords but swiftly arrested Bakhrom following the release of hostages. Rizvon, who was sidelined in the peace process by both the government and the opposition, kidnapped French aid workers in November 1997, calling on the government to free his brother. One of the hostages, a French citizen, Karine Mane, was shot when her captors detonated a grenade in an effort to commit suicide, and Rizvon was killed in a shootout with government troops days later. Little is known about the sources of revenue for the Sadirov contingent, but some argue that the gunmen were funded by the Taliban. Similar to the IMU, the Sadirov group

was well situated to benefit from the drug trade. Rizvon's militants operated from bases in northern Afghanistan and maintained cross-border con-
tract with the Taliban. Bakhrom's men were based in the mountain valley
of Garm in eastern Tajikistan, which was zigzagged by trafficking routes.
A refusal to co-opt these maverick warlords into postwar power-sharing
arrangements precipitated a cycle of terrorist violence. Some of the warlords'
supporters (including their two younger brothers) escaped the government's
offensive and continued posing a challenge to peace in the years to come.[20]

The convergence of criminal and terrorist agendas in Tajikistan, however, only lasted while the militant groups operated under the protection
of their political patrons in Afghanistan and Tajikistan. By 2001, the IMU
was driven out of Tajikistan (effectively losing its foothold in the region's
drug trade), and its leader, Namangani, was killed by U.S. forces in Afghanistan. Over the course of the 2000s, moreover, the Rahmon leadership
reasserted control within the government, dismissing many of the unruly
elites who had drawn the state apparatus into their criminal and commercial activities. This removed conditions that would have enabled the crime-
terror convergence to continue. Nor has there been an institutional legacy
of the IMU's particular combination of criminal and terrorist networks. As
we discuss in chapter 4, those who point to the dangers of intersecting organized crime groups, drug trafficking, and extremist groups today in Tajikistan contend that it is primarily an entirely new generation of youth (born
in 1995 or 1996) who are drawn to these activities.[21]

UZBEKISTAN: KEEPING CRIMINAL AND EXTREMIST
NETWORKS APART

Uzbekistan's presidential administration, confronting disturbances in the
late 1980s, invested early on in strengthening its security apparatus, devot-
ing resources to its National Security Service (SNB), police, and the military. Initially, the central government had determined that it needed a well-
trained and well-equipped security apparatus capable of exercising public
control. Over time, however, the leadership under President Islam Karimov
utilized this security apparatus to extend its reach into the regions
and check the growing power of regional elites who controlled important

industries, ran the agricultural sector, and delivered public services to the broader population. In addition, postindependence Uzbekistan inherited an ambition for regional dominance and used its security and military forces to carry out limited interventions in the sovereign affairs of its neighbors.[22] Consequently, Uzbekistan embarked on a state-building trajectory that centered on political control and social stability, underpinned by powerful security services.

At the same time, extensive state intervention in the domestic economy drew on these coercive offices to retain government control. Concessions granted to police, prosecutors, the SNB, and the tax inspectorate, among others—in exchange for their loyalty to Karimov—gave them license to exploit rent-seeking opportunities in these local economies and commodity exports.[23] Using (formal and informal) taxes, customs, and border controls, law enforcement and security offices became deeply involved in the country's lucrative agricultural, industrial, and resource extractive sectors. The government of Uzbekistan, therefore, was able to strike a revenue bargain that minimized security apparatus involvement in drug trafficking, compartmentalized rents from the drug trade, and forged hegemonic capacities that separated and effectively combated trafficking and terrorism.

COMPARTMENTALIZING DRUG RENTS

Uzbekistan's central leadership moved relatively early and aggressively to limit and control the flow of drugs through the country. As one former security official in the region noted, by the mid-1990s, Uzbekistan's leadership had made a political decision to remove the government from the drug trade and remain focused on other areas of the economy. As civil war and low-intensity violence grew on in Tajikistan, and the Taliban government consolidated its control in Afghanistan in the mid-1990s, Uzbekistan's presidential apparatus increasingly viewed drug trafficking as an amplifier of instability, criminality, and (potentially) Islamist insurgency. In particular, it was concerned about the conflict-enabling transborder activities of militant groups in Tajikistan at the time, especially those who later formed the IMU.[24] Although the drug trade had generated substantial (untaxed) income for regime insiders, Uzbekistan's leadership saw that remaining involved in this illicit economy created security risks and undermined their own state apparatus by exposing it to spheres of criminal activity.[25]

Several advantages facilitated Uzbekistan's control over the drug trade across and within its borders. First, it had only a ninety-mile border with Afghanistan, in its southernmost Surkhandarya Province. By the late 1990s, the government had "closed off" the high-risk province, instituting extra security measures at the region's border crossings with Afghanistan (as well as the region's northern border with Kashkadarya Province), appointing a former prosecutor as provincial governor, and requiring special permission to enter the region.[26] Second, the government of Uzbekistan concluded that open borders with its neighbors were a liability for its national security, and it moved swiftly to establish checkpoints and customs controls. By the late 1990s, the government had established restrictive passport controls and cumbersome customs inspections along its borders with Tajikistan and Kyrgyzstan. It expedited the delimitation of shared borders and unilaterally demarcated some contested border passages to legitimize the territorial frameworks of its new border regime. It mined some areas of its border with Kyrgyzstan, erected barbed-wire constructions on parts of the border with Kazakhstan, and decreased the number of border passages.[27]

With these security reforms in place, Uzbekistan moved to control its drug trafficking economy. As can be seen in figure 3.1, opiate seizures were already quite high in the 1990s, reflecting the government's concern with spillover threats from Taliban-controlled Afghanistan. After the arrival of U.S.-led coalition troops in 2001, the regime saw fewer threats emanating from Afghanistan and appeared to slightly loosen its controls over the drug trade. However, Uzbekistan had reclaimed its "leadership" in heroin seizures by 2010. According to the UNODC, Uzbekistan was the only Central Asian country in which heroin seizures increased by 25 percent due, in part, to the strength of its border guards, customs, police, and national security services.[28] There is anecdotal evidence, moreover, that while state authorities have been more lenient toward the smuggling of other goods (agricultural products, livestock, household items, chemicals and fertilizers, etc.), they have been more restrictive toward the smuggling of narcotics.[29] In fact, cross-border drug interdictions are widely publicized in the Uzbek media, feeding into the official narrative that has presented Uzbekistan as a last bastion against drug trafficking flows that its neighbors, Tajikistan in particular, were unable to infiltrate.[30]

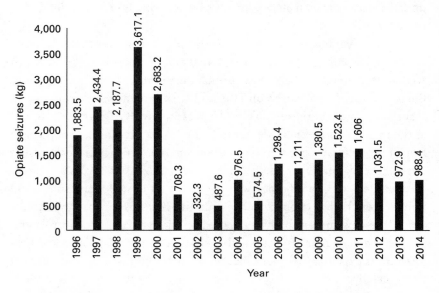

FIGURE 3.1 Opiate seizures (opium and heroin) in Uzbekistan, 1996–2014

Source: UNODC Regional Office for Central Asia, Paris Pact Initiative, *Illicit Drug Trends in Central Asia*, April 2008, https://www.unodc.org/documents/regional/central-asia/Illicit%20 Drug%20Trends_Central%20Asia-final.pdf; Paris Pact Initiative, the Afghan Opiate Trade Project of the United Nations Office on Drugs and Crime (UNODC), and the UNODC Regional Office for Central Asia, Drugs Monitoring Platform, http://drugsmonitoring.unodc-roca.org

In recent years, Uzbekistan has taken further measures to improve its technical capacity to combat drug trafficking by increasing the number of checkpoints equipped with modern technologies and equipment (e.g., mobile scanners). With the SNB taking over the interior forces and thus claiming its dominance over the national police, the Ministry of Internal Affairs (MVD), coordination and information exchange among the various security agencies improved. Uzbekistan has also developed a single database for exchanging information provided through international partnership projects. The National Center for Drug Control provides law enforcement and security personnel with training in informational analysis.[31] This is not to say that Uzbekistan's interdiction capacity has no weakness or that corruption has decreased. Drug trafficking continues to provide illicit income to senior members of the central leadership. However, it is not pervasive across the ruling elite nor has it broadly implicated the security apparatus, which remains enmeshed in rent seeking in other parts of the economy (but not in Central Asia's cross-border opiate trade). This has enabled Uzbekistan to limit the dependence of its security institutions on drug trafficking rents and prepare the way for its development of hegemonic state capacity in dealing with trafficking and terrorism intersections.

HEGEMONIC STATE CAPACITY

Having benefited early on from state investment and access to rent-seeking avenues in much of the formal economy, Uzbekistan's security institutions were well-positioned to entrench their place as a central pillar of state power. At the core of this effort were several initiatives. The first focused on extending a broader mandate to national security organs that focused their surveillance and control functions over many areas of society. The strengthening of security capabilities, particularly those of the SNB and the police, have also been justified as a necessary measure to avoid internal conflict, like the one ravaging Tajikistan, and to counter the purported threats posed by radical Islamic groups (ostensibly with external backing). Much of the central government's control is rooted in the SNB (formerly the KGB), which is embedded in local and regional governments, business, education, and other sectors. State control, of course, is limited, and regional and local governments have some autonomy from security apparatuses when it comes to allowing economic or social activity in their territories. Nonetheless, regional elites still have to negotiate a share of the profitable sectors of the economy under their purview with the security services. The influence of the SNB further grew after the 2005 Andijan uprising, when it won a turf war with the Ministry of Interior Affairs (the police) and further concentrated its power within the national leadership. It was only after 2016, when Shavkat Mirzoyoyev became president, that checks on the power of the SNB began to be imposed.

Following the 1999 incursions by IMU militants into Kyrgyz territory with the stated purpose of infiltrating Uzbekistan, the Karimov leadership decided to expedite an additional area of security: military reform. This centered on the introduction of changes to the management of the army and interagency coordination between the state security structures. The creation of well-equipped and trained mobile military formations deployable to any potential zone of military operations became a chief goal of reforming the army of Uzbekistan. Most of the changes to Uzbekistan's military introduced during the 1990s were brought by external assistance, largely through NATO's Partnership for Peace (PfP) program, which was used to foster the security capacity of former Soviet states and turn them into the reliable Western partners.[32]

U.S. military assistance featured prominently in the creation of a functioning border control system. The Export Control and Related Border Security program, for example, was initially used to train border security and customs personnel and supply the staff and border crossings with the necessary equipment. The U.S. Drug Enforcement Administration offered training in intelligence collection, the use of computerized databases, and basic analytical techniques as part of a broader regional strategy called Operation Containment. The U.S. Department of Defense offered other types of training at the operational and tactical levels to Uzbek security officials, army officers, border guards, and interior troops. The levels of assistance increased in response to Uzbekistan's help with U.S. counterterrorism efforts in the region (particularly in Afghanistan), but its focus shifted to the provision of more equipment.[33]

Although provision of equipment by the United States was interrupted by the curtailment of U.S. security assistance in the wake of the 2005 uprising in Andijan, the more limited counternarcotics training program continued.[34] The U.S.-Uzbekistan military aid relationship resumed in 2007 (while State Department–funded aid to Uzbekistan remained restricted) and intensified with the launch of the Northern Distribution Network into Afghanistan in 2008. In addition to the U.S.-funded programs, Uzbekistan has partnered with the UNODC, the Organization for Security and Cooperation in Europe (OSCE), the Shanghai Cooperation Organization (SCO), the European Commission, and the Russian Federation to improve its intelligence, drug interdiction, and counterterrorism capabilities, including through conducting joint training exercises in antitrafficking and counterterrorism measures.

A third arena of institutional reform entailed focusing law enforcement and security agencies on monitoring local governance and resource extraction within the main areas of the economy. The repercussions of Uzbekistan's weakened state infrastructure began to be felt at the national level, and the central leadership increasingly took steps to prevent its further loss of control over the regions. Made up of twelve provinces, one autonomous republic, and one independent capital city, Uzbekistan confronted long-standing pressures of regionalism.[35] By 1997, the central leadership in Uzbekistan initiated a concerted effort to strengthen state capabilities at local and regional levels. An array of measures was applied, including economic, political, and coercive controls. In principle, these offices were refashioned to serve as an internal check on concentrations of power within the executive branch, particularly against the economic influence of provincial and district governors (*hokims*). A number of laws and internal orders expanded the role of law enforcement in defending property rights (of farmers, entrepreneurs, business enterprises), strengthened top-down controls over local prosecutors (*prokurators*) at the district level, and took aim at economic crimes and political corruption.[36] In practice, these measures enabled law enforcement (police, prosecutors, tax inspectors, and other security organs) to target the legal economies in their jurisdiction. Many in the security apparatus (police, *prokurators*, customs control, SNB) built commercial empires based on their influence in these lucrative rent-seeking activities, including through taxes and customs, and also control over border security.[37]

As a result of the early withdrawal of the state from the drug trade, Uzbekistan's efforts to strengthen its security apparatus (supported by international actors), and its leadership's decision to root rent seeking by security services in the formal economy, Uzbekistan found itself in a position to craft hegemonic state capacity in combatting the intersection of terrorism and trafficking. The efforts of the Uzbek government to fill gaps in security personnel recruitment and training, acquire equipment and technology, and build military infrastructure spilled over into border control measures that resulted, over time, into a heightened capacity to interdict drug traffic and to detect, weed out, and respond to the real and imagined threats of militancy and terrorism.

UZBEKISTAN'S TRAFFICKING-TERRORISM NEXUS: COEXISTENCE BUT NO RELATIONSHIP

As a result of its state-building trajectory, the government of Uzbekistan has been able to keep extremist and criminal networks separate. While these two types of nonstate actors exist in the country, there is little or no relationship between them. Indeed, there have been some criminal and terrorist activities in Uzbekistan, but these have remained largely independent, sporadic attacks. On February 16, 1999, six bombs exploded within an hour and a half of each other in the center of Tashkent City, killing 16 people and injuring more than 120 others. The bombings targeted multiple government buildings, and it is possible that one of them targeted President Karimov (who was due to speak at one of the locations). No organization has claimed responsibility for the bombings, and the nature and motives of the attack remain a topic of speculation. Initially, the government blamed IMU militants for the blasts, and named IMU leaders Tohir Yoldosh and Juma Namangani as the masterminds behind the explosions. Later, the government added the opposition leader Muhammad Solih to the list of the suspects, and used the attacks as a pretext for a clampdown on religious and political dissent.[38] There is no evidence, however, of these attacks being linked to a terrorist-trafficking connection.

A second wave of violence occurred in 2004, first with a series of explosions and shoot-outs that occurred over three days in late March–April. This was followed by three suicide bombings targeting the U.S. and Israeli embassies and the Uzbek prosecutor-general's office, all taking place on the same day in June. According to official accounts, the first spate of violence claimed forty-seven lives, including thirty-three alleged terrorists, ten law enforcement personnel, and four civilians; the summer attacks killed three assailants and four security officials.[39] The government accused Hizb ut-Tahrir and the IMU for the attacks and arrested dozens in connection with the bombings. Responsibility for the explosions was later claimed by the Islamic Jihad Union (IJU), an offshoot of the IMU.

Several aspects of the 2004 bombings make us doubt the existence of connections between these explosions and the drug trade. First, the attackers lacked coordination and training and used primitive explosive devices filled with chemicals widely available in Uzbekistan. While the March–April bombings were preplanned, they were prematurely implemented, with several not taking place at all. Explosive devices used in the June bombings malfunctioned as well. Second, all of the attacks targeted government representatives and security officials. Even the suicide bombings at the Chorsu Bazaar in Tashkent occurred on a Monday, when the bazaar was closed and at a time when the police arrived at the place.[40] The IJU was formed in 2005, months after the 2004 bombings. Even if Hizb ut-Tahrir, a transnational Islamist organization that advocates the reestablishment of an Islamic caliphate (through nonviolent means), inspired the attackers, the group has not been implicated in the drug trade and a great deal of its operational expenses have been funded from abroad.[41]

A more plausible explanation for these attacks is that they were perpetrated by ordinary Uzbeks organized in local semi-autonomous cells of resistance to the increasingly authoritarian regime, and were at best loosely connected to the fledgling remnants of the IMU. According to analysts, the attacks were likely prompted by the growing popular frustration with flagrant corruption, abject poverty, and abuses of individual rights. For instance, some Tashkent residents blamed the government for imposing trade restrictions that stifled economic opportunities as a trigger for the suicide bombing at the Chorsu Bazaar. The majority of vendors at the bazaar operated illegally, unable to sustain legitimate business due to the restrictive trade regulations imposed by the Karimov government in 1999. As a consequence, they were vulnerable to abuses by police and security services.[42]

A third event occurred in May 2009, when a suicide bomber detonated an improvised explosive device that killed a police officer and wounded three civilians. The same day, several assailants fired rocket-propelled grenades and small arms at a police station, killing one police officer and wounding three others. Both attacks took place in the Andijan Province of Uzbekistan and were claimed by the IJU.[43] The Islamic Jihad Group rebranded itself as IJU in 2005, ostensibly to denote its broader operational outreach, closer ties to the Al Qaeda hierarchy, and an increasingly diversified ethnic makeup. Beginning in 2005, the IJU shifted its focus to plotting terrorist attacks in the Afghan-Pakistan region and Western Europe, particularly Germany. Although a substantial number of its members were from Central Asia and the Caucasus, it began attracting a growing following of Turkish and German Muslims. During the late 2000s, non-Uzbek ethnic groups came to dominate both the IJU and IMU. By then, the IMU had completely distanced itself from Uzbekistan and Central Asia and began operating primarily along the Afghanistan-Pakistan border.[44]

Overall, Uzbekistan has experienced little conflict between its political elites (as in Tajikistan) or nonstate criminal violence (as in Kyrgyzstan or Kazakhstan). Instead, Uzbekistan's trajectory, and the separate coexistence of trafficking and terrorism within its borders, have led to sporadic terrorist violence and have enabled state violence to predominate far more than any other forms of organized violence. Indeed, repression is consistently perpetrated by the regime for political purposes against independent opposition figures, civil society groups, and occasional local protests. This heavy use of repression reached a peak May 13–14, 2005, when Uzbekistan's state security forces suppressed an uprising in Andijan City, resulting in the deaths of hundreds—possibly seven hundred—civilians (including many women and children).[45] The crackdown after the uprising spread well beyond Andijan Province, resulting in a wave of arrests, a refugee crisis as protesters fled into neighboring Kyrgyzstan, and a low-intensity regime of repression of human rights defenders, local journalists, independent media outlets (including foreign organizations), civil society activists, and nearly every NGO and international organization office. Its use of repression against society notwithstanding, Uzbekistan's authorities have remained sufficiently strong to suppress most of the activities of the IMU and other potential extremists, and to stamp out other forms of dissent. The government's counterterrorism and antidrug efforts, in short, have succeeded in preventing the emergence of the relationship between drug trafficking and terrorism, and have kept levels of the latter low.

CONCLUSION

Through the examples of Uzbekistan and Tajikistan, this chapter has explored the effects of state-trafficker revenue bargains on the type of trafficking-terrorism nexus that can emerge. It began by emphasizing the broadest contrast between two drug transit states: the withdrawal of one from involvement in the drug trade and the near full immersion of the other. In Uzbekistan, political developments prepared the way for the central leadership to withdraw the state from the drug trade, secure political support by opening rent seeking in other economic sectors, and use its security apparatus to aggressively combat political threats, including terrorism, and their intersections with trafficking in the country. In Tajikistan, civil war forced the Rahmon government to rely on former commanders (progovernment and opposition alike) who had established interests in drug trafficking. This led the country into a period of open access to drug rents as key parts of the governing apparatus—especially its national political offices and security institutions—were subordinated to powerful regional and national elites. These developments enabled the convergence of terrorist, insurgent, and trafficking networks in Tajikistan in the 1990s, combining illicit economic activities with local, regional, and transnational terrorist initiatives.

The nature of the nexus in each case, in turn, strongly influenced the level and nature of terrorist violence. Uzbekistan experienced little nonstate violence (including terrorist attacks), though its state continues to exercise heavy-handed repression. In Tajikistan, the convergence of trafficking, insurgent, and terrorist groups has led to relatively higher levels of terrorist violence, with increases in both the frequency and intensity of attacks. In the majority of instances, these attacks arose directly from local or regional disputes over formal and informal authority, including control over the areas' political economy, but some might be linked to transnational terrorist agendas. Yet they were largely defined by interwoven extremist and criminal groups. In exemplifying the polar opposites of the nexus, therefore, this chapter illustrates the stark differences that state involvement in the drug trade can make in determining a country's state-building trajectory, its type of terrorism-trafficking nexus, and its vulnerability to organized terrorist violence.

4

EMERGING RELATIONSHIPS WITHIN THE NEXUS

Kazakhstan, Kyrgyzstan, and Tajikistan

During the Bakiev era, I had relatives in rural areas who, when they had a problem, would find that the police were not present and they would seek out criminal groups to intervene. . . . Many of us were frightened when we would see a TV advertisement openly stating that this group or that group could collect a debt you need collected or settle a dispute you have— something that many companies, businesses, and everyday people resorted to using when law enforcement, security, and legal institutions were no longer fulfilling this role since they were so corrupt and ineffective.

—NGO ACTIVIST AND POLITICAL ANALYST, BISHKEK, 2016

A lot of us have a real concern about this investment and advancement in security. What's it being used for? It's not for real security . . . it's actually being used by the Rahmon family to control the population and to eliminate internal rivals, yet many of us turn a blind eye.

—INTERNATIONAL NGO STAFF MEMBER, DUSHANBE, 2017

Though a region of infrastructurally weak states, Central Asia contains countries with law enforcement and security capabilities that vary in important ways. As the quotes above suggest, even countries that are otherwise similar, such as Kyrgyzstan and Tajikistan, have developed very different institutional capacities over the past two decades. In one country, despite a record of democratic reform and economic liberalization, law enforcement and other security institutions had become "so corrupt and ineffective" by the mid-2000s that they were even supplanted by criminal groups in certain localities. In the other, by contrast, those same offices received substantial investment and rapidly expanded their capabilities, but these advancements only enabled "the Rahmon family" leadership to consolidate a system of authoritarian rule. As we demonstrate, state security capacities in each country were shaped by their particular involvement in the illicit political economy, and these subtle differences came to have far-reaching consequences for their integration of criminal and militant networks.

This chapter examines the process by which partial state involvement in drug trafficking defines the nature of the trafficking-terrorism nexus and reduces levels of terrorist violence. It does so through a comparison of Kazakhstan, Kyrgyzstan, and Tajikistan (since 2000), three drug transit states in post-Soviet Eurasia whose political leaderships and coercive institutions have become partially engaged in the drug trade (i.e., providing political protection, managing trafficking routes, etc.) and have given rise to distinct forms of the nexus. In the first two states, fragmented control over drug trafficking and diminished state capacities provided opportunities for criminal and extremist actors to exploit spaces of weak governance and establish operational ties between them. In Tajikistan, the regime's deeper involvement in and consolidation of the drug trade has fueled an expanded, predatory state that has inserted itself in the forging of alliance relationships within the trafficking-terrorism nexus. These cases, in short, manifest two types of the nexus—one defined by operational and the other by alliance relationships. In starkly different ways, however, each has served to absorb and moderate terrorist violence.

For many observers, who point to similar historical, political, and economic conditions in Kazakhstan, Kyrgyzstan, and Tajikistan, these distinct paths are unlikely and puzzling. All three countries experienced broadly equivalent post-Soviet developments, such as a weakening of central political authority, ongoing economic problems, and new security challenges.[1] All three have become critical transit points for drug trafficking, organized criminal activity, and (in a few instances) insurgents based in Afghanistan. The past two decades have seen greater interrelations and collusion among organized criminal actors and state officials, producing a "state-crime nexus" that has extended across the region.[2] Similarly, the total volumes of foreign military aid flowing into these countries since the September 11, 2001, attacks are in fact quite comparable.[3] A focus on broad historical trends or international influences, however, misses the subtle, yet important, differences that have defined the trafficking-terrorism nexus emerging in Kazakhstan, Kyrgyzstan, and Tajikistan.

By carefully delineating the divergent paths of these countries, this chapter makes three contributions to our understanding of the intersections of drug trafficking and terrorism. First, it parses out two important causal paths that lead regimes to engage in drug trafficking in different ways. Specifically, it traces how regimes strike particular revenue bargains with drug traffickers, which shape state capacities and result in the rise of operational or alliance relationships within the trafficking-terrorism nexus. In one path, autocratic regimes consolidate their control over drug trafficking rents and become dependent on security apparatuses to deepen and maintain that control. As these regimes invest in their coercive apparatuses, their enhanced capabilities become highly predatory, drawing officials into the drug trade (and related criminal activity), promoting the cooptation of regional elites to shield their activities, and infusing repressive measures with targeted bribery and extortion. Ultimately, the rise of predatory state capacity promotes alliance relationships—durable, multifaceted associations between criminal and militant actors—within the trafficking-terrorism nexus. In another path, where regimes do not control illicit networks and drug trafficking rents, their revenue bargain does not depend on security offices as rent-seeking agents. Consequently, they invest comparatively little in coercive capacity, leading to degraded capabilities that leave security officials ill prepared to confront growing criminal activity, unable to consistently rely on local elites, and ineffectual in their use of state repression. In short, a fragmented drug trade and a state's degraded capacity opens up opportunities for traffickers and militants to appropriate one another's skill sets and resources on a limited, short-term basis—constituting operational relationships within the nexus.

Second, it demonstrates how partial state involvement in drug trafficking can have a dampening effect on terrorist violence, mitigating the frequency and intensity of attacks. As we demonstrate in chapter 3, Central Asia is a region in which trafficking and terrorism spatially and temporally overlap, with drug trafficking activity positively associated with increased frequency and intensity of terrorist violence. Moreover, certain economic, geographic, and demographic factors also account for increased patterns in violent attacks. Taken together, therefore, underlying conditions tend to favor higher levels of organized violence. This chapter elucidates how, even when underlying conditions may favor increased violence, the particular ways in which the state shapes the nexus has a powerful dampening effect and explains why many regions such as Central Asia continue to manifest relatively low levels of terrorist violence.

Third, this chapter's fine-grained analysis provides insight into the broader political economy of security in countries where formal and informal politics blend together in highly complex ways. Regimes in Kazakhstan and Kyrgyzstan command a perennially underfunded and weak security infrastructure that has accumulated a record of sporadic and ineffectual policing and opened a space for criminal and extremist actors to coordinate their activities. By contrast, Tajikistan has experienced a remarkably rapid development of its security apparatus that has enabled the formation of alliance relationships within the nexus. Despite a destructive civil war in the 1990s, Tajikistan's security institutions by the late 2000s came to possess advanced technical resources, employ extensive monitoring and surveillance capabilities, and reach far into society. These improvements, however, remain tethered to deep-seated corruption, predation, and participation in the drug trade. In what follows, we trace out these two causal pathways through the cases of Kazakhstan, Kyrgyzstan, and Tajikistan. In each case, we outline the partial immersion of the state in drug trafficking, the crystallizing of state capacities, and the type of trafficking-terrorism nexus that has emerged. We conclude the chapter with a discussion of how state involvement in the drug trade and this type of nexus have reduced levels of terrorist violence in Central Asia.

DEGRADED CAPACITY AND THE NEXUS IN KYRGYZSTAN

Marked by intra-elite divisions, state paralysis, and twice overwhelmed by elite-led protests (2005 and 2010), Kyrgyzstan has witnessed an intersection of organized criminal organizations, drug trafficking, and limited non-state violence. Having initiated political liberalization in the early 1990s,

Kyrgyzstan's national and regional elites remained influential actors, particularly in the parliament, where they were in frequent contestation with the first Kyrgyz president, Askar Akaev. By the early 2000s, moreover, Kyrgyzstan was suffering from the effects of Akaev's loosening grip on power and a shift from "foreign-aid wealth distribution to rent-seeking behavior."[4] Crime, demonstrations, and the breakdown of public services were increasingly detailed in the press, and growing corruption undermined economic progress as many of the country's political elite became linked to illicit businesses and mafia groups. While the inflow of foreign economic aid was initially diffuse, forcing Akaev to share with other members of the political elite, the gradual concentration of rent seeking under Akaev and his family undermined elite cohesion.[5] As their access to foreign aid diminished, local elites diversified their economic holdings. Many established ties with those in Kyrgyzstan's growing criminal underworld, while members of the latter sought positions in government and parliament (which afforded them prosecutorial immunity).[6] These changes further attenuated local elites' ties to the regime, as they were no longer dependent upon it for rents.

By Akaev's third term in office (from 2000 to 2005), trends of corruption and mismanagement had grown, feeding into a conflict in Aksy District in southern Kyrgyzstan when police opened fire on protesters who were storming several government buildings. Indicative of a now divided elite, the Aksy conflict was a turning point that led to the dissolution of the government in May 2002 and presaged the "Tulip Revolution" that brought Kurmanbek Bakiev to power in 2005.[7] Against this backdrop of a frequent rotation in and out of political positions, Kyrgyzstan has struggled to control its drug trade and advance the capabilities of its coercive institutions.

FRAGMENTED CONTROL OVER THE DRUG TRADE

The government of Kyrgyzstan—despite its long history of anti-drug-trafficking policing—has been unable to consolidate its control over this booming illicit economy. This is indicated by the consistently low levels of opiate seizures since the early 2000s, which have not risen or fallen much over time (see figure 4.1). As far back as the 1980s, Kyrgyzstan had sought to establish interagency relationships to address the multifaceted nature of trafficking, crime, and instability, but these efforts have been plagued by ongoing political change and continued competition (over both credit and rents).[8] As one informant noted, there are periods of time when agencies have a standing arrangement as to how payments are distributed. But after each external reshuffling of elites (i.e., after 2005 or 2010), or when one agency seeks to gain a greater share of the rents, indications of open competition can be seen in the charges of corruption or misuse of office that are brought by one or two agencies against another.[9]

The trafficking of opium and heroin through southern Kyrgyzstan has been fragmented since the early 1990s, when much of it was divided between Uzbek and Tajik criminal groups. Seeking to implement political and economic reform at the time, the government struck a bargain over illicit revenues with traffickers. The latter enjoyed protection from political and law enforcement interference but were excluded from positions within the central government apparatus. Over time, this patron-client relationship

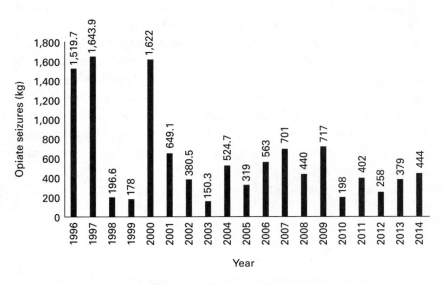

FIGURE 4.1 Opiate seizures (opium and heroin) in Kyrgyzstan, 1996–2014

Source: UNODC Regional Office for Central Asia, Paris Pact Initiative, *Illicit Drug Trends in Central Asia,* April 2008, https://www.unodc.org/documents/regional/central-asia/Illicit%20 Drug%20Trends_Central%20Asia-final.pdf; Paris Pact Initiative, the Afghan Opiate Trade Project of the United Nations Office on Drugs and Crime (UNODC), and the UNODC Regional Office for Central Asia, Drugs Monitoring Platform, http://drugsmonitoring.unodc-roca.org/

became further attenuated as a number of criminal groups who were initially working under "ruling family representatives" linked to President Akaev became more independent of their patrons—a development that further fragmented control over the drug trade. At best, drug trafficking was only partially consolidated under drug baron Bayaman Erkinbaev from the late 1990s until his assassination in September 2005.[10] His death, and the aftermath of the Tulip Revolution, though, opened the door to a return of Tajik and Uzbek groups, as well as different state agencies seeking entry into the drug trade via border control, police, and other points of access.[11] This ensured the continued fragmentation of Kyrgyzstan's drug trade. Between 2005 and 2010 there were reportedly thirty-one different criminal groups (relatively small, between five and fifteen members) in the country, many of which were operating under the patronage and protection of their own regional and local elites. These criminal groups were often able to operate with few checks from Kyrgyzstan's weakened law enforcement authorities.[12] Even though "there was open approval for drug trafficking" at the highest levels of Bakiev's presidential administration at the time, the state's revenue bargain with traffickers continued to exclude them from key posts in government.[13] In contrast to Tajikistan, where having large portions of the state apparatus involved in the drug trade led some to label it a "narco-state," there are only "key persons" within Kyrgyzstan's state—mostly within its law enforcement and security agencies—that provide protection over disparate parts of this economy.[14] Consequently, Bakiev's control over the drug trade in Kyrgyzstan was never consolidated. This trend continued, even when interethnic violence in 2010 in the Osh and Jalal-Abad Provinces enabled Kyrgyz criminal groups to replace their Uzbek and Tajik counterparts in the drug trade.[15]

THE CONTINUING CHALLENGES OF DEGRADED STATE CAPACITY

Kyrgyzstan's central authorities have long struggled to regain control over the country's main law enforcement agencies from regional and institutional (formal and informal) power brokers. The latter's resistance to police reform is understandable: by some accounts, profits from shadow and illicit economies, including gold mining; the ownership of hotels, casinos, restaurants, and gas stations; contraband; prostitution; and drug trafficking, far exceeded state revenues.[16] With very limited influence over the country's fragmented and changing commercial networks, including those transiting opium and heroin through Kyrgyzstan, ruling elites have had little incentive and capacity to develop enforcement and security capabilities that would channel potentially lucrative rents to the central leadership. Akaev, Bakiev, and Kyrgyzstan's current leadership, therefore, have seen little benefit in investing in the state's coercive institutions, which remain chronically underfunded, internally divided, and lacking technical and institutional capabilities. The Drug Control Agency (DCA) in Kyrgyzstan is a case in point. In contrast to its counterpart in Tajikistan, it has long had internal problems and external pressures that undermined its institutional capacity. The DCA was created in 2003, closed in 2009, reopened in 2010, and again disbanded in 2016 after being absorbed by the Ministry of Internal Affairs (MIA). Its seizures were markedly smaller than drug interdictions by the National Security Service and the MIA, and it eventually fell victim to a turf war with the latter.[17] Border and customs agencies remain marginally involved in counternarcotics efforts. Border officers were reportedly instructed not to make drug trafficking a priority (and to focus on espionage instead), while customs agents claimed their primary role was to enforce tariffs on cross-border transited goods.[18]

Moreover, there is also very limited strategic analysis involving the collection and systematic assessment of data on the drug trade and little interest by higher-ups to "modernize" in this regard. This varies from Tajikistan, where there is much greater institutional capacity in strategic analysis (though not necessarily in operations). Compared to Tajikistan's fifty-person strategic analysis unit, Kyrgyzstan has only ten persons (of whom only two individuals actually collect and analyze statistical data).[19] Law enforcement and security agencies continue to use a quota system in terms of arrests, seizures, and operations—as well as reported crimes in a province. As a result, there is a standard practice of having each month's (or year's) quota barely met, which stymies any effort to accurately analyze patterns of crime and security threats.[20]

Security incapacities were particularly acute in Kyrgyzstan's southern regions. There were even brief periods of time after the 2005 and 2010 uprisings when local security apparatuses manifested state failure (i.e., when law enforcement agencies lost their monopoly of violence, enabling criminal groups and drug trafficking networks to fill this void).[21] While these uprisings did not bring about a reorganization of security institutions, which remained intact while ministers or deputy ministers were replaced depending on their political ties,[22] there was a decline in capacity in the regions during President Bakiev's tenure (2005–2010).

Bakiev's regime used many security bodies to intervene in political matters and dismantled those that threatened his ruling circle's concentration of rents. This weakened and politicized security organs and ultimately contributed to many of these offices falling under the influence of criminal leaders and local elites during the 2010 violence.[23] Bakiev replaced all ministers of security institutions with his own close supporters and relatives (including his brother Janysh, who was appointed head of the National Security Service). He dissolved the U.S.-backed Drugs Control Agency (which many believed was getting too close to the regime in its investigations) and established a special unit to protect top government officials. These protected officials acquired greater influence over drug trafficking activities in the country.[24] In December 2009, Bakiev also disbanded the National Guard, Kyrgyzstan's elite military force that had trained with U.S. armed forces and had carried out counterinsurgency and counternarcotics operations. The National Guard was merged with Janysh Bakiev's National Security Service to form a presidential guard known as Arstan ("The Lion").[25] As a result, law enforcement's role at the local level visibly diminished, which empowered criminal groups willing to fill this vacuum. In rural areas where police were not present, people would seek out criminal groups to solve their problems. This became common enough that some groups even advertised on television openly, claiming that they could collect a debt or settle a dispute—something to which many companies and everyday people resorted. It was only when the rising political clout of these groups reached parliament and the presidency that the post-2010 government acted to crack down on them.[26]

A critical turning point in Kyrgyzstan came in April 2010, when a second uprising deposed Bakiev and brought to power an interim government. As an international commission's postviolence assessment report found, Bakiev's departure left a political vacuum that opened up a three-way struggle for power between Bakiev's erstwhile supporters, those who backed the interim government, and members of the Uzbek minority community. Over several days in June 2010, violence between Kyrgyz and Uzbeks led to more than 400 deaths, 100,000 people displaced into Uzbekistan, and widespread property destruction in Osh and Jalal-Abad Provinces. At the center of the 2010 violence were members of Kyrgyzstan's southern elite, who mobilized various ad hoc gangs, militias, and local security personnel in coordinated attacks against (largely unarmed) civilians as they sought to barricade themselves in their neighborhoods.[27] After several days of ethnic violence, the national government reasserted order in southern Kyrgyzstan, but the episode further weakened the country's degraded security capacities and exacerbated interethnic tensions.

Attempts at law enforcement reform after the 2010 violence, for instance, have been undermined by Kyrgyzstan's state incapacities. Efforts to enhance counternarcotics and other policing capabilities across security offices remain poorly coordinated. Although the police and other law enforcement organs have generally remained open to instituting reform in collaboration with civil society groups and international organizations, many of these efforts have not been implemented.[28] International organizations seeking to promote joint or interagency roundtables and trainings have been limited in that these efforts are solely sectoral in nature—focusing on how drug trafficking should be addressed or how to incorporate protections of human rights in prisons.[29] Moreover, each security ministry conducts its own training, and these are generally not coordinated. As a result, there is little information sharing across agencies and no effective top-down mechanism to coordinate them.[30] One attempt at interagency cooperation that has been formed is the Defense Council, which advises the president. As such, its work includes a focus on the intersection of trafficking and other security threats, and there are working groups established for each area or field in which there might be relevant threats.[31] However, the council is mainly a venue for actors to meet and it does not gather or analyze information, nor does it have the capability to implement policies formulated.[32] Major policy formulations must first be approved by Parliament (which has several factions) before being translated into law.[33] Following the 2010 violence, for example, it became evident that a coordinating mechanism would be needed should another mass violence episode or other crisis arise.[34] Several European governments supported establishing a "situation room" that would bring together different agencies during a crisis, but the donors pulled out after it became clear the government was not committed.[35]

Another proposal in the wake of the 2010 violence sought to establish an early warning system should interethnic violence recur. The Agency for Local Government and Ethnic Diversity that emerged worked well with civil society and local community leaders, but most security agencies were not involved, favoring a focus on investigation and prosecution of crimes over conflict prevention.[36]

Insufficiently funded, lacking morale, and plagued by low-level corruption, Kyrgyzstan's security apparatus has been less effective, therefore, in its use of repression, which has tended to target groups with sweeping arrests but few other measures. In the aftermath of the 2010 interethnic violence, some of those in the government sought to penalize members of the Uzbek minority, and there was also pressure from the public on security agencies to be more responsive in order to prevent another clash.[37] The use of sweeps in Uzbek neighborhoods was the primary means by which law enforcement and security agencies identified participants in the June 2010 interethnic violence—an action exacerbated by the ethnic makeup of security offices. There are few Uzbeks in security agencies and police in Osh City, and this does not reflect the 45 percent of the city's population that is Uzbek.[38] Security and law enforcement agencies reportedly target Uzbeks for searches, often using false claims of a search warrant to enter their homes. It is claimed that these policing strategies are carried out in order to preserve security, but they are often a means by which security offices extort payments of bribes.[39] Kyrgyzstan's coercive apparatus has also carried out blanket sweeps in crackdowns on religious activity. According to Ministry of Interior statistics, 1,822 people were arrested or detained for extremist activities in 2012 (of which 70 percent were from southern Kyrgyzstan), with the number of arrests increasing about 10 percent annually for the next two years.[40] These mass arrests, however, have not been accompanied by more focused forms of repression: the government has only occasionally sought to close mosques or religious meetings; there has been little attempt to regulate religious practices; and there is no publicly articulated policy to return to Kyrgyzstan citizens studying religion abroad (other than vague statements of concern by the central leadership). It was not until mid-2016, in a Defense Council session in which the branches of the security services met with senior religious authorities, that the government sought to design a joint initiative to have the state more involved with madrassas and mosques.[41]

KYRGYZSTAN'S TRAFFICKING-TERRORISM NEXUS:
AN OPERATIONAL RELATIONSHIP

Kyrgyzstan's degraded capacity has allowed (and at times enabled) the emergence of operational relationships between criminal and extremist actors. This is partly because the state's limited involvement in the drug trade, coupled with its diminished security capacities, has inadvertently created a space for the intersection of drug trafficking, organized crime, and terrorism. The emerging operational relationships within Kyrgyzstan's trafficking-terrorism nexus have, in turn, shaped the intensity and nature of outbreaks of violence.

In the space opened by Kyrgyzstan's degraded capacity, most nonstate violence has been primarily among criminal elements in society. Kyrgyzstan's law enforcement, citing the seizures of extremist literature during counternarcotics operations, has frequently identified the Islamic Movement of Uzbekistan (IMU) and its various factions as using the opiate trade to finance arms purchases and other operations.[42] However, Kyrgyzstan is far from spawning breeding grounds for extremist recruitment: the appropriation of criminal activities by extremist groups or the shift to political violence by criminal groups has remained rare and sporadic. In fact, while some former criminals may have become ideologically radicalized, the dominant discourse of "criminal-gang-turned-terrorist-cell" greatly exaggerates the extent of drug trafficking–terrorist connections.[43] Indeed, there have been reports of incidents in which criminal organizations' rank-and-file members peel off and attach themselves to influential local religious leaders (at times through their involvement in sports clubs and associations).[44] At the same time, the state's sweeping arrests in some areas have led some to contend that organized crime members may have adopted religious ideologies when they occupy the same prison cell as religious extremists (a relationship that continues after the former are released). Because arrest sweeps tend to pull in large numbers of individuals for trumped up charges, many of those imprisoned are not well known (either as criminals or as religious activists) by the authorities.[45] Instead, much of the radicalization appears to be originating from ineffectual uses of repression, particularly in the country's southern regions.

Since these searches and abuses tend to target ethnic Uzbeks, there has arisen considerable anger and distrust between the latter and these provinces' security and law enforcement offices.[46] Many of those expecting to be targeted (including religious groups that eschew violence but take stricter interpretations of Islam) have been "self-isolating," or going underground, in order to avoid the repressive tactics of state security agencies. This is especially true among the Uzbek minority, many of whom believe that they are targeted due to their ethnicity. This trend has intensified in recent years due to triggering events, such as the February 2015 arrest of the prominent cleric Imam Rashot Kamalov (which generated fear of arrest in other groups) and news from Syria that a suicide bomber had come from Jalal-Abad Province (which led many to fear an intensified crackdown in the region).[47] As a 2016 report by the NGO Search for Common Ground found, the state and the Uzbek minority are increasingly pulled into a cycle of perceived extremism, repression, marginalization, and extremism.[48] The report noted that the NGO's "survey revealed that the marginalized ethnic groups are also subject to radicalization. Those who have become isolated in their communities and not involved in social life and processes are especially vulnerable."[49] While these measures have led religious activists to become further marginalized, creating a number of "pull and push factors that could very quickly lead to violence," very few have taken up violence.[50]

Moreover, the limited involvement of the state in drug trafficking (and its relatively weak capacities) under the conditions of an operational relationship in Kyrgyzstan has tended to reduce levels of terrorist violence. This is because criminal groups, existing either independent of or linked to potential extremist actors, have benefitted much more from the symbiotic relationship with the state than from ties to extremist groups, and they have not acquired dominance over the state's coercive institutions. Although some individual political elites and parts of the coercive apparatus are directly involved in Kyrgyzstan's drug trade, they typically provide patronage and protection for criminal activity in exchange for payments. As a result, criminal organizations—including those with operational linkages to extremists—cannot marshal coercive resources (arms, ammunition, personnel). This has limited terrorist violence in the country to a relatively few, small-scale attacks. Despite the many arrests related to terrorism and religious extremism in Kyrgyzstan, especially in the south of the country (the Osh, Batken, and Jalal-Abad regions), much of the violence has involved criminal groups (settling scores or competing for resources with their rivals), politicians, or individuals spanning the two spheres.

There have been several small incidents alleged to have been carried out by extremist groups in Kyrgyzstan. As noted in chapter 2, however, most of these were either perpetrated by groups coming from outside the country or limited to individual attacks (such as political assassinations) or larger attacks inaccurately attributed to extremist groups. In 1999 and 2000, two separate incidents of hostage takings in rural areas of the country were carried out by IMU incursions from Tajikistan, which the government was poorly equipped to handle.[51] Approximately two to three bombings of police stations and other government buildings were carried out each year over the 2000s, though in most cases these were not claimed by any extremist groups. On November 30, 2010, an explosion took place outside the Bishkek Sports Palace, which was the venue for a trial of those accused of ordering and carrying out violence during the April 2010 anti-Bakiev protests.[52] The explosion at the Sports Palace injured two police officers and did not cause extensive damage to the building. While the government attributed the Sports Palace attack (and an attack on a police station) to a newly created group, Jayash al-Mahdi (JM, Army of the Redeemer), ultimately none of those arrested were convicted.[53] Human rights groups accused the government of using political instability in the country to exert pressure on the Muslim community of Kyrgyzstan, crackdown on dissent, and marginalize and silence political opposition. The majority of those detained on suspicion of membership in the JM were practicing Muslims and activists, whose legal defendants reported torture of their clients and extortion of confessions under duress.[54] In addition, the East Turkistan Liberation Organization was believed to have carried out a bombing at the front gate of the Chinese embassy in Bishkek in August 2016, although the group has not claimed responsibility.[55]

Instead, the majority of violent incidents in Kyrgyzstan have involved attacks targeting politicians (often linked to criminal activities) and law enforcement officials/offices. For example, a series of assassinations of famous Kyrgyz athletes-turned-businessmen-and-policymakers in the 1990s and 2000s were often carried out by criminal groups, including those involved in the drug trade.[56] The athletic criminal community has been an important part of Kyrgyzstan's criminal world.[57] A study carried out by

UNODC researchers found that Kyrgyz athletes—boxers and wrestlers—often provide "the muscle of organized crime," playing a critical role in extortion, fraud, the settlement of gang disputes, and money laundering through the sports foundations.[58] Some of these criminal organizations, especially those operating in the South, specialize in the drug trade. Many others, however, engage in other criminal activities and cross-border smuggling. These criminal groups may broaden their "specialization" whenever a demand for weapons, alcohol, cigarettes, or drugs arises.

This pattern of criminal groups, often with political ties, targeting their rivals and law enforcement officials, has continued in recent years. On July 16, 2015, the Kyrgyz capital of Bishkek saw heavy gunfire and explosions as special operations troops chased alleged members of an ISIS cell preparing for an attack on a mass religious gathering. Two of the alleged "terrorists" rounded up during the special operation turned out to be members of the criminal underworld known to law enforcement agencies for their involvement in robberies, possession of firearms, extortions, and the drug trade.[59] In a similar incident, "terrorists" were purportedly responsible for the murder of a policeman in November 2015 and were also liquidated in a special operation a month later. The alleged perpetrators of the terrorist attack turned out to be hardened criminals convicted for robbery, illegal arms possession, and inciting interethnic and religious hatred.[60] Despite claims of a "wave of terrorism," therefore, several alleged connections between criminals and militants were cases in which the label of "terrorist" was affixed to criminal, if politicized, activity.

Other examples of violence centered around intra-elite competition over political power, control of economic resources, and, in some instances, illicit activities, such as drug trafficking and smuggling in goods. Following Bakiev's ouster in April 2010, massive political unrest exposed a deep rift between the country's northern and southern elites vying for control over Kyrgyzstan and its limited resources. Bakiev's allies in the Osh region were quickly dispossessed of the advantages they had enjoyed under the president. A large and heterogeneous group of Bakiev supporters were reportedly involved in the drug trade, and the fall of their patron opened up competition for control over trafficking rents in the South that at times escalated into violence. Indeed, some of the interethnic clashes that occurred in June 2010 in the streets of Osh and Jalal-Abad were criminally motivated, as Kyrgyz criminal-political groups tried to assume predominance over ethnic Uzbek criminal groups in controlling the drug routes through this part of the country.[61] Overall, though, much of the violence committed during the Bakiev regime and over the course of the current administration has had little or no connection to terrorism, and has been linked to the efforts of criminal and criminal-political organizations to take over the control of criminal networks, including trafficking in drugs.[62]

DEGRADED CAPACITY AND THE NEXUS
IN KAZAKHSTAN

Defined by a territory too expansive to monitor using its underfunded coercive apparatus, Kazakhstan has served as a critical link in the region's drug trade by channeling narcotics from its Central Asian neighbors into Russia. Kazakhstan's role in the drug trade has been decisively shaped by its geographic and demographic landscape. It is the world's ninth-largest country, with a land area of 2.7 million square kilometers (approximately 1 million square miles), yet it also has one of the lowest population densities in the world. Though much of Kazakhstan's population is concentrated in the south of the country in the cities of Almaty, Shymkent, and Taraz, and a number of urban centers (Astana, Pavlodar, Ust-Kamonogorsk, and others), these are separated by long distances. These factors have been complicated by (sub)ethnic and regional identities that have hindered the unification of Kazakhstan.[63] As others have shown elsewhere, expansive and inhospitable terrains pose challenges to states' ability to broadcast their power over their territory.[64] In Kazakhstan, these conditions have become major obstacles to the consolidation of the drug trade (by cartels or the state), and its steppe and prairie landscape is conductive to multiple routes and groups involved in trafficking.[65]

In addition, Kazakhstan is a resource-rich country, which offers far greater opportunities for rent seeking than the drug trade. This has given rise to a revenue bargain rooted in fossil fuels with little incentive to seek out drug trafficking routes (and develop the coercive capacity to respond to the drug trade or attempt to control it). Kazakhstan's Tengiz oil and gas field is the sixth-largest oil field in the world, and its proven gas reserves rank fifteenth in the world.[66] Kazakhstan has an abundance of other mineral resources—copper, iron ore, coal, gold, and bauxite—available for use in domestic production and for export. Kazakhstan's postindependence politics were marred in the competition over control of these lucrative resources and the industries that extracted, processed, or otherwise used them. By the end of the 1990s, Kazakhstan witnessed unprecedented growth in its energy sector, revitalized with help from the Western investors. Kazakhstan's long-standing president, Nursultan Nazarbayev, managed to steer his family members and loyalists into control of the country's strategic industries and resources and extended patronage to other clients to stabilize his rule.[67] Nazarbayev's frequent reshuffling of cadres, likened by journalists to "the movement of pawns on the chessboard" also characterized Kazakhstan's state politics.[68]

Although acutely aware of the threat of drug trafficking to the country and the deleterious impacts of drug consumption on productivity and health, the Nazarbayev administration has not made the reform and modernization of border security, customs, and police a priority. Instead, the country's copious resources were invested in a political project, the creation of the superpresidential party Nur Otan in 2006, which allowed Nazarbayev to fully consolidate the power of the presidential office. Kazakhstan has also sought to bolster its international image by modernizing parts of its military and special operations forces, and creating a peacekeeping brigade. Kazakhstan has the best-paid, best-trained, and best-equipped elite military and special operations formations in the region, yet weak and underfunded border troops and police. As a result, Kazakhstan has a low record of drug seizures, which has opened a space for the emergence of an operational relationship between drug trafficking and terrorism.

FRAGMENTED CONTROL OVER THE DRUG TRADE

Similar to the drug trade in Kyrgyzstan, the opium and heroin trafficking routes through Kazakhstan have been fragmented since the early 1990s. The postindependence period saw a rise in the number of organized criminal groups, and the drug trade continues to be dominated by smaller-size criminal groupings. There have been fewer transnational criminal groups with ties to organized criminal cartels in Russia participating in the transborder drug trade. The majority of these transnational groups specialize in transborder criminal activity, including human trafficking, smuggling counterfeit goods and arms, and stealing vehicles. There are also criminal organizations participating in the functional division of labor along the drug trafficking chain, including transportation between specific parts of the route within the country, wholesale, and distribution, while being only nominally parts of the transnational criminal chains. Individuals independent from organized crime are also frequent participants in the trade and transit of small quantities of drugs. Many of these individual actors come to Kazakhstan from other Central Asian republics or outside the region and engage in a variety of legal commercial activities as a cover-up for the trade in illicit drugs.[69]

Much of the fragmentation in the drug trade has to do with the sheer size of the country's territory, which has hampered state control over this and other illicit economies. In addition, several institutional developments have further undermined state ability to rise to the position of dominance in the drug trafficking business. The first has to do with the frequent reorganizations of Kazakhstan's Border Troops Command. Formed on the basis of the Eastern Border Troops Districts of the former Soviet Union in 1992, Kazakhstan's Border Guards were initially placed under the National Security Committee (KNB), formerly the Kazakhstan Committee for State Security (KGB). However, in 1995, the Border Troops were transformed into an independent agency—the State Committee on the Protection of the Border—only to be moved under the Defense Department's jurisdiction in 1997. In 1999, the overall control of border security was returned to the KNB. The frequent changes affected the discipline, morale, preparedness, and staffing of the Border Troops. This exacerbated corruption at official border crossings, especially in areas of high economic activity like the borderland in the South of Kazakhstan. The border officers in Kazakhstan, Uzbekistan, and Kyrgyzstan have all been known to abuse their authority and receive considerable income from illegal border crossings.[70] The transformations in the Kazakhstan Border Guards also meant changes in oversight that precluded the consolidation of control over transborder illicit activity within any state security agency.

Second, President Nazarbayev carried out frequent reshufflings and purges of personnel in the KNB, as well as other agencies tasked with combating drug trafficking in Kazakhstan, including the Ministry of Internal Affairs (MVD) and the Customs Control Committee (CCC) of the Ministry of Finance. The MVD oversees regional counternarcotics divisions and police involved in the majority of drug interdictions in the territory of Kazakhstan, while the CCC is present on the border along with the Border Troops. The primary goal behind these reshufflings, which affected every level of the state administration—from national to local— was to ensure that the security apparatus remained a stabilizing force for President Nazarbayev, especially during the period of heightened intra-elite competition (1998–2006).[71] Purportedly, Nazarbayev also sought to create a system of "checks and balances" within the security apparatus to thwart the politicization and criminalization of any individual agency. As a result, no security agency was directly empowered to consolidate its control over the illicit transborder activities and markets.

Lastly, political order in Kazakhstan has rested on intra-elite stability, and resource sharing has been central to forestalling the emergence of a disaffected counterelite challenging the political and economic power of the president. Elites in Kazakhstan are diverse and decentralized, and they typically include members of the presidential family, oligarchs, and powerful bureaucrats. Nazarbayev's family in particular has acquired control over Kazakhstan's strategic industries, such as its lucrative oil and gas sector. Oligarchs have made their fortunes in Kazakhstan's mining sector, agribusiness, and the burgeoning banking, finance, and communication institutions. Powerful bureaucrats have enriched themselves by controlling the appointment of cadres and the distribution of state resources to the private sector and regional authorities.[72] Legal profits and rents from these activities surpassed revenue from the drug grade. The state and its elites therefore have little incentive to pursue consolidation of control over the riskier and less profitable business of the drug trade. Instead, to counter the threat posed by oppositional elite, Nazarbayev sought to create a strong and unified political block, the superpresidential party Nur Otan. This propresidential consolidation ensured that Nazarbayev was in a position to shape and control the country's political and economic processes and resources.

THE CONTINUING CHALLENGES OF DEGRADED STATE CAPACITY

Since Nazarbayev's ability to strike a revenue bargain with the state elites did not depend on drug trafficking rents and security offices responsible for collecting them, his regime invested comparatively little in security agencies tasked with combating the drug trade. This, in turn, led to the state having a reduced antidrug capacity, despite the presence of the Nazarbayev government's genuine political will to wipe out drug-related abuses by state authorities.[73] Members of all law enforcement agencies have certainly been implicated in the drug trade, but there has not been the systemic state collusion in drug trafficking that characterizes Tajikistan.

After the dissolution of the Soviet Union, Kazakhstan inherited a large (if antiquated) military technical base, professional cadres, and one of two Soviet border troop–training facilities—the Almaty Border Troops School—that provided the foundation for creating the republic's Border Troops. As discussed above, the Border Troops Command was reorganized multiple times during the 1990s, and these frequent changes undermined the capacity, technical base, and prestige of the Border Troops service. During this period, the Border Troops were headed by representatives of the KNB rather than career border guards. The KNB staff viewed these assignments as temporary appointments necessary for transitioning into higher-level positions. This determined their attitude toward the work with the Border Troops, including their neglect of the needs of the agency in terms of proper training and living conditions for the Border Guards, their material and technical base, and the modernization of sensitive border crossings.

Low wages and poor living standards caused many border guards and mid-range officers to turn to trafficking and other abuses of authority. Hazing and suicides among the conscripts climbed. Having lost the prestige that it had during the Soviet era, the Border Troops Service had a difficult time staffing its mid ranks with professional officers. The majority of ethnic Russian military personnel left the republic by the mid-1990s. Exacerbating the severe shortage of trained military cadres was the lack of higher-level Border Troops training facilities. The Border Troops Academy in Almaty was capable of graduating only a handful of junior officers a year.

The problems with the Border Troops Service appeared publicly in the early 2000s with a series of tragic events, including the killing of fifteen border guards at the Arkankergen border post in the Almaty region, the crash of a military plane that killed leading border guards, and the suicide of the director of the Border Service Academy. The Nazarbayev government immediately responded with a series of legislative and institutional measures that redefined the conditions of recruitment into the Border Service's ranks, delineated the responsibilities of a border protection commission that would act as a consultative body under the Kazakh government, and called for organizing comprehensive exams for the border protection officials currently in service. The latter measure resulted in the departure of more than sixteen thousand police officers considered to be unfit for their demanding duties.[74]

Acknowledging the challenges of safeguarding Kazakhstan's long border, multiple international agencies provided the Kazakh government with support to modernize border equipment and to train and reform border management. The European Union's Border Management Programme in Central Asia and the U.S. Embassy offered Kazakhstan's Border Guards a variety of training programs and a sophisticated technical base for equipping its border posts and crossings.[75] The sustainability of the infrastructure provided by international organizations, especially the training centers, equipment, and technology, has been undermined by the inability of the Kazakh security services tasked with combating drug trafficking to manage it effectively.

The influx of petroleum dollars to Kazakhstan's coffers has allowed the Kazakh government to begin investing more aggressively in modern inspection equipment for its border posts. However, the quality of the equipment has varied, and the human aspect continues to receive insufficient attention.[76] On balance, a bulk of security funding has gone to modernize, train, and equip Kazakhstan's elite special operations formations,[77] including Kazakhstan's National Guard, to restructure and modernize its armed forces, to transform the national system of military education, and to rejuvenate the country's military-science institutions.[78] President Nazarbayev has periodically appeared at the exercises and training of the country's elite special operations and military formations. These agencies' personnel are carefully selected, at times hired on a contractual (rather than conscript) basis, and are routinely trained in the military establishments in the United States, Russia, Germany, and other countries. In 2000, President Nazarbayev announced the creation of Kazakhstan's own peacekeeping battalion (KAZBAT), with the express goal of achieving NATO interoperability.[79] In subsequent years, the government invested in training, exercises, and equipment for KAZBAT to progress swiftly to this goal. Trained with U.S. and NATO assistance programs, KAZBAT received interoperability status with the NATO peacekeeping force in 2008.

Kazakhstan has been the largest recipient of U.S. foreign military assistance in Central Asia, with 3,341 Kazakh officers receiving training through programs such as Foreign Military Education and Training, Foreign Military Financing, Combating Terrorism Fellowship Program, and International Narcotics Control and Law Enforcement, among others, between 1994 and 2015. It has been the most active participant in regional and international security initiatives, taking part in the annual Steppe Eagle exercises with the United States, annual joint military exercises "Rubezh" and counternarcotics operations "Kanal" within the Collective Security Treaty Organization (CSTO) framework (which is discussed in the book's conclusion), and others. This foreign assistance has not, however, trickled down to the rank-and-file members of the Border Troops Service and police. While the special operations troops have become the most combat-ready units of Kazakhstan's Armed Forces, the Border Troops, interior troops, and police continue to lack preparedness for interdicting organized criminals, traffickers, and violent extremists. The CSTO trainings and operations have been heavily staffed and funded by Russia, and, despite their temporary success in drug interdictions or joint exercises, they have not resolved the problems of interagency information sharing and cooperation between border guards, military units, and police in Kazakhstan.

The slow reform of the Kazakh police has also been a factor in the low level of drug interdictions around the country. While police have received better equipment and financing since the 2000s, little has been done to overcome the Soviet legacy of acting as an instrument of state power and the resultant abuse of authority. The existence of patronage networks within the Interior Ministry interested in covering up corruption and illicit activities has been named as a chief factor in the slow pace of police reform. To date, the MVD remains the only state agency spared of a broad overhaul.[80] Despite its international engagement and openness to addressing the drug trade, Kazakhstan's coercive apparatus remains underfunded, lacks interagency coordination, and suffers from limited information sharing, which have undermined its institutional capabilities to address drug trafficking, terrorism, and their intersections.

KAZAKHSTAN'S TRAFFICKING-TERRORISM NEXUS: AN OPERATIONAL RELATIONSHIP

The degraded capacity of Kazakhstan's border troops and police have left security and law enforcement officials ill prepared to confront challenges to the country's stability. For the most part, however, patterns of violence in Kazakhstan have been rooted in tensions arising from the state's resource-based development (particularly in its western provinces). These growing tensions were well illustrated in the police crackdown in Janoazen on miner protests that morphed into riots in December 2011. Yet this particular conflict was part of a series of ongoing labor disputes in the region extending as far back as the late 2000s.[81] Moreover, these socioeconomic tensions are part of a broader trend in Kazakhstan, placing new demands on its security and law enforcement agencies.[82]

In addition, the state has seen sporadic outbreaks of criminal violence, such as conflicts or attacks arising from organized criminal groups and their involvement in the growing drug trade. For instance, the country's first suicide bombing occurred in May 2011, in the western city of Aktobe, which was carried out by a member of an organized criminal group. A target of several investigations, the assailant attacked the regional department of the National Security Committee, killing himself, wounding two bystanders, and damaging the building.

The emerging operational relationship in Kazakhstan's nexus, however, has led to only a handful of cases that fit the narrative of radical groups recruiting members who have criminal pasts and links to the drug trade.[83] In addition, it has generated several attacks by a terrorist group in late 2011. Members tied to a local cell of Jund al-Khalifa (JaK, Army of the Caliphate) carried out two failed bombings on October 31, 2011; a shooting rampage targeting police that ended in a suicide bombing attack (killing eight people including the shooter) in November 2011; and two shootouts in December 2011 between members of the JaK and security forces attempting to arrest them.[84] Independent of the transnational terrorist organization, this local cell, based in an Almaty suburb, carried out a couple of uncoordinated, small-scale attacks before being identified by security agencies. Two additional extremist attacks, in the summer of 2016, do not appear to be linked to transnational terrorist organizations (though they may have been inspired by ISIS). One was carried out by a group that stormed two gun shops and attacked a local National Guard base. After this loosely coordinated attack, members of the group were tracked down and arrested within a week.[85] Yet there remain questions as to whether these attacks were truly driven by extremist motivations. As one report noted, "Several Astana-based diplomats asserted that little about the attacks, or the groups alleged to be behind them, made sense. As a result, they tended to ascribe the incidents to criminal turf wars or localised domestic political spats."[86] As in Kyrgyzstan, therefore, the emerging operational relationship in Kazakhstan has led to attacks linked more to the criminal world than to extremists and has generally dampened terrorist violence.

COERCION, PREDATION, AND THE NEXUS IN TAJIKISTAN IN THE 2000S

By the early 2000s, Tajikistan's formula for postwar political order—ceding control over parts of the state apparatus to commanders-turned-politicians—had given President Emomali Rahmon room to maneuver and consolidate power. Playing powerful political opponents against one another, Rahmon was able to push many of them out of his government while keeping the "power ministries" related to security under the control of his relatives or close associates. This was aided by his large family: approximately 150 close and distant relatives were appointed across various parts of the government.[87] Rahmon secured foreign support through promises that he would ensure domestic stability and provide assistance in Afghanistan (after 2001), and his tightening authoritarian rule was conveniently overlooked. In this context, the country's senior leadership seized opportunities to consolidate their control over the lucrative drug trade and invest in the technical and institutional capabilities of its security apparatus.

CONSOLIDATED CONTROL OVER DRUG TRAFFICKING

In the course of concentrating power, the regime gradually shifted its revenue bargain with traffickers, enabling it to consolidate and exploit its control over the drug trade. As in Kyrgyzstan, the drug trade in Tajikistan in the mid-1990s was somewhat fractured, made up of several competing medium-sized groups that were residual formations of warlord militias from the civil war period. The heads of drug trafficking operations were also former commanders of militias during the civil war—leaders such as Yaqub Salimov and Mirzo Ziyoev.[88] As part of the postconflict power-sharing and reintegration process, these commanders were appointed to senior positions in government, which enabled them to conduct the drug trade from within state structures. This not only allowed these political elites to use their positions to influence countertrafficking efforts, eliminate rivals, and centralize the drug trade; it also enabled President Rahmon to exert control over the drug trade by gradually removing (and at times arresting) those senior officials and replacing them with persons beholden to him.[89]

As indicated in figure 4.2, drug seizure patterns illustrate the state's consolidation of the drug trade. The rise of seizures in the late 1990s and early 2000s occurred as the regime eliminated small-scale, independent traffickers and established control over trafficking routes under its own supporters. It is generally believed that government-connected dealers and sellers are protected, and in return smaller dealers and traffickers are turned over to keep up an image of regular seizures and arrests.[90] Thus, larger organized syndicates remained untouched, allowing the central government to continue to benefit from large profits generated from the drug trade. Once the

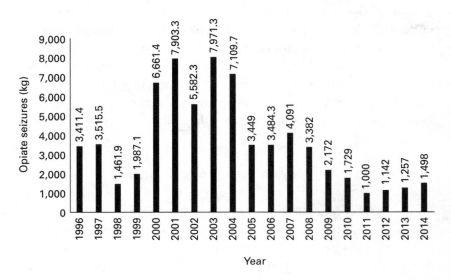

FIGURE 4.2 Opiate seizures (opium and heroin) in Tajikistan, 1996–2014

Source: UNODC Regional Office for Central Asia, Paris Pact Initiative, *Illicit Drug Trends in Central Asia*; Paris Pact Initiative, the Afghan Opiate Trade Project of the United Nations Office on Drugs and Crime (UNODC), and the UNODC Regional Office for Central Asia, Drugs Monitoring Platform

regime consolidated its control by the mid-2000s, the level of seizures declined precipitously. Indeed, most observers attribute this decline to the consolidation of drug trafficking by senior Tajikistan government officials vis-à-vis their opponents.[91]

THE RAPID RISE OF RAHMON'S PREDATORY CAPACITY

Over the past twenty years, Tajikistan's security apparatus has markedly changed, shaped by an increasingly closed political environment in which the authoritarian regime seeks to retain its control over the drug trade. The regime has supported substantial domestic and foreign investment in Tajikistan's security apparatus generally and on its border with Afghanistan. Stark advancements in security capabilities emerged in specific areas, resulting in extensive closed-circuit TV monitoring throughout parts of Dushanbe, forensic resources, border infrastructure, and improved technical capacity of special forces.[92] These increased technical and human capabilities have improved Tajikistan's overall security, providing more professionalized policing, reducing crime rates, and creating a greater sense of security among the public. They have also enabled more extensive monitoring and surveillance of religious activity as well as extensive crackdowns that proponents claim have reduced insurgent/terrorist attacks in the country.[93] In fact, there has been a significant decline in the number of terrorist attacks and episodes of instability. While several prominent attacks occurred in 2010, 2012, and 2014 and were indicative of weak state capacity in certain security areas, such events have decreased and no longer appear to many experts interviewed to be a significant issue.[94]

Building on domestic and international investment in technical resources, training, and the infrastructure of its security apparatus, Tajikistan has witnessed gradual improvement in capacity and coordination among its various agencies. Despite a number of drawbacks, international organization staff have found that capacity building in Tajikistan has been greatly aided by the long-term presence of senior officials, limited elite turnover, and continued support from central leadership. The Security Council and other security ministries are reportedly engaged in more robust and substantive efforts to impose coherence across Tajikistan's security institutions.[95] The government has invested in other specialized areas of its security apparatus. Backed by U.S. financial support, the Drug Control Agency has built up its strategic analysis section, staffed with approximately fifty analysts that collect, analyze, and use statistics on criminal activity and security threats.[96] The government also has designed rapid alert response systems to enhance its emergency response (via the Ministry of Emergency Situations). In addition, the regime has sought to extend the reach of its security apparatus into the Rasht Valley and the Gorno-Badakhshan Autonomous Oblast (GBAO)—two areas of Tajikistan that supported the opposition in the civil war and have since been difficult for the Rahmon government to control. Among other tactics, the regime has drawn on security officials from Hatlon Province when filling security posts in the GBAO's capital city (Khorog) and its outlying villages—a Soviet-era strategy in which the center seeks to more reliably monitor and police potentially independent regions.[97]

This investment in Tajikistan's security capabilities, however, has given rise to increased abuses of authority, widening repression, and more systemic predation. Indeed, many have concluded that these developments have produced tactical and technical skills useful in effecting the state repression necessary for the regime's longevity, while weakening norms of transparency and accountability to the public. After several years of creeping authoritarianism, the discovery of a reputed coup attempt in 2015 led to a significant intensification of repression against political and religious groups. In the wake of the coup attempt, the regime arrested more than 150 members of the country's main opposition party, the Islamic Renaissance Party (IRP), which caused another one thousand IRP activists to flee the country. Members of Group 24, another opposition group living abroad, were targeted with arrests or assassinations (and their families in Tajikistan were harassed as well).[98] Repression against political opponents to the regime has been highly focused on specific individuals and organizations.[99]

Intensified repression of religious activists between 2013 and 2015 led to the closure of 1,032 independent (unregistered) mosques, requiring 2,543 imams and clerics to take "refresher" courses, installation of video cameras in virtually every mosque and madrassa in the country, the return of 3,008 of 3,360 students who were studying abroad (who the regime feared were receiving illegal education), and the detention of hundreds of citizens each year for their supposedly unlawful religious dress and appearance.[100] While more arrests occurred in Sughd Province (which had experienced a hand-ful of localized extremist attacks), they also occurred nationwide.[101] The potential backlash effect of the state's heavy-handedness has led even some security professionals in Tajikistan to question this approach.[102] Govern-ment officials, however, saw little reason to scale back the regime's more tar-geted approach to monitoring and policing religious activists, as there have been numerous cases of its successful prevention of attacks. The only way the regime might change course would be if there were several attacks that clearly demonstrated the negative consequences of the current harsh approach.[103]

Most important, increased capabilities have led to the institutionaliza-tion of systematic predation that has deeply engaged law enforcement and security organs in drug trafficking. While petty corruption by police street patrols had declined, the regime focused its coercive reach on consolidat-ing and extracting drug trafficking rents. By the early 2000s, it was widely believed that drug trafficking was supported and protected by a range of officials, including border officers, customs officials, and those in the DCA and MIA. Advance payments to secure senior government and military (border patrol) positions led officials to engage in the drug trade to recoup costs. As one National Security Service official noted, there are many "hid-den hands" aiding the drug trade that serve as intermediaries enabling for-mer warlords and others in this illegal activity.[104] Technical advancements, moreover, had not led to broad-based anticorruption efforts. And there remained a deficit in the "human resources" of these institutions because the people being trained lacked basic education, which left many agencies vulnerable to absorption into the drug trade.[105]

TAJIKISTAN'S TRAFFICKING-TERRORISM NEXUS: AN EMERGING ALLIANCE

Although it has benefited from increased funding, new technical resources, and advanced training, much of Tajikistan's coercive apparatus has also become immersed in drug trafficking and closely interwoven with the coun-try's corrupt political establishment. These two postwar developments have forged the government's predatory capacity and fostered the rise of a set of alliance relationships between the country's criminal and extremist actors. In contrast to Kazakhstan and Kyrgyzstan, the state's deeper involvement in Tajikistan's drug trade, coupled with its expanded security capacities, has inserted its coercive apparatus into the country's intersection of drug trafficking, organized crime, and regional politics. The emerging alliance relationships within Tajikistan's trafficking-terrorism nexus, in turn, significantly diminished levels of terrorist violence. The deep involvement of state security institutions in these lucrative illicit economies meant conflict tended not to involve disparate groups of criminals or extremists but rather centered around well-connected insider politicians and security officials who commanded territory, arms, and personnel that made them dangerous if they should break from the regime. In fact, a few low-level terrorist attacks notwithstanding, most organized violence has been embedded in struggles among elites and security officials over local resources (including drug trafficking networks), regional power centers, or national governmental posts. While subnational power networks of former militants-turned-state-officials often have residual contacts with extremist groups, the IMU and other transnational terrorist organizations no longer operate in Tajikistan as they had in the 1990s. Instead, most potential homegrown extremists became integrated into these regional networks of drug traffickers, former militants, and government officials.

As a result, terrorist violence in Tajikistan has remained quite low over the past two decades. Only a handful of disconnected, small-scale terrorist attacks have occurred. The first terrorist attack recorded by the Global Terrorism Database during the period examined in this study occurred in April 2009 in Isfara in Sughd Province. Two unidentified assailants fired on a police officer, injuring him. In a similar fashion, three police officers were seriously wounded a year earlier in the city. The authorities blamed the IMU for these attacks and began conducting searches for IMU members in early 2009.[106] In September 2010, another town in Sughd Province, Khujand, just sixty miles away from Isfara, saw a car packed with explosives driving into the building of the organized crime department of the regional police, killing two officers and two civilians, and wounding twenty-eight people. Although the authorities blamed the IMU for the attack, a previously unknown group—Jamaat Ansurallah—later claimed the responsibility for this incident.[107]

These were relatively rare events, which also may reflect local conditions in northern Tajikistan. Isfara City stands out from the rest of Tajikistan for the greater religiosity of its population.[108] A number of Central Asian detainees in the global war on terror hail from this region, and the IRP of Tajikistan enjoyed overwhelming support in this territory.[109]

At the same time, efforts by the Rahmon administration to use combinations of cooptation and coercion against some former opposition politicians and senior officials (nationally and regionally) have generated several prominent episodes of violence. Many of these figures in the Rasht Valley and GBAO were believed to be heavily involved in the drug trade (as well as other industries). It is widely held that these regime insiders mobilized networks of supporters (often former militants) when they were dismissed or preemptively broke from the regime. In fact, collaborations between drug traffickers, criminal groups, and militants that had evolved under the protection and patronage of the dismissed figures devolved into violent confrontations with the regime.[110] These conflicts not only predominated in Tajikistan, they also absorbed most of the nonstate militant activity, thereby minimizing the frequency and intensity of religiously inspired terrorist violence.

Attempts to squeeze former opposition figures out of power began with the 2003 dismissal (and 2005 arrest) of Mahmadruzi Iskandarov (former head of Tajikgaz energy company) and the 2006 dismissal of Mirzo Ziyoev (former minister of emergency situations), who were both implicated in the drug trade and seen as potential threats to Rahmon's leadership. These efforts to incrementally push out opposition elites spurred cycles of violence between forces loyal to the central government and groups backing excluded elites.[111] In May 2009, a government operation against regional leaders in the Tavildara District, triggered by the kidnapping of three soldiers in nearby Darvoz District, led to dozens of arrests and the deaths of Ziyoev and his nephew Nehmat Azizov (a prominent local leader who was head of the Tavildara division of the Ministry of Emergency Situations). When twenty-five of those arrested escaped from one of Tajikistan's maximum-security prisons later that year, and a military convoy was sent in to recapture the escapees, the convoy was ambushed and suffered heavy losses. Among those blamed for the ambush were Alouviddin Davlatov (a deputy police captain in Rasht District) and Abdullo Rahimov (called "Mullo Abdullo"), who had escaped to Afghanistan in 2000 but had returned to Tajikistan in 2009 and was joined by other ex-commanders and fighters who formed his militant unit.[112] Government sources allege that Rahimov left the country and forged ties with the Al Qaeda, Taliban, and IMU networks. However, many experts maintain that he had tenuous connections to these groups and was known primarily for running drug trafficking networks.[113] Rahimov's group, which itself exhibited features of a militant and criminal organization, developed weak alliance relationships with other militant and criminal groups. In 2010 and 2011, large-scale government operations hunted down the escapees, killing Rahimov and Davlatov. Since 2011, after the government established control over the Rasht Valley, this cycle of violence ceased.

Similar events occurred in the GBAO. In July 2012, the chairman of the State Committee for National Security in the GBAO, Abdullo Nazarov, was murdered in a brawl at the Ishkashim border.[114] Tajikistan's authorities accused Tolib Ayombekov, a former warlord and a chief of the Ishkashim border unit, in Nazarov's murder. Ayombekov had a history of criminal activities, including human trafficking, drug smuggling, trading in contraband cigarettes, and other crimes. Dushanbe's special operation forces poured into the area, killing several dozen militants and capturing forty more. Shortly afterward, Ayombekov, who escaped the government's raid, turned himself in.[115] Rather than being part of an insurgency, the incident is emblematic of the struggle between the government and smuggling networks run by former members of the opposition to the regime. During the 2012 military operations that followed the murder of the security chief, Dushanbe's authorities tried, but mostly failed, to unseat several local elites in what has been seen as part of a turf war.

The 2010 violence in the Rasht Valley and the 2012 conflict in the GBAO represent the predominant forms of violence in Tajikistan: the central government's struggle to assert control over regional networks of local politicians, security officials, and former militants that control territory and access to drug trafficking routes. As these networks are challenged, divided, and eliminated by the regime, the groups targeted by the center largely consist of bands of former militants who have been effectively absorbed into these regional structures as part of the postwar reintegration. As a result, these former militants have not been organized into decentralized, nonstate terrorist organizations, but were drawn into this spate of larger-scale regional conflicts that overshadowed the relatively few and local-level episodes of terrorist violence.

CONCLUSION

This chapter has traced out two intermediate paths that several of Central Asia's drug transit states have taken within the terrorism-trafficking nexus. Through the examples of Kazakhstan, Kyrgyzstan, and Tajikistan, it found that autocrats whose revenue bargains exclude drug traffickers from the state apparatus (and diffuse rents from their control) have less incentive to build coercive institutions, creating conditions for operational relationships within the nexus that involve the short-term and sporadic tactical exchange of skills and resources between criminal and terrorist actors. Conversely, autocrats who strike a revenue bargain that concentrates control over the drug trade (and concentrates drug trafficking rents directly to the regime) invest in coercive capacity to maintain control over those rents. This, in turn, lays the foundation for alliance relationships within the nexus that give rise to the creation of more durable and wide-ranging associations between terrorism and crime.

The first path is demonstrated by Kazakhstan and Kyrgyzstan, whose political and economic reforms excluded drug traffickers from top posts in government, leaving its drug trade fragmented. With little incentive to develop its coercive apparatus to access these rents, both regimes have seen their weakened security agencies leave open a space in which criminal violence significantly exceeds attacks by extremists. The second trajectory is illustrated by Tajikistan, whose postconflict power-sharing arrangement initially brought drug barons into the state, but this room to maneuver enabled its new president to consolidate control over drug trafficking wealth and invest in building an empowered coercive apparatus in place of one that had been decimated by civil war. Deeply enmeshed in the narcotics business, however, a predatory apparatus emerged, drawing the state into a web of drug trafficking, organized crime, and regional politics. As Tajikistan shows, this path also diminishes levels of terrorist violence, which is often subsumed under intra-elite disputes, conflicts over territory and resources, and local insurgencies.

Beyond Central Asia, this exposition carries implications for our more fine-grained analysis of the complex intersections that define the terrorism-trafficking nexus. It demonstrates how similar weak states can travel down divergent paths as a consequence of their differential control over the drug trade within their borders. Across many countries, a government's strategy to control or not control the most lucrative areas of its illicit economy strongly shapes the resources and responsibilities it gives to its coercive apparatus. This in turn defines how organized violence emerges in a country—either as criminalized violence opened up in a space or as criminal and extremist violence absorbed into conflicts within the state apparatus (between state officials and regional politicians). These are markedly different outcomes that arise from what appear, but are quite clearly not, similar conditions of state weakness.

This chapter also demonstrates that a state's partial immersion in illicit economic activity—whether its control over that sphere is consolidated or fragmented—has the effect of dampening levels of terrorist violence. A state's partial involvement in illicit economies such as drug trafficking does not promote a proliferation of terrorist attacks, but instead leads to other forms of nonstate violence that sideline or absorb them. Moreover, we believe that the trajectories outlined in this chapter are quite common in weak states around the globe. Therefore, these cases provide a sobering contrast to studies contending that terrorism and trafficking constitute a mutually reinforcing relationship that fosters terrorist attacks.

CONCLUSION

Since the 1980s, the traditional understanding of terrorist and criminal groups has been that they are separate actors with distinct strategies, goals, and organizational structures. It was widely held that, while terrorist groups sought to force political change, organized criminal organizations supported a status quo that favored their illegal profit-making activities. If terrorists' goals were to stage "terror" (i.e., strike fear in the population through indiscriminate attacks on crowded locations), organized criminal groups were said to use more selective targeting and calibrated violence against competitors or uncooperative governments.[1] And if criminal groups built an organizational structure to facilitate access to suppliers, transit routes, and markets, then terrorist groups typically functioned as networks or cells to avoid detection and carry out surprise attacks on political targets.[2] With such differences, terrorist groups and criminal organizations had been deemed mutually exclusive and unlikely to collaborate.[3] These assumptions had shaped states' counterterrorist and counternarcotics responses so that national security and law enforcement agencies combated these two transnational threats separately.[4]

Several important changes in the post–Cold War era have made this thinking obsolete. The end of the Cold War abruptly cut a major source of funding for terrorist groups, namely state sponsorship, compelling them to look for alternative sources of cash to finance their operations. Concurrently, the advent of globalization, particularly the cross-border fluidity of people, information, goods, and services, provided new opportunities for organized criminal groups across the world.[5] Organized criminal activities, in turn, have offered new access points to revenue for those terrorist groups willing to adopt criminal modus operandi or to forge alliances with criminals to further their political agendas. Advances in information and communication technologies and globalized business practices have also transformed the structure of many organized criminal groups, changing them from formal, regional, and hierarchical organizations to informal, decentralized, transborder networks.[6] In light of these developments, the lines between the two traditionally separate phenomena of organized crime and terrorism have begun to blur.

Consequently, the trafficking-terrorism nexus is now widely viewed as a prevalent feature of our interconnected, globalized world. Indeed, individual examples portray this perceived trend as our new reality. In 1993, the Sicilian Mafia carried out a series of terrorist attacks on the government and tourist sites in Italy using cars packed with explosives to openly challenge the political elite for passing anti-Mafia legislation.[7] The Lebanese group Hezbollah initiated an elaborate cross-continental drug-and-weapons-trafficking scheme in the late 2000s involving the Los Zetas Mexican drug cartel during 2005–2007.[8] In 1993, the Medellín cartel in Colombia hired the National Liberation Army of Colombia to plant car bombs on its behalf, while Irish Republican Army operatives reportedly helped the FARC to design gas-cylinder bombs and other urban warfare devices in the early 2000s.[9] Focusing on these individual cases, however, tells us little about how prevalent these complex intersections of criminal and terrorist activities actually are. In fact, questions persist about how and under which conditions the nexus of trafficking and terrorism is more likely to emerge: Why do terrorism, trafficking, and crime intersect in some areas but not in others? What is the nature of trafficking-terrorism connections, and how do they vary across countries? Does the trafficking-terrorism nexus amplify or mitigate the threat of terrorist violence posed by extremist groups and drug trafficking organizations? Answering these questions accurately is important to understanding how states respond to these challenges, and the roles that states and international organizations can play by providing external security sector assistance.

Using cases in Central Asia, this book has sought to address these questions about the trafficking-terrorism nexus. Central Asia is a natural location to explore these security issues. Because of its geographic position between the major narcotics-producing territories (Afghanistan and Pakistan) and the large narcotics markets in Russia and Europe, the five states of Central Asia (Kazakhstan, Kyrgyzstan, Tajikistan, Turkmenistan, and Uzbekistan) serve as one of the world's largest transit areas for drugs. Afghanistan and Pakistan are also home to several homegrown and international terrorist organizations, including the Islamic Movement of Uzbekistan (IMU), Islamic Jihad Union (IJU), and Al Qaeda, some of which have purportedly carried out attacks in Central Asia. This has led many observers to view the region as a hub in which terrorism and drug trafficking intersect. To systematically examine the nexus in Central Asia, we employed a three-staged research design. To determine when and where the nexus was likely to occur, we applied GIS-enabled tools to map terrorist-criminal connections and presented a series of maps visualizing locational patterns of trafficking and terrorism in Central Asia. We then used statistical models to test the impact of a number of geographic and socioeconomic factors on the prevalence of the nexus in some locations, and its absence in others. While this enabled us to better understand where trafficking-terrorism connections were more likely to occur, it was quite clear that the nexus took different forms over time, across the region, and even within individual countries. Therefore, we utilized process tracing in a series of in-depth case studies to define the causal paths through which the state's involvement in the drug trade produced different types of the nexus.

We here summarize the conclusions of this book and endeavor to apply these conclusions more broadly. We proceed in three steps. First, we recap the central findings of our analysis. In doing so, we identify the conditions that make the trafficking-terrorism nexus more likely to occur, explain how the state defines the various forms it assumes, and elaborate on the nature of terrorist violence it produces. Second, we apply the findings of the book to selected cases beyond Central Asia, demonstrating the wider application of our model to countries in southern Europe, South Asia, Latin America, and the Middle East that also manifest forms of the nexus. Finally, this conclusion outlines several policy implications of our analysis for states and international organizations seeking to address the trafficking-terrorism nexus.

THE TRAFFICKING-TERRORISM NEXUS IN CENTRAL ASIA

Through our study of trafficking, terrorism, and their intersections in Central Asia, the book makes several conclusions. First, it finds that terrorism and drug trafficking do not intersect randomly but in patterned ways. Using maps of drug seizures and terrorist activity across the states of Central Asia and statistical analyses, we found that certain geographic, topographic, socioeconomic, and demographic factors make the nexus more likely to emerge in some localities than in others. Proximity to international borders, urban centers, and capitals as well as the presence of dense rail and road infrastructure facilitate drug trafficking and tend to be associated with higher probabilities of the nexus occurring, while difficult mountainous or desert terrain serves as an obstacle to these intersections. Analyses of socioeconomic variables showed that territories where the nexus developed tended to have been beleaguered by inadequate living standards, including poverty, wealth disparity, low income, and a lack in the quality and availability of employment. Demographic factors were mixed, with the nexus emerging in both populous and sparsely populated areas in Central Asia. Our analysis also found an inverse relationship between the nexus and education, affirming other scholarship that argues that disaffected youth who are lacking opportunities for education and self-actualization are more likely to be drawn to crime, trafficking, and militant groups.[10] While it is an oversimplification to identify a particular profile of a locality where the trafficking-terrorism nexus occurs, our analysis suggests that centrally located urban areas with low standards of living and fewer educational opportunities have a greater probability of having the nexus materialize.

While the book finds compelling evidence supporting the presence of a drug trafficking–terrorism nexus in Central Asia, it also cautions that this nexus has not replaced the functioning of criminal organizations driven by the consideration of profit and of violent groups driven by political motives. There is an important variation in the volume, size, and nature of criminal groups' activities across the region, with many specializing in different types of contraband, human trafficking, extortion, and looting of natural resources, and who are unaffiliated with extremist groups of any kind. Some criminal groups, especially in Kyrgyzstan and Kazakhstan, which are characterized by a greater fragmentation of the criminal world, have added drug trafficking to their portfolio of illicit activities when an opportunity to earn profits presented itself. It has also been common for drug trafficking organizations to engage in other types of smuggling and contraband. Therefore, criminal and militant actors operating in Central Asia have not limited their illicit operations to the lucrative business of the drug trade. Yet, in all of the cases considered in the book, drug trafficking was featured as a prominent activity of criminal and extremist organizations.

In fact, a type of intersection that is most common in Central Asia is one where drug trafficking and violent groups do not interact but coexist within the same areas. This suggests that the conditions that give rise to both types of illicit activities are the same. We also urge against hasty conclusions, recognizing several methodological issues embedded in any study of the trafficking-terrorism nexus. For one, crime-related violence has sometimes been mistaken for terrorist activity (and Central Asian governments have deliberately framed violent incidents as terrorist acts), in this way contributing to the overassessment of the gravity of the Islamist threat and the role of international factors in the radicalization of Islam in Central Asia. The amplification of the terrorist threat in the region can be found in early analyses and research on Central Asia that ignored the varied and complex nature of the sources of violence in the region. After a close study of the quantitative and qualitative evidence before us, we find that most of the violent attacks attributed to terrorist groups have been committed by local militant/political and criminal formations, some with tenuous connections to transnational terrorist groups, who are fighting for control over the space in which they operate against the state and among themselves.

Second, the book concludes that, while socioeconomic and geospatial factors do matter, it is the state—specifically its collusion in the drug trade—that fundamentally defines intersections of organized crime, trafficking, and terrorism. To uncouple the integrative impact of the state on the trafficking-terrorism nexus, we proposed a typology of state capacity to prevent and respond to the trafficking-terrorism nexus based on two dimensions: (1) capabilities of state institutions; and (2) willingness to utilize these capabilities. From these two dimensions, we conceptualized four ideal types of state capacity—hegemonic, degraded, predatory, and captured—that provided the basis of our model explaining the nature of trafficking-terrorism connections. There are multiple ways, moreover, in which the state becomes involved in drug trafficking. It provides protection for organized crime and trafficking, which enables the proliferation of illegal funding central to the nexus. In other cases, it uses control over drug trafficking spheres as instruments of cooptation and control of local elites (which fosters fluid relationships of collusion with, disaffection from, and opposition to regimes). It also may foster the rise of violent and predatory law enforcement/security institutions that can dampen terrorist violence in the short term, but strengthen the appeal of radicalization and push certain populations toward extremism in the long run.

By withdrawing the state from the drug trade and investing early in its coercive institutions, Uzbekistan, examined in chapter 3, developed a hegemonic state capacity to deal with the problems of trafficking and terrorism that allowed the state to prevent the emergence of their intersections. On the other hand, Tajikistan of the 1990s, also examined in chapter 3, saw full immersion of the state in the drug trade, which allowed for the integration of various criminal and militant networks into a single entity. The extensive involvement of the state in drug trafficking led to captured state capacity, and the state became the mechanism by which criminal and militant networks became integrated. By the 2000s, the Tajik government managed to consolidate its control over the drug trade but became dependent on its security apparatus to deepen and maintain this influence. As we discuss in chapter 4, Tajikistan has experienced a remarkably rapid development of its security apparatus, assisted by an influx of foreign security aid, but its enhanced capabilities became highly predatory, drawing officials even deeper into the drug trade and other illicit activities. Ultimately, the rise of the predatory state in Tajikistan, accompanied by the cooptation and control of local elites that fostered their collusion with, disaffection from, and opposition to the regime, promoted the development of an alliance relationship within the trafficking-terrorism nexus. In another path exhibited by Kyrgyzstan and Kazakhstan, also examined in chapter 4, the fragmented control over drug trafficking made these regimes less dependent on border patrol officers and police tasked with drug-related interdictions. Consequently, these governments invested comparatively little in their coercive capabilities, leading to a degraded capacity that left security officials ill prepared to confront growing criminal activity, unable to consistently rely on local elites, and ineffectual in their use of state repression. Kyrgyzstan's and Kazakhstan's degraded capacities gave rise to operational relationships between violent and criminal actors within the nexus. In short, the deeper the state collusion in the drug trade is, the more complex a relationship the trafficking-terrorism nexus tends to assume.

A third conclusion of this book is that, in most types of the nexus, the involvement of the state reduced rather than increased levels of terrorist violence. This was true even when underlying conditions in a country favored increased violence. For example, when the state has a predatory capacity characterized by a strong coercive apparatus and state control over the drug trade, it effectively limits the space for independent drug trafficking groups and, therefore, precludes the formation of convergence relationships between traffickers and terrorists. In states with predatory and hegemonic capacity, the strong coercive apparatus is used to suppress violence, dissent, and terrorism, including through the penetration of society by security institutions. Even in states with degraded capacity, criminal groups, which have not gained an upper hand over the coercive institutions of state violence, have a stronger incentive to increase their margin of profits by exploiting the loopholes in the state security infrastructure rather than engage with transnational terrorist groups. Only in the states with captured capacity characterized by extremely weak central rule and the subordination of the coercive apparatus to competing political-criminal interests, does the convergence of these actors translate into higher rates of violence and terrorism.

The book comes to several broader conclusions as well. It finds that terrorists are far from being the biggest fish in drug trafficking ponds. Numerous other actors, including members of the political establishment, play an important role in the drug trade. At times, official charges of the links between drug trafficking and terrorism serve to obscure the role of state actors in allowing organized crime to grow. In fact, in some Central Asian contexts, local authorities have probably reaped greater profit from the drug trade than those identified by regimes as insurgent or terrorist groups. The collusion of the state in illicit economies remains at the core of the region's underdevelopment and internal conflicts. State involvement in the drug trade is also an obstacle to regional cooperation in counternarcotics operations and counterterrorism. The states of Central Asia have never developed a strong regional identity due in part to countervailing claims to territory, religious and cultural heritage, and regional leadership. Their involvement in the drug trade further undermines the trust among these states and discourages them from genuine international cooperation.[11]

Our research also shows that, although drug trafficking facilitates terrorism, the magnitude of the drug trade's impact on the frequency and intensity of terrorist violence is very small compared to other determinants of terrorist activity. Our case studies suggest that this limited effect is because drug trafficking does not constitute the only or even a major source of funding for any terrorist organization. The drug trade more often constitutes an important resource for localized militant movements and insurgent groups motivated by different criminal-political agendas. These motives, which can only be understood in light of the attitudes of these groups to the locality and their relationship with the state and society, determine their choice of tactics. Such tactics rarely involve indiscriminate use of force against large numbers of citizens but involve targeted attacks on representatives of the government.

The available evidence analyzed in this book, then, does not mesh with official explanations. Instead of the existence of extensive networks of terrorist groups linked to global jihadist movements and using drug trafficking to fund their needs, there have been only a small number of local militant movements, radicalized citizens, and disaffected political elites engaged in insurgent violence—and very few of those were connected to transnational terrorist groups. Central Asian state authorities have named these particular areas—such as the Ferghana Valley and eastern Tajikistan—as breeding grounds for extremist recruitment. Since these are the same areas where large volumes of trafficking in drugs have been observed, the IMU and other groups have been identified as using the opiate trade for arms purchases and financing their operations.[12] While such a nexus exists, it varies greatly across Central Asia. More broadly, our book finds that much of Central Asia's internal violence has involved intra-elite struggles or fierce competition among criminal groups resorting to violence to settle scores with their rivals.

THE TERRORISM-TRAFFICKING NEXUS IN COMPARATIVE PERSPECTIVE

Our model characterizes the trafficking-terrorism nexus as a set of complex relationships between criminal and political actors. These relationships not only vary spatially and temporally within a country, but they are fundamentally shaped by the integrative effect of the state. Having explored the empirical implications of this model in Central Asia, we now utilize it to explain the nexus in other parts of the world. Organized by the different types of the nexus, we examine cases in Sri Lanka, Kosovo, and Syria.

SHIFTING BETWEEN OPERATIONAL AND CONVERGENCE RELATIONSHIPS: THE TAMIL TIGERS

The trafficking of heroin into Sri Lanka is a fairly recent phenomenon, originating in the late 1970s, when criminal groups smuggling contraband between India and Sri Lanka began diverging into the drug trafficking business. With the heightened demand for more potent drugs brought by the growing tourism industry, the drug trade soon became lucrative. A number of fishing communities on the western and northern coasts of Sri Lanka took part in the smuggling operations, especially in Northern Province, which left the trafficking business fragmented across several well-established smuggling cartels. Moreover, trafficking of drugs (and arms) hinged on the use of speedboats and other small vessels in order to evade Sri Lanka's coastal surveillance and law enforcement. By the 1980s, the turbulent conditions in the North that engulfed the country in a burgeoning ethnic crisis made it all but impossible for the state to closely monitor the drug trade.[13] While the coercive apparatus of the Sri Lankan government was generally repressive (impacting the Tamil population), it had a degraded capacity to curb the fragmented drug trade. The drug control activities of the government agencies—the National Dangerous Drugs Control Board under the Ministry of Defense, the Police Narcotics Bureau under the Ministry of Interior, and others—were poorly coordinated and further undermined through a system of patronage politics. This, in turn, opened up opportunities for the emergence of an operational relationship between drug trafficking and militancy in the North of the country.

The northern coast of Sri Lanka, especially the town of Velvettiturai, has also been regarded as the cradle of the Liberation Tigers of Tamil Eelam (LTTE), one of the most significant groups among the militant Tamil Tigers. The founders of the LTTE regularly met in this town to develop their political strategy, plan attacks, and mobilize and organized recruits. In the context of Sri Lanka's degraded state capabilities over the 1970s, the LTTE (and other insurgent groups in the area) was quickly drawn into the drug trade. Indeed, a host of factors promoted the development of operational relationships between Tamil militants and traffickers: ongoing competition among more than three dozen Tamil militant groups; their strategic location along drug trafficking and smuggling routes linking Sri Lanka to the "Golden Triangle" hub in Southeast Asia; and strong ties that militant organizations had forged with smugglers, fishermen, and traders in towns like Velvettiturai.[14]

The LTTE continued relying on the drug trade alongside other criminal activities, such as piracy, arms smuggling, and human trafficking, to fund its operations. At the height of its activities, the LTTE became a "state" within the Sri Lankan state with elements of civil administration, courts, police, social services, and banks established in the territory under its control. The LTTE Sea Tigers controlled regional waters, and this enabled the LTTE to smuggle high volumes of contraband, low-technology arms, and heroin. Trafficking in heroin peaked in the late 1990s when Burma (Myanmar), Sri Lanka's southwest neighbor across the Bay of Bengal, became the world's largest source of opium and heroin, accounting for over 90 percent of the entire Golden Triangle opium production. The LTTE had also developed contacts with senior elements in the Burmese military involved in the Golden Triangle heroin trade. The collusion of the Burmese state in drug trafficking contributed to the emergence of a complex political economy where various government-led and antigovernment militant activities became intertwined with the drug trade. Owing to the collusion of LTTE military and political wings in the drug trade and other types of organized crime, the organization had developed a network of relationships with criminal gangs and various Islamist groups in other parts of the world.[15] For more than a decade, therefore, Sri Lanka's degraded coercive capacities sustained a set of alliance relationships linking LTTE to smuggling and drug trafficking.

Sri Lanka manifested convergence relationships in the late 1980s when the breakdown of state authority and the country's descent into full-scale civil war enabled criminal and insurgent groups to subordinate state offices in the North. Much of the worst violence perpetrated by the LTTE took place during this period.[16] With the exception of several major incidents that the LTTE militants carried out outside Tamil-controlled territory, the majority of terrorist attacks took place in Northern Province. Most attacks occurred at the height of the civil war in the late 1980s when the LTTE retaliated against the Sri Lankan government's advances with a campaign of suicide attacks on military, economic, and civilian targets within the government-held areas. This heightened level of terrorist violence is consistent with our hypothesis of captured state capacity, which enabled the LTTE political wing to subordinate coercive offices to criminal and terrorist intersections. This convergence of criminality and organized violence was fleeting, however, and lasted for several years from the late 1980s to the early 1990s. As hostilities diminished and the Sri Lankan state reasserted some limited authority in northern and western regions, degraded state capacity allowed a return to more limited operational ties between traffickers and militants, with considerably fewer terrorist attacks.

AN ALLIANCE RELATIONSHIP IN THE BALKANS

The relationship between the Albanian Mafia and the Kosovo Liberation Army (KLA) during the Kosovo conflict (1999–2000) provides an example of an alliance between criminal and terrorist groups that was centered on heroin smuggling operations.[17] Both the Albanian Mafia and the KLA have been considered "hybrid" groups based on the nature of their activities in the 1990s.[18] The Albanian Mafia gained control over Balkan heroin-trafficking routes following the fall of the Albanian government in 1997. Taking advantage of the political crisis, criminal groups armed themselves and took control of entire cities. Captured by the criminal gangs, the Albanian state became a main drug outpost and a place mired in violence as criminal groups fought among themselves and with what was left of the government.

The KLA was established around the same time, with the goal of seeking Kosovo's independence from Serbia. Before Yugoslavia's descent into war, heroin was funneled from Turkey via Serbia, Croatia, and Slovenia to Western Europe. Yugoslavia's turbulent fragmentation shut down that traditional Balkan route toward Albania but left a network of ethnic criminal groups who had been long-standing participants in drug trafficking operations. What followed was the establishment of smoothly operating "drugs-for-arms" arrangements between the KLA and Albanian groups smuggling heroin.[19] While former Yugoslavian president Slobodan Milošević publicly criticized Kosovan and Albanian mafias as the key conduits of narcotics to European drug markets, investigations conducted by Serbian police into the Milošević regime concluded that senior government figures were also implicated in the drug trade.[20]

Since the days of the federal republic of Yugoslavia, the ethnic mafias controlled much of the illicit market in the Balkans. While the broader criminal milieu in the region was more fragmented, ethnic-based criminal groups had a near monopoly on illicit business and the drug trade within the boundaries of their respective provinces and later independent states. The consolidation of the ethnic mafias' control over the drug trade would not have been possible without state collusion in the trafficking business. Political authorities in Slovenia, Serbia, and Kosovo traded political patronage of the criminal groups in exchange for rents from the drug trade. The Serbian government, while colluding in the drug trade, also had the strongest security and military apparatus in the former federal republic of Yugoslavia. Its military and security forces committed egregious crimes against ethnic minorities. Yet top military and security brass have been tied to the Balkan drug trade that fostered alliances between drug traffickers and terrorists. Serbia, however, saw very little terrorist violence during the Yugoslav wars, including the Kosovo conflict. Most of the violent attacks perpetrated on Kosovo's territory targeted law enforcement institutions and were marked by a low rate of civilian casualties. This, too, supports the integrative role of the state colluding in the drug trade in both facilitating alliances between criminals and insurgents and reducing levels of terrorist violence.

After the fall of Yugoslavia, former rebels and criminals who had frequently changed roles and formed intricate webs of alliances during the Balkan wars maintained connections to the new governments. Some of the former republics of Yugoslavia, including Serbia and Kosovo, have retained varied degrees of state involvement in the drug trade, impacting the relationship between militant, terrorist, and criminal organizations. Kosovo's former prime minister, and current foreign minister and parliament deputy—Hashim Thaçi—and his underlings have long been engaged in drug smuggling. Pervasive corruption and organized crime activities in Kosovo, including the drug trade, have led to the emergence of complex networks of connections between criminal elements in Kosovo, Serbia, Montenegro, Macedonia, Turkey, Albania, and other countries with local militant groups and international jihadist organizations.

There are numerous reports suggesting that militants linked to Al Qaeda established connections with Bosnian criminal organizations to establish a route for trafficking Afghan heroin into Europe. Radicalization of Kosovo Muslims has become a growing problem for Kosovar and European authorities. Kosovo has produced the highest number of foreign fighters per capita among European countries. As scores of radicalized Kosovars have left the country for the Middle East, radical elements have infiltrated its underworld. Cooperation between ethnic Albanian drug cartels and ISIS remains a concern. Lavdrim Muhaxheri, a notorious ISIS member from Kosovo, served for many years as the link between Albanian drug trafficking operations and ISIS recruitment.[21] This marks "an increasingly violent and religiously-oriented drug-smuggling outfit in the region, with ties to the Italian and other mafias."[22]

NO RELATIONSHIP WITHIN THE NEXUS: STATE POWER IN HAFIZ AL-ASSAD'S SYRIA

Having come to power through a coup in 1970, Hafiz al-Assad pursued a state-building trajectory that incorporated the geographic and ethnic periphery into its security apparatus. Syria's top military council shifted from being dominated by Sunni Arabs in the years after independence to a broader representation of Alawite, Ismaili, Druze, and Sunni Arabs under Assad's leadership (1970–2000).[23] At the same time, Assad enhanced the resources and technical capabilities of Syria's security apparatus. The number of people working in security and army institutions grew to make up nearly half (roughly 43 percent) of Syria's total public-sector employment.[24] Most of the organs within the Ministry of Defense, moreover, worked closely with the Baath Party to exercise local surveillance through regional branches and a central branch in Damascus. The security apparatus under Assad was also given access to lucrative rent-seeking opportunities within Syria's state-dominated economy and in its control over economic assets in Lebanon. The Ministry of Defense, for instance, owned two of the country's largest companies, Military Construction Establishment and Military

Housing Establishment, employing nearly 10 percent of the country's population.[25] The army also received cushy benefits, such as access to cheap imported goods, interest-free loans to buy real estate, high salaries, and generous benefits.[26] Syrian intervention in the Lebanese civil war in 1976, moreover, opened up new rent-seeking opportunities within its security institutions.[27] Large, well-funded, and integrated deeply into rent-seeking opportunities in the country's main economic sectors, Syrian security institutions saw little incentive for getting involved in drug trafficking or other transnational illicit economic activities. With its technical capabilities and institutional reach greatly enhanced by government support, and its loyalty to the regime shored up through domestic rent seeking, Syria exemplified hegemonic state capacity that enabled it to effectively separate and counter potential intersections of terrorist and criminal networks.

Like Uzbekistan, the Syrian state was involved in the drug trade, but had compartmentalized drug rents so that its security apparatus was not dependent on that income. A large opiate trade did involve the Syrian military but it was almost entirely located in Syria-occupied Lebanon (from the late 1980s into the 1990s) and therefore did not permeate into the armed forces and political leadership. While lucrative, moreover, it was a fraction of the rents the military and security services accessed from the rest of Syria's economy.[28] Although involved in an extensive drug trade, therefore, the Syrian government and its security services were by no means dependent on it. Moreover, there are very few ties linking this industry to nonstate terrorist networks, since it is controlled and monitored by an effective security apparatus. In fact, in the twenty years between the end of the Cold War and the onset of the 2011 Arab Spring protests, Syria had seen only seven terrorist attacks (of which two were significant in scale and intensity). Moreover, virtually none of the attacks targeted the Syrian state or its offices: three were small-scale attacks targeting diplomatic offices (U.S. Embassy, UN personnel, etc.); one ostensibly targeted the Kurdish Workers' Party (PKK) leader Abdullah Ocalan in a failed assassination attempt; one targeted Syrian Air Force facilities (reportedly carried out by the PKK); one targeted a passenger bus (killing fifteen people); and one targeted civilians in a residential neighborhood near a Shia shrine (killing eighteen people).[29] There were no terrorist-trafficking connections in these cases, which demonstrates how the Syrian security apparatus, rooted in rent seeking in the main economy, effectively separated and combated intersections between extremist and criminal worlds.

POLICY IMPLICATIONS OF THE NEXUS

Our analysis also has potentially important implications for policy, especially the provision of security sector assistance (SSA) to address the trafficking-terrorism nexus. From 2001 through 2016, the U.S. government spent $1.9 billion in security assistance to Central Asia. Spread across various programs, this aid was designed to increase professionalism of the Central Asian ground troops, focusing on training and equipping Central Asian security personnel for counterterrorism and counternarcotics operations. All Central Asian states have seen some improvement in their internal security forces as a result of American (and other countries') security aid. External security assistance has not yielded immediate results in combating the nexus, however, in part because it has frequently unintentionally facilitated opium trafficking from Afghanistan and reinforced authoritarian tendencies on the rise across the region.

While the U.S. government has sought to reduce the misuse of security equipment and training that it has transferred to Central Asia, it has not been able to ensure that government authorities in the region deploy security aid for its intended use. This has had direct implications for the trafficking-terrorism nexus in each recipient country. Major crossings between Tajikistan and Afghanistan have had border posts constructed, staffed, and equipped, but they have done little to rein in the drug trade.[30] The U.S.-funded "Friendship Bridge" between Uzbekistan and Afghanistan, for instance, was equipped with drive-through scanners and modern customs offices at both ends. Yet large volumes of opiates continue to transit the bridge via trucks and railroad cars.[31] While the defection of Tajikistan's Lieutenant-Colonel Gulmurod Khalimov (who benefited from five U.S.-funded training courses) to ISIS garnered attention, the failure of external counternarcotics aid to prevent the region's security agencies from colluding in the drug trade is just as damaging. Security assistance benefiting political regimes has strengthened the coercive capabilities of authoritarian regimes in four of the five Central Asian republics. As has been widely recognized, building state capacity without requiring accountability, transparency, and anticorruption programs can result in security assistance being redirected to enhancing repression, sidelining rivals, and concentrating illicit rents. In Central Asia, sizable investments in training for counterterrorism operations have played into governments' narratives about the risks of terrorism, which are used to justify regimes' human rights abuses, lackluster political and economic reform, and weak investment in depleted public services.

The challenges of crafting SSA to address trafficking and terrorism intersections, however, can be partially met by tailoring assistance to the type of nexus that emerges in each case. In countries with predatory capacity, enhanced security can bring significant advances to addressing the nexus in the short term, but specific risk factors—eroded governance and accountability, arms/weapon diffusion, widespread abuses of authority, and moral hazard problems—pose important long-term vulnerabilities to the trafficking-terrorism nexus. In the short term, enhanced technical resources and training certainly aid a regime in addressing particular areas of the trafficking-terrorism nexus: professionalized policing can reduce crime, advanced surveillance tracks religious activity, and technical capabilities can thwart insurgent/terrorist attacks. Such improvements extend the center's control across its territory and may reduce regional tensions if different groups in society are absorbed within security institutions. Several risks, however, threaten to undermine predatory states over the long run. First, enhanced security sector capabilities appear to significantly undermine governance by reinforcing a regime's dependence on elite military units under presidential control (i.e., "praetorian guards"), increasing rent-seeking behavior within law enforcement, and fostering a general lack of accountability to the public. This applies to states with hegemonic capacity, like Uzbekistan, as well. Although it has withdrawn from the drug trade, Uzbekistan's security apparatus partakes in rent-seeking behavior in the various sectors of the country's economy. These emerging trends have made it more difficult for the regime to engage the public, especially religious or ethnic communities that have been targeted by repression in the past. Likewise, defection from and clashes within security institutions—including defection to insurgent or extremist organizations—are an ongoing concern.

Moreover, deep fissures within security institutions can be spurred by corruption and conflict over control of illicit economies (such as drug trafficking), which substantially and directly affects a country's security capacity to deal with the nexus. Enhanced security may also lead to a number of abuses of authority, including unlawful applications of forced extortion, and targeting of religious or ethnic groups. This poses a prevalent risk to addressing the nexus, as it potentially drives those estranged by the state into criminal activity (especially drug trafficking) or toward religious communities professing extreme views. Lastly, moral hazard problems—in which security actors forgo actions against particular threats in order to encourage continued investment in their agencies—are a concern given security offices' simultaneous dependence on profits from drug trafficking and external security sector assistance (which is often specifically designed to combat this problem). As the case of Tajikistan suggests, external SSA from states and international organizations alike should: (1) continue to provide technical support for developing a security infrastructure but make institutional support (training, increased staff pay, anticorruption efforts) even across agencies; (2) make all current and future support contingent on measures that eliminate abuses of authority, diminish predatory rent-seeking behavior, and end violations of civil and religious rights; and (3) develop independent means of assessing security agencies' activities to deter moral hazard problems.

In countries with degraded state capacity, inroads into addressing intersections of criminal and extremist groups over the long term are possible, yet these countries confront short-term vulnerabilities to the nexus. These states possess potential for improving their long-term capacity to address the nexus for several reasons. First, investing in security sector capabilities is less likely to undermine governance through dependence on "praetorian guards," increasing predatory behavior, and fostering a lack of accountability. These countries, particularly if they have pursued democratic reforms, are better poised to enact tighter security measures with less risk of extensive corruption or abuses of authority. Several short-term risks, however, exist. First, enhanced security has inadvertently exacerbated regional and ethnic tensions in divided societies with weakened state apparatuses that are ill prepared to integrate claims from competing groups. In such contexts, enhancing security capabilities may promote one group at the expense of another and generate rumors, misconceptions, and conspiracies that feed internal tensions. As Kyrgyzstan demonstrates, ethnic tensions, weak coercive apparatuses, and a criminalization of the state can interact to cause unexpected diffusions of arms, persons, and expertise to nonstate actors (through corruption, illicit sales of arms, and defections) and inadvertently lead to increased criminal violence that may exacerbate elements of the trafficking-terrorism nexus. Accordingly, external SSA from states and international organizations alike should: (1) incrementally increase technical and institutional support for developing security infrastructure; (2) make that support contingent on measures that reduce regional or ethnic tensions (i.e., incorporate groups into local security and government offices proportional to their size in the population, end abuses targeting minorities, and focus on drug trafficking hubs); and (3) remain vigilant of emerging moral hazard problems.

In countries with hegemonic state capacity, short-term gains in preventing intersections of criminal and extremist groups hold particular promise in addressing the trafficking-terrorism nexus. In building coercive institutions, these countries may also absorb regional and ethnic divisions, reduce levels of criminality in society, and counteract the diffusion of arms, persons, and expertise to nonstate actors. Much like countries with predatory state capacity, however, advancing security sector capabilities threatens to undermine governance over the long term by creating unaccountable elite military units that protect the interests of a ruler, by increasing predatory behavior and entrenched rent seeking, by fostering a culture of limited accountability to the public, and by promoting state violence. As Uzbekistan demonstrates, inherent in hegemonic state capacity is a powerful security apparatus removed from illicit economies, yet this is often achieved by entrenching security institutions in rent-seeking relationships in other economic sectors. A central challenge for those providing SSA is to support short-term accomplishments in addressing the trafficking-terrorism nexus while simultaneously advocating for substantive institutional checks on the executive, for an independent media presence, and for a robust civil society. Accordingly, many of the policy recommendations for external SSA mirror those for states with predatory capacity: (1) aid should provide technical and institutional support for maintaining the security apparatus; (2) support should be contingent on measures that institutionalize checks on the independent use of state violence; and (3) support should be wary of potential moral hazard problems.

Finally, in countries with captured state capacity, where a convergence of criminal and terrorist groups emerges, short-term demands on regimes to ensure political order predominate over long-term goals. With state offices subordinated to local powerbrokers enmeshed in illicit economies, these countries have high levels of criminal and terrorist violence, regular outflows of arms and persons to nonstate actors, and ongoing threats to political stability. As Tajikistan's experience suggests, strong incentives push rulers to assert control over unruly elites and shore up their regimes by using their security apparatuses to consolidate their control over the country's illicit economy. A central objective of SSA, therefore, is to couple technical and institutional support to security offices with economic and political incentives that remove them from illicit economic activities. At the same time, this will likely raise the long-term challenge of inculcating the recipient country's dependence on foreign security assistance.

Our analysis of Central Asia also finds commonalities across the cases that suggest two broad lessons. First, the complicity of the state in illicit economic activity and the framing of security threats for political purposes strongly suggests that donor governments can do better in developing their own indicators of threat assessment and security aid performance instead of relying on the claims and evidence provided by the recipients of the security aid. All Central Asian governments have arguably overstated the threat of extremism and terrorism in the region, and the heightened levels of the counterterrorism and counterdrug aid feed into and reinforce a securitization narrative long employed by Central Asian governments in pursuit of their particularistic agendas. Second, our book suggests a more finely tuned approach to providing security assistance to the region so that donor governments can carefully calibrate their use of security aid to Central Asian governments. Instead of the quid pro quo "aid for access" approach used since 2001, we recommend that countries such as the United States, China, and Russia use security assistance strategically, which entails transcending their immediate interests in geopolitical influence and status concerns. Instead, foreign donors should consider the sources of regional instability in the long term, the underlying conditions in each country, and how each country's government is involved in illicit economic activity. This approach not only benefits the region but also better situates foreign governments as they confront new and persistent security challenges in Central Asia.

At the international level, two regional organizations—the Collective Security Treaty Organization (CSTO) and Shanghai Cooperation Organization (SCO)—have identified links between terrorism and transnational crime as an issue of primary concern. With its origin in the 1992 Collective Security Treaty, the CSTO was established in 2002 under the framework of the Commonwealth of Independent States (CIS) to serve as a mutual defense alliance among Russia, Armenia, Belarus, and the four Central

Asian states (except Turkmenistan). Kyrgyzstan is home to a permanent military base of the CSTO's Collective Rapid Deployment Force (CRDF), designed to support "collective security" in the region. Another CRDF division is staged at the 201st Military Base in Tajikistan. The SCO evolved from the "Shanghai Five," a forum of Russia, Kazakhstan, Tajikistan, Kyrgyzstan, and China established in 1996 to discuss security and confidence-building measures. With the incorporation of Uzbekistan, the regular meetings of the "Shanghai Five" grew into the present-day SCO. By 2002, the organization expanded its objectives to the fight against the "three evils" of terrorism, Islamism, and separatism to assuage the security concerns of its founding members. The SCO's Regional Anti-Terrorism Structure (RATS) was established in Tashkent in 2004. Conjoint antiterrorist operations, military exercises, and security drills held under the auspices of the SCO and CSTO have become a regular feature of Russia–Central Asia security cooperation.[32]

A number of declarations adopted by the CSTO and SCO in recent years acknowledge the importance of disrupting funding sources in the fight against terrorism. However, the SCO's efforts at counteracting the trafficking-terrorism nexus have focused on providing political support for member states' counterterrorism measures and drafting programmatic documents that express the need to coordinate their military and political steps. The CSTO, on the other hand, has set up a multilevel system of collective responses to address threats posed by the nexus. The CRDF, created in 2009 to counter external aggression, terrorist attacks, and drug trafficking operations within the territory of member states, has staged regular joint combat exercises and special operations and has provided tactical training. In the area of antidrug trafficking, the CSTO has implemented an annual international counternarcotics operation, "Kanal" (Channel), involving drug control, security, and internal affairs agencies; border and customs services; and units of CSTO financial intelligence services. The SCO's RATS has also staged joint counterterrorism maneuvers but has been less active in organizing member states' operations aimed at disrupting terrorism financing and money laundering. Importantly, the CSTO's and SCO's conventional war games, counterterrorism, and antinarcotics exercises are each organized separately, reflecting a dominant position within these organizations treating terrorism, insurgency, and organized crime as discrete, rather than deeply intertwined.

Still, both CSTO and SCO are currently lacking the sustainable capacity to provide an effective collective response to regional security challenges. From an operational standpoint, their military and security personnel have insufficient experience of interagency cooperation and training to differentiate traffickers' operations from Islamists' maneuvers. Their operational capacity to address complex emergencies, such as those unfolding in Afghanistan's northern regions, is limited by a shortage of military and security resources in these regional organizations. Instead, Russia's forces dominate the CSTO's training and special operations. The Kremlin's military and technological advancements in recent years have widened the gap between it and other CSTO member states' security forces. This means that Moscow will be called on to do more to address the nexus in the region. Indeed, through collective exercises and military aid, Moscow has sought to convince the regional capitals that Russia is the only guarantor of stability and security in Central Asia. The Kremlin's ability to successfully deliver on this promise in the future is in question, as Russia's economy entered a stagnation period following the 2014 economic crisis brought about by plummeting crude oil prices and Western economic sanctions.

The absence of Uzbekistan and Turkmenistan in the CSTO leaves another major crack in the regional security architecture, and their unwillingness to deepen bilateral security cooperation with Russia is emblematic of diverging interests and deep distrust between the member states of the CSTO and SCO. Fearing Russia's military presence and China's growing economic influence, the leaderships of Central Asian republics have been wary of committing to these regional arrangements. They have also repeatedly altered the official narrative about the nature and extent of national security threats.[33] Tajikistan, for example, has sought to cast itself as the frontline against the spillover of Afghanistan's insurgency and has employed this narrative to secure international military aid. On the other hand, the Tajik government has occasionally dismissed the threat of Islamist violence and insisted that its security forces are prepared to counter any security threat. Similar to Tajikistan, Kyrgyzstan has used its membership in regional organizations to gain access to modern security equipment and training and buy diplomatic leverage with the United States. For Kazakhstan, CSTO and SCO membership has been integral to its multivector foreign policy and external image building. These relationships between states complicate political willingness to address the nexus collaboratively. For all these reasons, the CSTO and SCO leadership has tended to overlook the important domestic undercurrents conducive to the rise of the nexus in Central Asia.

———— ∞ ————

This book has investigated the trafficking-terrorism nexus in Central Asia and the particular forms it assumes in each country. As emphasized in the preceding pages, the type of nexus varies widely, depending on the nature of state involvement in a country's illicit economy. Having used the Central Asia cases to outline four types of the nexus—coexistence, operational, alliance, and convergence—the book has specified many of the relationships between criminal and terrorist networks that underpin it. This chapter, after summarizing these four outcomes, has explored the comparative scope of our argument to countries in other parts of the world. Through the illustrative cases of Syria, Sri Lanka, and Kosovo, it demonstrated the model's applicability beyond Central Asia.

Our empirical findings and conclusions also have relevance for those in positions to address the various manifestations of the nexus. Specific policy implications, we contend, must relate to the individual types of the trafficking-terrorism nexus, so that security sector assistance from governments and international organizations can be shaped (with important conditions attached to that aid) to best fit the circumstances of each country. Perhaps the most significant conclusion of the book, however, is a general one: that trafficking-terrorism connections rarely increase or intensify terrorist attacks. In fact, the relationships we unpack within the nexus are far more likely to diminish terrorist violence, even as they permit other forms of nonstate violence.

APPENDIX 1

SOCIOECONOMIC PREDICTORS OF
THE TRAFFICKING-TERRORISM NEXUS

G iven the structure of the data (our outcome variable is a binary
response variable, with "1" denoting province-years experiencing
terrorism and "0" otherwise), we used standard logistic regression
with a cluster robust variance estimator to test for the impact of the predictor variables on the trafficking-terrorism nexus. The clustered variance
estimator that indexes groups of observations by province assumes that
observations within provinces may be correlated in some unknown way and
adjusts the standard errors accordingly.

Some studies use fixed or random effects to address the problem with
the within-group correlation. Using fixed effects in the case of observational
data requires an exact modeling of the structure of disturbances in the data.
If the disturbance process is incorrectly modeled, then the Beta estimates
are inefficient.[1] The random effects model, on the other hand, assumes normal distribution of the error terms, meaning errors and regressors are
uncorrelated at all levels. With large-N data sets, this assumption of the random effects model is counteracted by the sheer amount of observations at
each level to satisfy asymptotic theory concerning maximum likelihood.[2]
However, this data set contains only 240 observations across 30 groups,
which may not allow enough observational information to maintain the
assumption of a normal distribution of errors. For this reason, the logistic
regression model with a robust cluster variance estimator is most appropriate for modeling these particular data.[3]

TABLE A.1 Socioeconomic Predictors
of the Trafficking-Terrorism Nexus

Infant mortality rate	−0.098*
	(0.034)
Population	−0.0006
	(0.0004)
Interaction term (Youth unemployment and professional education)	0.0039*
	(0.001)
Net migration	0.00002
	(0.00003)
Crime	−0.00003**
	(0.00001)
Public service employment	−17.05*
	(4.42)
Gender ratio	−0.061*
	(0.023)
Constant	6.91**
	(2.72)
N	240
Wald Chi2 (8)	33.00
Prob > chi2	(0.000)

*$p < 0.01$

**$p < 0.05$

Note: Robust standard errors in parentheses

Source: Author's own data

APPENDIX 2

THE IMPACT OF DRUG TRAFFICKING ON TERRORISM

Opiates	0.0018*
	(0.00045)
Cannabis	0.00002*
	(2.14e-06)
Forest area	−0.0666*
	(0.0243)
Infant mortality	0.0023***
	(0.0013)
Time to the nearest city	−0.0007*
	(0.00023)
Distance to border	−0.009*
	(0.003)
Urban area	0.21***
	(0.11)
Constant	0.282
	(0.757)
N	34
Wald Chi2(8)	400.08
Prob > chi2	(0.000)
Pseudo R2	0.55

*p < 0.01

**p < 0.05

***p < 0.1

Note: Robust standard errors in parentheses

Source: Author's own data

NOTES

INTRODUCTION

1. Charles Lister, "Cutting Off ISIS' Cash Flow," Brookings Institution, last modified October 24, 2014, http://www.brookings.edu/blogs/markaz/posts/2014/10/24-lister-cutting-off -isis-jabhat-al-nusra-cash-flow.

2. Yaya J. Fanusie and Alex Entz, *Islamic State: Financial Assessment*, Center on Sanctions and Illicit Finance, Foundation for Defense of Democracies, last modified March 2017, https://s3.us-east-2.amazonaws.com/defenddemocracy/uploads/documents/CSIF_TFBB _IS_Finance.pdf.

3. Hezbollah has also raised funds through smuggling and the illegal diamond trade. See Shawn Teresa Flanigan, "Terrorists Next Door? A Comparison of Mexican Drug Cartels and Middle Eastern Terrorist Organizations," *Terrorism and Political Violence* 24, no. 2 (2012): 286, https://doi.org/10.1080/09546553.2011.648351.

4. Yaya J. Fanusie and Alex Entz, *Boko Haram: Financial Assessment*, Center on Sanctions and Illicit Finance, Foundation for Defense of Democracies, last modified May 2017, https://s3.us-east-2.amazonaws.com/defenddemocracy/uploads/documents/CSIF_Boko _Haram.pdf.

5. Vanda Felbab-Brown, "Afghanistan: When Counternarcotics Undermines Counter- terrorism," *Washington Quarterly* 28, no. 4 (2005): 55–72, https://doi.org/10.1162/016366 0054798735; Jonathan Goodhand, "From Holy War to Opium War? A Case Study of the Opium Economy in Northeastern Afghanistan," *Central Asian Survey* 19, no. 2 (2000): 265–280, https://doi.org/10.1080/02634930050079354.

6. ISIS has been taxing drug production and trafficking networks in Syria and Iraq and, more recently, in Lebanon. See Sarah Graveline, "Is ISIS Making Inroads in East Africa?," IDA Africa Watch, last modified September 22, 2016, https://www.ida.org/idamedia/Corpo rate/Files/Publications/AfricaWatch/africawatch-September-22–2016-vol12.ashx.

7. James G. Stavridis, "Foreword," in *Convergence Illicit Networks and National Security in the Age of Globalization*, ed. Michael Miklaucic and Jacqueline Brewer (Washington, D.C.: National Defense University Press, 2013), vii.

8.   We define drug trafficking as illicit activity involving the cultivation, manufacture, distribution, and sale of substances that are subject to drug-prohibition laws (including opiates, cocaine, cannabis, amphetamine-type stimulants [ATS], and new psychoactive substances [NPS]). To be considered part of organized crime, drug trafficking must be carried out by a group of three or more persons, exist for a sustained period of time, and act in concert with the goal of obtaining a financial or other material benefit. See UNODC, "Drug Trafficking," accessed April 22, 2017, https://www.unodc.org/unodc/en/drug -trafficking/; UNODC, "The United Nations Convention Against Transnational Organized Crime and the Protocols Thereto," accessed April 22, 2017, https://www.unodc.org /documents/treaties/UNTOC/Publications/TOC%20Convention/TOCebook-e.pdf.

9.   Svante Cornell and Michael Jonsson, "The Nexus of Crime and Conflict," in *Conflict, Crime, and the State in Post-Communist Eurasia*, ed. Svante Cornell and Michael Jonsson (Philadelphia: University of Pennsylvania Press, 2014), 3.

10. Juan Miguel del Cid Gómez, "A Financial Profile of the Terrorism of Al-Qaeda and Its Affiliates," *Perspectives on Terrorism* 4, no. 4 (2010): 3–27, http://www.terrorismanalysts .com/pt/index.php/pot/article/view/113/html.

11. UNODC, "Research Report: Estimating Illicit Financial Flows Resulting from Drug Trafficking and Other Transnational Organized Crimes," last modified October 2011, https:// www.drugsandalcohol.ie/16151/1/Illicit_financial_flows_2011_web.pdf.

12. William F. Wechsler and Gary Barnabo, "The Department of Defense's Role in Combating Transnational Organized Crime," in *Convergence: Illicit Networks and National Security in the Age of Globalization*, ed. Michael Miklaucic and Jaqueline Brewer (Washington, D.C.: National Defense University Press, 2014), 233–242.

13. White House, "National Strategy to Combat Transnational Organized Crime, Addressing Converging Threats to National Security," last modified July 19, 2011, https://obam awhitehouse.archives.gov/sites/default/files/Strategy_to_Combat_Transnational_Orga nized_Crime_July_2011.pdf.

14. Azhar Ibrahim et al., *Afghanistan Interprovincial Opiate Trafficking Dynamics* (Kabul: Islamic Republic of Afghanistan Ministry of Counter Narcotics, 2013).

15. As cited in James A. Piazza, "The Opium Trade and Patterns of Terrorism in the Provinces of Afghanistan: An Empirical Analysis," *Terrorism and Political Violence* 24, no. 2 (2012): 213–234. According to a different estimate by Vanda Felbab-Brown, poppy cultivation makes up around 30 to 40 percent of the Taliban's income of "tens of millions of dollars a year," with the lion's share coming from fund-raising in the Gulf and Pakistan. As reported in Max Daly, "No, Your Drug Use Is Not Funding Terrorism," *Vice*, last modified September 20, 2016, https://www.vice.com/en_us/article/is-the-drug-trade-really -bank-rolling-terrorists.

16. Angel Rabasa et al., *Counternetwork: Countering the Expansion of Transnational Criminal Networks* (Santa Monica, Calif.: Rand Corporation, 2017).

17. Liana Eustacia Reyes and Shlomi Dinar, "The Convergence of Terrorism and Transnational Crime in Central Asia," *Studies in Conflict & Terrorism* 38, no. 5 (2015): 380–393.

18. Robert I. Rotberg, ed., *Burma: Prospects for a Democratic Future* (Washington, D.C.: Brookings Institution, 1998); Bertil Lintner, *Burma in Revolt: Opium and Insurgency Since 1948* (Chiang Mai, Thailand: Silkworm Books, 1999).

19. See, for example, John Rollins and Liana Sun Wyler, "Terrorism and Transnational Crime: Foreign Policy Issues for Congress," Congressional Research Service, last modified June 11, 2013, http://www.fas.org/sgp/crs/terror/R41004.pdf; Thomas M. Sanderson,

"Transnational Terror and Organized Crime: Blurring the Lines," *SAIS Review of International Affairs* 24, no. 1 (2004): 49–61.

20. Like other scholars in the field, we question the utility of a popular analytical distinction between "strong" and "weak" states. The categories of "failed," "fragile," and "weak" conceal immense variation among states designated with these labels. These generalizations add little to our understanding as to why some states designated as "weak" experience some types of threats but not others. It is more productive to think of the states along a continuum or continua in terms of their relative institutional strengths as well as political will. For further discussion, see John Heathershaw and Edward Schatz, "The Logics of State Weakness in Eurasia: An Introduction," in *Paradox of Power: The Logics of State Weakness in Eurasia*, ed. John Heathershaw and Edward Schatz (Pittsburgh: University of Pittsburgh Press, 2017), 3–24; Stewart Patrick, *Weak Links: Fragile States, Global Threats, and International Security* (Oxford: Oxford University Press, 2011).

21. Robert I. Rotberg, ed., *When States Fail: Causes and Consequences* (Princeton, N.J.: Princeton University Press, 2003); Joel S. Migdal, *Strong Societies and Weak States: State-Society Relations and State Capabilities in the Third World* (Princeton, N.J.: Princeton University Press, 1988); Catherine Boone, *Merchant Capital and the Roots of State Power in Senegal, 1930–1985* (Cambridge: Cambridge University Press, 1992); Frances Hagopian, *Traditional Politics and Regime Change in Brazil* (Cambridge: Cambridge University Press, 1996).

22. Crawford Young, "Deciphering Disorder in Africa: Is Identity the Key?," *World Politics* 54, no. 4 (2002): 532–557.

23. Alexander A. Cooley and John Heathershaw, *Dictators Without Borders: Power and Money in Central Asia* (New Haven, Conn.: Yale University Press, 2017); Sarah Chayes, *Thieves of State: Why Corruption Threatens Global Security* (New York: Norton, 2015).

24. United Nations Security Council, Resolution 2195, December 19, 2014, http://unscr.com/en/resolutions/doc/2195.

25. Mónica Medel, *Narco Violence in Mexico: A Spatial Analysis of Drug-Related Bloodshed* (Austin: University of Texas, 2011); Ryan Clarke and Stuart Lee, "The PIRA, D-Company, and the Crime-Terror Nexus," *Terrorism and Political Violence* 20, no. 3 (2008): 376–395.

26. Helena Carraico, Daniella Irrera, and Bill Tupman, *Criminals and Terrorists in Partnership: Unholy Alliance* (Abingdon, UK: Routledge, 2016); Jennifer L. Hesterman, *The Terrorist-Criminal Nexus: An Alliance of International Drug Cartels, Organized Crime, and Terror Groups* (Boca Raton, Fla.: CRC Press, 2013); Michael Miklaucic and Jacqueline Brewer, eds., *Convergence: Illicit Networks and National Security in the Age of Globalization* (Washington, D.C.: National Defense University Press, 2013); Lyubov Grigorova Mincheva and Ted Robert Gurr, eds., *Crime-Terror Alliances and the State: Ethnonationalist and Islamist Challenges to Regional Security* (New York: Routledge, 2013); Louise Shelley, *Dirty Entanglements: Corruption, Crime, and Terrorism* (Cambridge: Cambridge University Press, 2014).

27. David Lewis, "Crime, Terror and the State in Central Asia," *Global Crime* 15, nos. 3–4 (2014): 337–356.

28. Thomas J. Biersteker and Sue E. Eckert, *Countering the Financing of Terrorism* (London: Routledge, 2008).

29. Tuesday Reitano, Colin Clarke, and Laura Adal, *Examining the Nexus Between Organized Crime and Terrorism and Its Implications for EU Programming* (The Hague: International Center for Counter-Terrorism, 2017), accessed December 28, 2017, https://icct.nl

/publication/examining-the-nexus-between-organised-crime-and-terrorism-and-its-impli cations-for-eu-programming/.

30. Cornell and Jonsson, "Nexus of Crime and Conflict," 3; Alexander Kupatadze, *Organized Crime, Political Transitions and State Formation in Post-Soviet Eurasia* (New York: Macmillan, 2012), 142–114.

31. UNODC, *An Assessment of Transnational Organized Crime in Central Asia* (New York: UNODC, 2007), https://www.unodc.org/documents/organized-crime/Central_Asia _Crime_Assessment.pdf.

32. UNODC, *Assessment of Transnational Organized Crime in Central Asia*; Saltanat Berdikeeva, "Organized Crime in Central Asia: A Threat Assessment," *China and Eurasia Forum Quarterly* 7, no. 2 (2009): 75–100.

33. More than three-quarters of this amount are destined for the Russian market, with a small portion (approximately three to four tons) continuing to eastern and northern Europe. There are also challenges posed by homegrown drugs such as cannabis as well as the increasing use of synthetic drugs that are trafficked from other countries. Rustam Burnashev, "Terrorist Routes in Central Asia: Trafficking Drugs, Humans, and Weapons," *Connections: The Quarterly Journal* 6, no. 1 (2007): 65–70; Maral Madi, "Drug Trade in Kyrgyzstan: Structure, Implications and Countermeasures," *Central Asian Survey* 23, nos. 3–4 (2004): 249–273; UNODC, *Opiate Flows Through Northern Afghanistan and Central Asia: A Threat Assessment* (Vienna: UNODC, 2012), accessed May 4, 2017, https://www .unodc.org/documents/data-and analysis/Studies/Afghanistan_northern_route_2012 _web.pdf.

34. Kupatadze, *Organized Crime*, 1; See also Alisher Latypov, "Drug Dealers, Drug Lords and Drug Warriors-cum-Traffickers: Drug Crime and the Drug Trade in Kyrgyzstan," in *Drug Trafficking, Drug Abuse, Money Laundering, Judicial Corruption in Central Asia. Collection of Brief Summaries* (Bishkek: Altyn Print, 2012), 23–41.

35. Svante Cornell, "The Narcotics Threat in Greater Central Asia: From Crime-Terror Nexus to State Infiltration?," *China and Eurasia Forum Quarterly* 4, no. 1 (2006): 37–67.

36. Luke Falkenburg, "Trafficking Terror Through Tajikistan," *Military Review* 93, no. 4 (2013): 7–15, http://usacac.army.mil/CAC2/MilitaryReview/Archives/English/MilitaryReview _20130831_art005.pdf; Madi, "Drug Trade in Kyrgyzstan," 249–273; Tamara Makarenko, "Crime, Terror and the Central Asian Drug Trade," *Harvard Asia Quarterly* 6, no. 3 (2002): 28–38.

37. Rohan Gunaratna, "Introduction," in *Handbook of Terrorism in the Asia-Pacific*, ed. Rohan Gunaratna and Stefanie Kam (London: Imperial College Press, 2016), xxiii.

38. Gunaratna, "Introduction," xxiii.

39. Vanda Felbab-Brown, "Blood and Faith in Afghanistan: A June 2016 Update," Brookings Institution, last modified June 2016, https://www.brookings.edu/wp-content/uploads/2016 /06/Felbab-Brown-Paper-BLOOD-AND-FAITH-IN-AFGHANISTAN-May-2016.pdf.

40. Russell D. Howard and Colleen Traughber, "The 'New Silk Road' of Terrorism and Organized Crime: The Key to Countering the Terror-Crime Nexus," in *Armed Groups: Studies in National Security, Counterterrorism, and Counterinsurgency*, ed. Jeffrey H. Norwitz (Newport, R.I.: U.S. Naval War College, 2008), 374.

41. UNODC, *Addiction, Crime, Insurgency: The Transnational Threat of Afghan Opium* (Vienna: UNODC, 2009), 3, https://www.unodc.org/unodc/en/data-and-analysis/addic tion-crime-and-insurgency.html.

42. National Consortium for the Study of Terrorism and Responses to Terrorism (START), Global Terrorism Database, 2018, https://www.start.umd.edu/gtd/.

43. Chris Dishman, "Terrorism, Crime, and Transformation," *Studies in Conflict & Terrorism* 24, no. 1 (2001): 43–58; Tamara Makarenko, "The Crime-Terror Continuum: Tracing the Interplay Between Transnational Organized Crime and Terrorism," *Global Crime* 6, no. 1 (2004): 129–145; Peng Wang, "The Crime-Terror Nexus: Transformation, Alliance, Convergence," *Asian Social Science* 6, no. 6 (2010): 11.

44. Filippo De Danieli, "Counter-Narcotics Policies in Tajikistan and Their Impact on State Building," *Central Asian Survey* 30, no. 1 (2011): 129–145; Sébastian Peyrouse, "Drug Trafficking in Central Asia: A Poorly Considered Fight?," PONARS Eurasia Policy Memo No. 218, last modified September 2012, http://www.ponarseurasia.org/sites/default/files/policy-memos-pdf/pepm_218_Peyrouse_Sept2012.pdf.

45. This argument is consistent with David Lewis, "High Times on the Silk Road: The Central Asian Paradox," *World Policy Journal* 27, no. 1 (2010): 39–49.

46. Claire Adida, David Laitin, and Marie-Anne Valfort, *Why Muslim Integration Fails in Christian-Heritage Societies* (Cambridge, Mass.: Harvard University Press, 2016).

47. Lubov Mincheva and Ted Gurr, "Unholy Alliances? How Trans-state Terrorism and International Crime Make Common Cause," in *Crime-Terror Alliances and The State: Ethnonationalist and Islamist Challenges to Regional Security*, ed. Lyubov Grigorova Mincheva and Ted Robert Gurr, 1–23 (New York: Routledge, 2013). See also Chris Dishman, "The Leaderless Nexus: When Crime and Terror Converge," *Studies in Conflict & Terrorism* 28, no. 3 (2005): 237–252.

48. For instance, Svante Cornell and Michael Jonsson argue in "The Nexus of Crime and Conflict" that collapsing Soviet state institutions provide the context for their accounts of how grievances and disorder within post-Soviet conflicts create a "crime-conflict nexus" across the region.

49. Kupatadze, *Organized Crime, Political Transitions*; Erica Marat, *The State-Crime Nexus in Central Asia: State Weakness, Organized Crime, and Corruption in Kyrgyzstan and Tajikistan* (Washington, D.C.: Central Asia-Caucasus Institute Silk Road Studies Program, 2006).

50. Bob Jessop, "Territory, Politics, Governance and Multispatial Metagovernance," *Territory, Politics, Governance* 4, no. 1 (2016): 8–32.

51. Heathershaw and Schatz, "Logics of State Weakness in Eurasia."

52. Among the many works on this theme, see Pauline Jones Luong, *Institutional Change and Political Continuity in Post-Soviet Central Asia: Power, Perceptions and Pacts* (Cambridge: Cambridge University Press, 2002); Edward Schatz, *Modern Clan Politics: The Power of "Blood" in Kazakhstan and Beyond* (Seattle: University of Washington Press, 2004); Kathleen Collins, *Clan Politics and Regime Transition in Central Asia* (New York: Cambridge University Press, 2006); Olivier Roy, *The New Central Asia: Geopolitics and the Creation of Nations* (London: I. B. Tauris, 2007); Scott Radnitz, *Weapons of the Wealthy: Predatory States and Elite-Led Protests in Central Asia* (Ithaca, N.Y.: Cornell University Press, 2010).

53. UNODC, *Opiate Flows Through Northern Afghanistan and Central Asia*. Countries in the region have already agreed, in principle, to cooperate on counternarcotics with the establishment of the Central Asian Regional Information and Coordination Centre (CARICC). While this is a fundamental step, some countries are not making use of available cooperation mechanisms through CARICC; others are still developing their border

security policy largely in isolation. The resulting lack of professional trust makes it difficult to create relationships strong enough to support effective cooperation.

54. John Rollins, Liana Sun Wyler, and Seth Rosen, "International Terrorism and Transnational Crime: Security Threats, U.S. Policy and Considerations for Congress," Congressional Research Service, last modified January 5, 2010, https://fas.org/sgp/crs/terror/R41004
-2010.pdf.

55. On the inflation and mischaracterization of terrorism as a threat to the region's authoritarian regimes, see Nick Megoran, "Framing Andijon, Narrating the Nation: Islam
Karimov's Account of the Events of 13 May 2005," *Central Asian Survey* 27, no. 1 (2008):
15–31; Nick Megoran, "The Critical Geopolitics of Danger in Uzbekistan and Kyrgyzstan,"
Environment and Planning D: Society and Space 23, no. 4 (2005): 555–580; Sarah Kendzior, "Inventing Akromiya: The Role of Uzbek Propagandists in the Andijon Massacre," *Demokratizatsiya* 14, no. 4 (2006): 545–562; Stuart Horsman, "Themes of Official
Discourses on Terrorism in Central Asia," *Third World Quarterly* 26, no. 1 (2005): 199–213;
John Heathershaw and Nick Megoran, "Contesting Danger: A New Agenda for Policy
and Scholarship in Central Asia," *International Affairs* 87, no. 3 (2011): 589–612.

56. John Heathershaw and David W. Montgomery, "The Myth of Post-Soviet Muslim
Radicalisation in Central Asian Republics" (research paper, Chatham House, London,
2014).

57. Lewis, "Crime, Terror and the State in Central Asia."

58. By different estimates, between two thousand and four thousand Central Asian fighters
have joined the conflict since 2012, adding an element of extraterritoriality to the phenomenon of Central Asia terrorism. The majority of those (about 80 percent) who left for
the Middle East were recruited while working abroad as labor migrants in Russia, and
family members constitute about one-fifth of the total. Despite the strength of numbers,
Central Asian jihadists have been unable to unite into an autonomous, effective, and sustainable movement capable of staging a campaign of terrorist violence in their home
states or abroad. See Noah Tucker, *Central Asian Involvement in the Conflict in Syria and
Iraq: Drivers and Responses* (Arlington, Va.: Management Systems International, 2015),
http://pdf.usaid.gov/pdf_docs/PBAAE879.pdf. See also Soufan Group, "Foreign Fighters:
An Updated Assessment of the Flow of Foreign Fighters into Syria and Iraq," last modified
December 2015, http://soufangroup.com/wpcontent/uploads/2015/12/TSG_ForeignFighters
Update3.pdf

59. Lewis, "Crime, Terror and the State in Central Asia."

60. Evan S. Lieberman, "Nested Analysis as a Mixed Method Strategy for Comparative
Research," *American Political Science Review* 99, no. 3 (2005): 435–452.

61. John Gerring, "Is There a (Viable) Crucial-Case Method?," *Comparative Political Studies*
40, no. 3 (2007): 231–253.

62. UNODC Individual Drug Seizure reports, https://data.unodc.org/.

63. Paris Pact Initiative, the Afghan Opiate Trade Project of the United Nations Office on
Drugs and Crime (UNODC), and the UNODC Regional Office for Central Asia, Drugs
Monitoring Platform, http://drugsmonitoring.unodc-roca.org/.

64. Initial attempts at traditional geocoding failed in large part because of the sheer variety
of names for each given place. For example, a single city might have dozens of possible
names due to not only the variations in spelling and translation but also the number of
languages (many of the states in the study group have multiple official languages) and the

waves of renaming that have occurred over time with changes in governance. Therefore, we had to come up with a more robust geocoding solution using SAS.

65. START, Global Terrorism Database.

1. THEORIZING THE TRAFFICKING-TERRORISM NEXUS

1. Ryan Clarke and Stuart Lee, "The PIRA, D-Company, and the Crime-Terror Nexus," *Terrorism and Political Violence* 20, no. 3 (2008): 376–395.

2. Tamara Makarenko, "The Crime-Terror Continuum: Tracing the Interplay Between Transnational Organized Crime and Terrorism," *Global Crime* 6, no. 1 (2004): 129–145. Examples of activity appropriation abound in the literature. See, for example, Shawn Teresa Flanigan, "Terrorists Next Door? A Comparison of Mexican Drug Cartels and Middle Eastern Terrorist Organizations," *Terrorism and Political Violence* 24, no. 2 (2012): 279–294; Steven Hutchinson and Pat O'Malley, "A Crime-Terror Nexus? Thinking on Some of the Links Between Terrorism and Criminality," *Studies in Conflict and Terrorism* 30, no. 12 (2007): 1095–1107; Sylvia Longmire and John Longmire, "Redefining Terrorism: Why Mexican Drug Trafficking Is More Than Just Organized Crime," *Journal of Strategic Security* 1, no. 1 (2008): 35–51; Phil Williams, "The Terrorism Debate over Mexican Drug Trafficking Violence," *Terrorism and Political Violence* 24, no. 2 (2012): 259–278.

3. John T. Picarelli, "Osama bin Corleone? Vito the Jackal? Framing Threat Convergence Through an Examination of Transnational Organized Crime and International Terrorism," *Terrorism and Political Violence* 24, no. 2 (2012): 180–198.

4. Paolo Pontonier, "In Italy, Al Qaeda Turns to Organized Crime for Protection," New American Media, October 2005, http://www.freerepublic.com/focus/f-news/1507005/posts.

5. Williams, "Terrorism Debate."

6. Makarenko, "Crime-Terror Continuum"; John Rollins and Liana Sun Wyler, "Terrorism and Transnational Crime: Foreign Policy Issues for Congress," Congressional Research Service, last modified June 11, 2013, http://www.fas.org/sgp/crs/terror/R41004.pdf.

7. Makarenko, "Crime-Terror Continuum"; Lyubov Mincheva and Ted Robert Gurr, "Unholy Alliances? How Trans-State Terrorism and International Crime Make Common Cause," in *Crime-Terror Alliances and the State: Ethnonationalist and Islamist Challenges to Regional Security*, ed. Lyubov Grigorova Mincheva and Ted Robert Gurr (New York: Routledge, 2013), 1–23.

8. Makarenko, "Crime-Terror Continuum."

9. Nikita Malik, *Trafficking Terror: How Modern Slavery and Sexual Violence Fund Terrorism* (London: Henry Jackson Society, 2017), http://henryjacksonsociety.org/wp-content/uploads/2017/10/HJS-Trafficking-Terror-Report-web.pdf.

10. Svante E. Cornell, "The Narcotics Threat in Greater Central Asia: From Crime-Terror Nexus to State Infiltration?," *China and Eurasia Forum Quarterly* 4, no. 1 (2006): 471.

11. Karl Popper, *The Logic of Scientific Discovery* (London: Routledge, 1959); see also Gary King, Robert O. Keohane, and Sidney Verba, *Designing Social Inquiry* (Princeton, N.J.: Princeton University Press, 1994), 99–113.

12. David Lewis, "Crime, Terror and the State in Central Asia," *Global Crime* 15, nos. 3–4 (2014): 337–356.

13. Hutchinson and O'Malley, "Crime-Terror Nexus?"

14. Tuesday Reitano, Colin Clarke, and Laura Adal, *Examining the Nexus Between Organized Crime and Terrorism and Its Implications for EU Programming* (The Hague: International Center for Counter-Terrorism, 2017), https://icct.nl/publication/examining-the-nexus-between-organised-crime-and-terrorism-and-its-implications-for-eu-programming/.

15. Joseph J. Easson and Alex P. Schmid, "Appendix 2.1: 250-plus Academic, Governmental and Intergovernmental Definitions of Terrorism," in *The Routledge Handbook of Terrorism Research*, ed. Alex P. Schmid (London: Routledge, 2011), 99–200.

16. Bruce Hoffman, *Inside Terrorism* (New York: Columbia University Press, 2006), 3.

17. Martha Crenshaw, *Explaining Terrorism: Causes, Processes, Consequences* (London: Routledge, 2011).

18. Cornell, "Narcotics Threat in Greater Central Asia," 50.

19. Rajan Basra and Peter R. Neumann, "Criminal Pasts, Terrorist Futures: European Jihadists and the New Crime-Terror Nexus," *Perspectives on Terrorism* 10, no. 6 (2016): 25–40.

20. "Saudi Arabia: Terror Groups Rely on Drugs to Recruit Suicide Bombers," *Arab News*, last modified July 13, 2016, http://www.arabnews.com/node/952996/saudi-arabia.

21. Divine Ntaryike Jr., "Drug Trafficking Rising in Central Africa, Warns Interpol," Voice of America, September 8, 2012, http://www.voanews.com/content/drug-trafficking-rising-incentral-africa-warns-interpol/1504026.html.

22. Yaroslav Trofimov, "Al Ansari Exchange Finds Itself Embroiled in Terror Investigation," *Wall Street Journal*, November 1, 2001, http://www.wsj.com/articles/SB1004652055539 614360; U.S. Department of the Treasury, "Treasury Designates New Ansari Money Exchange," last modified February 18, 2011, https://www.treasury.gov/press-center/press-releases/Pages/tg1071.aspx.

23. Ibáñez Luis de la Corte, "To What Extent Do Global Terrorism and Organized Criminality Converge? General Parameters and Critical Scenarios," *Journal of the Spanish Institute of Strategic Studies* 1, no. 1 (2013): 11.

24. Matthew Levitt, "The Political Economy of Middle East Terrorism," *Washington Institute for Near East Policy* 6, no. 4 (2002): 49–65.

25. Glenn E. Curtis and Tara Karacan, *The Nexus Among Terrorists, Narcotics Traffickers, Weapons Proliferators, and Organized Crime Networks in Western Europe* (Washington, D.C.: Library of Congress, 2002), 4; Mincheva and Gurr, "Unholy Alliances?"

26. O'Brien McKenzie, "Fluctuations Between Crime and Terror: The Case of Abu Sayyaf's Kidnapping Activities," *Terrorism and Political Violence* 24, no. 2 (2012): 320–336.

27. Maral Madi, "Drug Trade in Kyrgyzstan: Structure, Implications and Countermeasures," *Central Asian Survey* 23, no. 3–4 (2004): 249–273; Tamara Makarenko, "Crime, Terror and the Central Asian Drug Trade," *Harvard Asia Quarterly* 6, no. 3 (2002): 28–38.

28. Michael Fitzpatrick and Stephen F. Lynch, "Stopping Terror Finance: Securing the U.S. Financial Sector," Task Force to Investigate Terrorism Financing, Committee on Financial Services, U.S. House of Representatives, 114th Congress, last modified December 20, 2016, https://financialservices.house.gov/uploadedfiles/terror_financing_report_12–20–2016.pdf.

29. See, for example, Ana Bela Santos Bravo and Carlos Manuel Mendes Dias, "An Empirical Analysis of Terrorism: Deprivation, Islamism and Geopolitical Factors," *Defense and Peace Economics* 17, no. 4 (2006): 329–341; James A. Piazza, "The Opium Trade and Patterns of Terrorism in the Provinces of Afghanistan: An Empirical Analysis," *Terrorism and Political Violence* 24, no. 2 (2012): 213–234.

30. MoonSun Kim, "Geographies of Crime," in *Encyclopedia of Theoretical Criminology*, ed. J. Mitchell Miller (Hoboken, N.J.: John Wiley and Sons, 2014), 1–4.

31. The geographies of terrorism are a relatively new area of research defined by a range of perspectives—cultural, critical geopolitical as well as empirical/quantitative—seeking to locate terrorism in space, identify its root causes, and investigate imaginaries of terror and representations of terrorism. See, for example, Karim Bahgat and Richard M. Medina, "An Overview of Geographical Perspectives and Approaches in Terrorism Research," *Perspectives on Terrorism* 7, no. 1 (2013), http://www.terrorismanalysts.com/pt/index.php/pot /article/view/242; Daanish Mustafa and Julian R. Shaw, "Geography of Terrorism," in *Oxford Bibliographies* (New York: Oxford University Press, 2013), http://www .oxfordbibliographies.com/view/document/obo-9780199874002/obo-9780199874002 -0066.xml.

32. Victor Asal, Milward H. Brinton, and Eric W. Schoon, "When Terrorists Go Bad: Analyzing Terrorist Organizations' Involvement in Drug Smuggling," *International Studies Quarterly* 59, no. 1 (2015): 112–123; Charlie Edwards and Calum Jeffray, "The Growing Nexus Between Terrorism and Organized Crime in the Atlantic Basin," in *Dark Networks in the Atlantic Basin: Emerging Trends and Implications for Human Security*, ed. Daniel S. Hamilton (Washington, D.C.: Center for Transatlantic Relations, 2015), 57–74.

33. Edwards and Jeffray, "Growing Nexus Between Terrorism and Organized Crime."

34. Asal, Brinton, and Schoon, "When Terrorists Go Bad," 112–123; James D. Fearon and David Laitin, "Ethnicity, Insurgency, and Civil War," *American Political Science Review* 97, no. 1 (2003): 75–90.

35. Stephen C. Nemeth, Jacob A. Mauslein, and Craig Stapley, "The Primacy of the Local: Identifying Terrorist Hot Spots Using Geographic Information Systems," *Journal of Politics* 76, no. 2 (2014): 304–317.

36. Reitano, Clarke, and Adal, *Examining the Nexus*.

37. Julie A. Cirino, Silvana L. Elizondo, and Geoffrey Wawro, "Latin America's Lawless Areas and Failed States," in *Latin American Security Challenges: A Collaborative Inquiry from North and South*, ed. Paul D. Taylor (Newport, R.I.: Naval War College, 2004).

38. Fearon and Laitin, "Ethnicity, Insurgency, and Civil War," 75–90; Nemeth, Mauslein, and Stapley, "Primacy of the Local," 304–317.

39. James L. Zackrison, "La Violencia in Colombia: An Anomaly in Terrorism," *Journal of Conflict Studies* 9, no. 4 (1989): 5–18.

40. See, for instance, Sarah Kenyon Fisher, *Dangerous Sanctuaries: Refugee Camps, Civil War, and the Dilemmas of Humanitarian Aid* (Ithaca, N.Y.: Cornell University Press, 2006).

41. Peter Andreas, *Border Games: Policing the U.S.-Mexico Divide* (Ithaca, N.Y.: Cornell University Press, 2000); George Gavrilis, *The Dynamics of Interstate Boundaries* (Cambridge: Cambridge University Press, 2008).

42. Cirino, Elizondo, and Wawro, "Latin America's Lawless Areas and Failed States," 18.

43. Patrick R. Keefer, "The Geography of Badness: Mapping the Hubs of the Illicit Global Economy," in *Convergence: Illicit Networks and National Security in the Age of Globalization*, ed. Michael Miklaucic and Jacqueline Brewer (Washington, D.C.: National Defense University Press, 2013), 97–110.

44. Peter Andreas, "Transnational Crime and Economic Globalization," in *Transnational Organized Crime and International Security*, ed. Mats Berdal and Mónica Serrano (Boulder, Colo.: Lynne Rienner, 2002), 42; James Mittelman and Robert Johnston, "The Globalization of Organized Crime, the Courtesan State, and the Corruption of Civil Society," *Global Governance* 5, no. 2 (1999): 103–126.

45. Nemeth, Mauslein, and Stapley, "Primacy of the Local."

46. See, among others, Paul R. Ehrlich, "Some Roots of Terrorism," *Population and Environment* 24, no. 2 (2002): 183–192; Andreas Frevtag, Jens Krüger, Daniel Meierrieks, and Friedrich Schneider, "The Origins of Terrorism: Cross-Country Estimates of Socio-Economic Determinants of Terrorism," *European Journal of Political Economy* 27 (2011): S5–S16; Gary LaFree and Laura Dugan, "How Does Studying Terrorism Compare to Studying Crime?," in *Terrorism and Counterterrorism: Criminological Perspectives*, ed. Donald Black and Mathieu Deflem (Bingley, UK: Emerald Group Publishing Limited, 2004), 53–74; Krisztina Kis-Katos, Helge Liebert, and Gunther G. Schulze, "On the Origin of Domestic and International Terrorism," *European Journal of Political Economy* 27 (2011): S17–S36.

47. Richard M. Medina, Laura K. Siebeneck, and George F. Hepner, "A Geographic Information Systems (GIS) Analysis of Spatiotemporal Patterns of Terrorist Incidents in Iraq 2004–2009," *Studies in Conflict and Terrorism* 34, no. 11 (2011): 862–882; James Piazza, "Rooted in Poverty? Terrorism, Poor Economic Development, and Social Cleavages," *Terrorism and Political Violence* 18, no. 1 (2006): 159–177.

48. Nemeth, Mauslein, and Stapley, "Primacy of the Local."

49. Ted Gurr provides the classic work on this perspective (*Why Men Rebel* [Princeton, N.J.: Princeton University Press, 1970]). See also Ehrlich, "Some Roots of Terrorism"; and Frevtag, Krüger, Meierrieks, and Schneider, "Origins of Terrorism."

50. See, for example, Alan Krueger, *What Makes a Terrorist: Economics and the Roots of Terrorism* (Princeton, N.J.: Princeton University Press, 2008); James A. Piazza, "Does Poverty Serve as a Root Cause of Terrorism? No, Poverty Is a Weak Causal Link," in *Debating Terrorism and Counterterrorism: Conflicting Perspectives on Causes, Contexts and Responses*, ed. Stuart Gottlieb (Washington, D.C.: Congressional Quarterly Press, 2009), 34–51.

51. Rajan Basra and Peter R. Neumann, "Criminal Pasts, Terrorist Futures: European Jihadists and the New Crime-Terror Nexus," *Perspectives on Terrorism* 10, no. 6 (2016): 25–40; Reitano, Clarke, and Adal, *Examining the Nexus*.

52. Quoted in Max Daly, "No, Your Drug Use Is Not Funding Terrorism," *Vice*, last modified September 20, 2016, https://www.vice.com/en_us/article/is-the-drug-trade-really-bank-rolling-terrorists.

53. Wibke Hansen and Judith Vorrath, "Atlantic Basin Countries and Organized Crime: Paradigms, Policies, Priorities," in *Dark Networks in the Atlantic Basin: Emerging Trends and Implications for Human Security*, ed. Daniel S. Hamilton (Washington, D.C.: Center for Transatlantic Relations, 2015), 101–120.

54. See, for example, Svante Cornell and Michael Jonsson, "The Nexus of Crime and Conflict," in *Conflict, Crime, and the State in Postcommunist Eurasia*, ed. Svante Cornell and Michael Jonsson (Philadelphia: University of Pennsylvania Press, 2014), 1–22; Alexander A. Cooley and John Heathershaw, *Dictators Without Borders: Power and Money in Central Asia* (New Haven, Conn.: Yale University Press, 2017); Alan Dupont, "Transnational Crime, Drugs and Security in East Asia," *Asian Survey* 39, no. 3 (1999): 433–455; Richard M. Gibson and John B. Haseman, "Prospects for Controlling Narcotics Production and Trafficking in Myanmar," *Contemporary Southeast Asia* 25 (2003): 1–19; Patrick L. Clawson and Rensselaer W. Lee III, *The Andean Cocaine Industry* (New York: St. Martin's Press, 1998).

55. Cornell, "Narcotics Threat in Greater Central Asia," 37–67; Alexander Kupatadze, *Organized Crime, Political Transitions and State Formation in Post-Soviet Eurasia* (New York: Macmillan, 2012); Alexander Kupatadze, "Political Corruption in Eurasia:

Understanding Collusion Between States, Organized Crime and Business," *Theoretical Criminology* 19, no. 2 (2015): 198–215.

56. Patrick Meehan, "Drugs, Insurgency and State-Building in Burma: Why the Drugs Trade Is Central to Burma's Changing Political Order," *Journal of Southeast Asian Studies* 42, no. 3 (2011): 376–404.

57. Meehan, "Drugs, Insurgency and State-Building in Burma."

58. Only Afghanistan, Iraq, and Pakistan, which rank within the twenty top states on the Fragile States Index, exhibit a marked presence of terrorist organizations, while more than half of those twenty states are free of foreign terrorist groups (as designated by the U.S. Department of State). J. J. Messner, ed., "Fragile States Index Annual Report 2016," Fund for Peace, last modified April 10, 2017, http://fundforpeace.org/fsi/2016/06/27/fragile-states -index-2016-annual-report/fragile-states-index-annual-report-2016-ver-3e/; Aidan Hehir, "The Myth of the Failed State and the War on Terror: A Challenge to the Conventional Wisdom," *Journal of Intervention and Statebuilding* 1, no. 3 (2007): 307–332.

59. Edward Newman, "Weak States, State Failure, and Terrorism," *Terrorism and Political Violence* 19, no. 4 (2007): 463–488.

60. Cornell, "Narcotics Threat in Greater Central Asia," 37–67; Kupatadze, *Organized Crime.*

61. Keefer, "Geography of Badness."

62. Alexander Cooley, *Logics of Hierarchy: The Organization of Empires, States, and Military Occupations* (Ithaca, N.Y.: Cornell University Press, 2005); George Gavrilis, *The Dynamics of Interstate Boundaries* (Cambridge: Cambridge University Press, 2008); Lawrence P. Markowitz, *State Erosion: Unlootable Resources and Unruly Elites* (Ithaca, N.Y.: Cornell University Press, 2013).

63. Kupatadze, *Organized Crime*; Alisher Latypov, "Drug Dealers, Drug Lords and Drug Warriors-cum-Traffickers: Drug Crime and the Drug Trade in Kyrgyzstan," in *Drug Trafficking, Drug Abuse, Money Laundering, Judicial Corruption in Central Asia. Collection of Brief Summaries* (Bishkek: Altyn Print, 2012), 23–41; Steven Levitsky and Lucan A. Way, *Competitive Authoritarianism: Hybrid Regimes After the Cold War* (Cambridge: Cambridge University Press, 2010).

64. Messner, "Fragile States Index Annual Report 2016."

65. Richard Snyder, "Does Lootable Wealth Breed Disorder? A Political Economy of Extraction Framework," *Comparative Political Studies* 39, no. 8 (2006): xx.

66. G. M. Easter, *Capital, Coercion, and Postcommunist States* (Ithaca, N.Y.: Cornell University Press, 2012).

67. Meehan, "Drugs, Insurgency and State-Building in Burma," 377; David Keem, *Complex Emergencies* (Cambridge: Polity Press, 2008), 182; Robert I. Rotberg, *State Failure and State Weakness in a Time of Terror* (Washington, D.C.: Brookings Institution Press, 2003).

68. Alex McDougall, "State Power and its Implications for Civil War in Colombia," *Studies in Conflict and Terrorism* 32, no. 4 (2009): 325.

69. This relationship between weak state capacity—particularly coercive capacity—and the drug trade is found in areas as diverse as Eastern Europe, Central America, and the Caribbean. Felia Allum and Jennifer Sands, "Explaining Organized Crime in Europe: Are Economists Always Right?," *Crime, Law, and Social Change* 41, no. 2 (2004): 133–160. See also John Engval, "The State Under Siege: The Drug Trade and Organised Crime in Tajikistan," *Europe-Asia Studies* 58, no. 6 (2006): 827–854; Erica Marat, "Impact of Drug Trade and Organized Crime on State Functioning in Kyrgyzstan and Tajikistan," *China and Eurasia Forum Quarterly* 4, no. 1 (2006): 93–111; Rotberg, *State Failure and State Weakness.*

70. Asal, Brinton, and Schoon, "When Terrorists Go Bad."
71. David M. Luna, "Trans-Africa Security: Combating Illicit Trafficking and Organized Crime in Africa," Remarks to the Bureau of International Narcotics and Law Enforcement Affairs of the Under Secretary for Civilian Security, Democracy, and Human Rights, May 12, 2017, https://www.state.gov/j/inl/rls/rm/2017/270858.htm.
72. Mariya Y. Omelicheva and Lawrence P. Markowitz, "When the Crime-Terror Nexus Does Not Materialize: Drug Trafficking, Militants and the State in Russia" (presented at the annual security conference Crime-Terror Nexus and Intelligence-Led Responses, University of Kansas, Lawrence, April 2018).
73. Johann Graf Lambsdorff, "Making Corrupt Deals: Contracting in the Shadow of the Law," Journal of Economic Behavior & Organization 48, no. 3 (2002): 227.
74. David C. Jordan, Drug Politics: Dirty Politics and Democracies (Norman: University of Oklahoma Press, 1999); Raphael F. Perl, "State Crime: The North Korean Drug Trade," Global Crime 6, no. 1 (2004): 117–128.
75. For more information on the nature of informal networks in Central Asia, see Idil Tuncer-Kilavuz, "Political and Social Networks in Tajikistan and Uzbekistan: 'Clan', Region, and Beyond," Central Asian Survey 28, no. 3 (2009): 323–334.
76. Charles Tilly, "War Making and State Making as Organized Crime," in Bringing the State Back In, ed. Peter Evans, Dietrich Rueschemeyer, and Theda Skocpol (Cambridge: Cambridge University Press, 1985), 169–191.

2. MAPPING HOW TRAFFICKING AND TERRORISM INTERSECT

1. Rustam Burnashev, "Terrorist Routes in Central Asia: Trafficking Drugs, Humans, and Weapons," Connections: The Quarterly Journal 6, no. 1 (2007): 65–70; Maral Madi, "Drug Trade in Kyrgyzstan: Structure, Implications and Countermeasures," Central Asian Survey 23, nos. 3–4 (2004): 249–273; UNODC, Opiate Flows Through Northern Afghanistan and Central Asia: A Threat Assessment (Vienna: UNODC, 2012), 68–70, accessed May 4, 2017, https://www.unodc.org/documents/data-and analysis/Studies/Afghanistan_northern_route_2012_web.pdf.
2. David Lewis, "High Times on the Silk Road: The Central Asian Paradox," World Policy Journal 27, no. 1 (2010): 39–49.
3. Svante E. Cornell and Niklas L. P. Swanström, "The Eurasian Drug Trade: A Challenge to Regional Security," Problems of Post-Communism 53, no.4 (2006): 10–28; Nalin Kumar Mohapatra, "Political and Security Challenges in Central Asia: The Drug Trafficking Dimension," International Studies 44, no. 2 (2007): 157–174.
4. UNODC, The Opium Economy in Afghanistan: An International Problem (New York: UNODC, 2003), https://www.unodc.org/documents/afghanistan//Counter_Narcotics/The_Opium_Economy_in_Afghanistan_-_2003.pdf.
5. Svante E. Cornell, "The Narcotics Threat in Greater Central Asia: From Crime-Terror Nexus to State Infiltration?," China and Eurasia Forum Quarterly 4, no. 1 (2006): 37–67; Ikramul Haq, "Pak-Afghan Drug Trade in Historical Perspective," Asian Survey 36, no. 10 (1996): 945–963; Fariba Nawa, Opium Nation: Child Brides, Drug Lords, and One Woman's Journey Through Afghanistan (New York: Harper Perennial, 2011).
6. Cornell, "Narcotics Threat in Greater Central Asia," 37–67.

7.   Joel Hernandez, "Terrorism, Drug Trafficking, and the Globalization of Supply," *Perspectives on Terrorism* 7, no. 4 (2013): 49.

8.   UNODC, *Global Illicit Drug Trends 2002* (United Nations Publications, 2002), https://www
     .unodc.org/pdf/report_2002-06-26_1/report_2002-06-26_1.pdf.

9.   Some top-ranking Taliban officers were involved in regional trade, but this was due to
     their personal ties to the drug mafia and warlords and for limited personal gain. Tamara
     Makarenko, "Crime, Terror and the Central Asian Drug Trade," *Harvard Asia Quarterly*
     6, no. 3 (2002): 28–38.

10. John Cooley, *Unholy Wars: Afghanistan, America and International Terrorism* (London:
     Pluto Press, 1999); Jonathan Goodhand, "From Holy War to Opium War? A Case Study of the
     Opium Economy in North Eastern Afghanistan," *Central Asian Survey* 19, no. 2 (2000): 265–
     280, https://doi.org/10.1080/02634930050079354; UNODC, *Opium Economy in Afghanistan.*

11. Makarenko, "Crime, Terror and the Central Asian Drug Trade," 28–38.

12. Tamara Makarenko, "The Crime-Terror Continuum: Tracing the Interplay Between
     Transnational Organized Crime and Terrorism," *Global Crime* 6, no. 1 (2004): 137.

13. Saltanat Berdikeeva, "Organized Crime in Central Asia: A Threat Assessment," *China and
     Eurasia Forum Quarterly* 7, no. 2 (2009): 75–100; Bakhyt M. Nurgaliyev, Kanat S. Lakbayev,
     and Alexey V. Boretsky, "Organized Crime in Kazakhstan: The Past, the Present, Development
     Tendencies and Social Consequences," *Journal of Applied Sciences* 14, no. 24
     (2014): 3436–3445; UNODC, *Opiate Flows Through Northern Afghanistan and Central
     Asia,* 68–70.

14. UNODC, *Opiate Flows Through Northern Afghanistan and Central Asia,* 68–70.

15. Makarenko, "Crime, Terror and the Central Asian Drug Trade."

16. U.S. Department of State, "Designated Foreign Terrorist Organizations," last modified
     June 1, 2017, https://www.state.gov/j/ct/rls/other/des/123085.htm.

17. Alexander Kupatadze, *Organized Crime, Political Transitions and State Formation in Post-
     Soviet Eurasia* (New York: Macmillan, 2012); Madi, "Drug Trade in Kyrgyzstan"; Makarenko,
     "Crime, Terror and the Central Asian Drug Trade."

18. Kupatadze, *Organized Crime, Political Transitions.*

19. Makarenko, "Crime, Terror and the Central Asian Drug Trade."

20. Murat Laumulin, "Islamic Radicalism in Central Asia," in *Religion and Security in South
     and Central Asia,* ed. K. Warikoo (Abingdon, UK: Routledge, 2011), 139–149.

21. However, the group's connection to the Taliban's Haqqani network, which funds its operations
     through the drug trade, and its location in the areas of opium production and
     trafficking make the argument that IJU militants are involved in the drug trade likely.
     Liana Eustacia Reyes and Shlomi Dinar, "The Convergence of Terrorism and Transnational
     Crime in Central Asia," *Studies in Conflict and Terrorism* 38, no. 5 (2015): 386.

22. These include the Shir Khan Bandar–Panji Poyon crossing, Ishkashim (Gorno-
     Badakhshan), the Khorog–Shegnan bridge, Kukul–Ali Khanoum, and the Kupruki
     Vanch–Jomarji Bolo bridge over the River Panj.

23. UNODC, *The Global Afghan Opium Trade: A Threat Assessment* (Vienna: UNODC, 2011),
     http://www.unodc.org/documents/data-and-analysis/Studies/Global_Afghan_Opium
     _Trade_2011-web.pdf.

24. UNODC, *Opiate Flows Through Northern Afghanistan and Central Asia.*

25. There are several other routes for transporting drugs from Tajikistan to Uzbekistan (e.g.,
     through the neighborhoods of the Namangan area and settlements of the Surkhondaryo
     region).

26. The only religious party in Central Asia—the Islamic Renaissance Party of Tajikistan—was banned and declared a terrorist organization in September 2015.

27. UNODC, *Opiate Flows Through Northern Afghanistan and Central Asia*, 68–70.

28. Madi, "Drug Trade in Kyrgyzstan," 251.

29. Redo Slawomir, *Organized Crime and Its Control in Central Asia* (Huntsville, Tex.: Office of International Criminal Justice, 2004), 98.

30. Catherine Putz, "Kyrgyz and Tajiks Clash along Disputed Border," *The Diplomat*, August 4, 2015, http://thediplomat.com/2015/08/kyrgyz-and-tajiks-clash-along-disputed-border/.

31. Other Uzbekistan exclaves in Kyrgyzstan are the town of Shakhimardan and the small areas of Qalacha and Khaimion. Tajikistan lays claim to Chorkuh village, which is also in Kyrgyzstan.

32. Madi, "Drug Trade in Kyrgyzstan."

33. Osh City, an administrative capital of the Osh region, became a separate administrative unit in Kyrgyzstan in 2003.

34. Madi, "Drug Trade in Kyrgyzstan"; UNODC, *Opiate Flows Through Northern Afghanistan and Central Asia*, 68–70. Also note that Tajik citizens do not need visas to cross into Kyrgyzstan.

35. Stina Torjesen and S. Neil MacFarlane, "R before D: The Case of Post Conflict Reintegration in Tajikistan," *Conflict, Security & Development* 7, no. 2 (2007): 311–332.

36. Kupatadze, *Organized Crime, Political Transitions*.

37. Burnashev, "Terrorist Routes in Central Asia"; Makarenko, "Crime, Terror and the Central Asian Drug Trade."

38. Mariya Y. Omelicheva, "Islam in Kazakhstan: A Survey of Contemporary Trends and Sources of Securitization," *Central Asian Survey* 30, no. 2 (2011): 243–256.

39. The East Turkistan Liberation Organization unites ethnic Uighurs, Muslims of Turkic decent who reside in the northwestern region of China and seek to establish an independent state.

40. The defendants of those prosecuted in the trial maintain that their clients confessed to the charges under duress. See Franco Galdini and Zukhra Iakupbaeva, "The Strange Case of Jaysh al-Mahdi and Mr. ISIS: How Kyrgyzstan's Elites Manipulate the Threat of Terrorism," Central Asia Fellows Papers, no. 179, Central Asia Program, last modified October 2016, https://app.box.com/s/svs8g9nybpsrhfwjgtrwnsgv1igzdnbt; "Kyrgyz Court Jails Members of Terrorist Group," Radio Free Europe/Radio Liberty, July 19, 2013, http://www.rferl.org/a/kyrgyzstan-terrorism-sentencing/25051277.html.

41. John Heathershaw and David W. Montgomery, "The Myth of Post-Soviet Muslim Radicalization in the Central Asian Republics," Research Paper, Chatham House, London, 2014, last modified November 11, 2014, https://www.chathamhouse.org/publication/myth-post-soviet-muslim-radicalization-central-asian-republics.

42. UNODC, *Addiction, Crime and Insurgency: The Transnational Threat of Afghan Opium* (Vienna: UNODC, 2009), https://www.unodc.org/unodc/en/data-and-analysis/addiction-crime-and-insurgency.html.

43. UNODC, *Opiate Flows Through Northern Afghanistan and Central Asia*, 68–70.

44. Institute for War and Peace Reporting Central Asia, "Kazakhstan Cannabis Klondike," last modified November 20, 2005, https://iwpr.net/global-voices/kazakstans-cannabis-klondike; UNODC, *World Drug Report*, vol. 1, *Analysis* (Geneva: United Nations Publications, 2006), https://www.unodc.org/unodc/en/data-and-analysis/WDR-2006.html.

45. Burnashev, "Terrorist Routes in Central Asia."

46. U.S. Department of State, "Kazakhstan," in *International Narcotics Control Strategy Report*, vol. 1, *Drug and Chemical Control* (Washington, D.C.: Bureau of International Narcotics and Law Enforcement Affairs, 2015), https://www.state.gov/j/inl/rls/nrcrpt/2015/vol1/238985.htm. Until it ceased production in 1991, Kazakhstan's Shymkent plant was the Soviet Union's only supplier of medicinal opiates.

47. Sergey Golunov, "Drug-Trafficking Through the Russia-Kazakhstan Border: Challenge and Response," in *Empire, Islam, and Politics in Central Eurasia*, ed. Uyama Tomohiko (Sapporo: Slavic Research Center of Hokkaido University, 2007), 331–350, http://src-home.slav.hokudai.ac.jp/coe21/publish/no14_ses/13_golunov.pdf; UNODC, *Opiate Flows Through Northern Afghanistan and Central Asia*, 68–70.

48. Golunov, "Drug-Trafficking Through the Russia-Kazakhstan Border."

49. U.S. Department of State, "Kazakhstan."

50. "Kazakh Police Suspect Uighur 'Separatists' of Murdering Two Policemen," BBC Monitoring Central Asia Unit, last modified September 2000, http://www.start.umd.edu/gtd/search/IncidentSummary.aspx?gtdid=200009240004.

51. Omelicheva, "Islam in Kazakhstan."

52. Erlan Karin, "Dilemmy Bezopasnosti Tsentral'noi Azii," *Russie.Net.Visions*, no. 98, February 2017, Institut français des relations internationales (Ifri), https://www.ifri.org/sites/default/files/atoms/files/rnv98_erlan_karin_dilemmy_bezopasnosti_centralnoy_azii_rus_2017.pdf.

53. While the key aspects of these groups' ideologies have appealed to a small number of Central Asian Muslims, these groups have sought to capitalize on the country's deteriorating economic situation, corruption, religious illiteracy, and ethnic discrimination by adapting their message to local contexts to appeal to vulnerable segments of the Kazakh population.

54. Mariya Y. Omelicheva, "Kazakhstan," in *World Almanac of Islamism*, American Foreign Policy Council, 2017, http://almanac.afpc.org/Kazakhstan.

55. Terrorism Research and Analysis Consortium (TRAC), http://www.trackingterrorism.org/groups.

56. Christian Bleuer and Said Reza Kazemi, "Between Co-operation and Insulation: Afghanistan's Relations with the Central Asian Republics," Afghanistan Analysts Network, June 2014, https://www.afghanistan-analysts.org/wp-content/uploads/2014/06/20140608-Bleuer_Kazemi-Central_Asia.pdf.

57. Tajikistan and Uzbekistan delimited about 90 percent of their shared border by 2002. Disputes about the remaining border stretches slowed down the delimitation and demarcation process, and all negotiations were tabled in 2009. An attempt at reviving those negotiations was undertaken in 2015. "Tajikistan, Uzbekistan Resume Border Delimitation Talks," Fergana News Agency, last modified November 22, 2016, http://enews.fergananews.com/news.php?id=3181&mode=snews.

58. U.S. Department of State, *International Narcotics Control Strategy Report* (Washington, D.C.: Bureau for International Narcotics and Law Enforcement Affairs, March 1995), http://dosfan.lib.uic.edu/ERC/law/INC/1995/02.html.

59. Vitaly V. Naumkin, *Radical Islam in Central Asia: Between Pen and Rifle* (Lanham, Nd.: Rowman & Littlefield, 2005), 96–97; Mariya Y. Omelicheva, "The Multiple Faces of Islamic Rebirth in Central Asia," in *Area Studies in the Global Age: Community, Place, Identity*, ed. Edith Clowes and Shelly Bromberg (DeKalb: Northern Illinois University Press, 2015),

143–158; Sébastien Peyrouse, "Islam in Central Asia: National Specificities and Postsoviet Globalisation," *Religion, State and Society* 35, no. 3 (2007): 245.

60. Gokalp Bayrmli, "Uzbekistan Bombing Allegations Raise Tensions with Turkey," Radio Free Europe/Radio Liberty, July 8, 1999, http://www.rferl.org/nca/features/1999/07/F.RU .990708132919.html.

61. Cerwyn Moore, "The Rise and Fall of the Islamic Jihad Union: What Next for Uzbek Terror Networks?," *Terrorism Monitor* 8, no. 14 (2010), https://jamestown.org/program/the -rise-and-fall-of-the-islamic-jihad-union-what-next-for-uzbek-terror-networks/.

62. U.S. Department of State, "Individuals and Entities Designated by the State Department under E.O. 13224," Bureau of Counterterrorism, accessed November 15, 2018, https://www .state.gov/j/ct/rls/other/des/143210.htm.

63. National Consortium for the Study of Terrorism and Responses to Terrorism (START), Global Terrorism Database, Incident Summary, Incident ID: 200905260013, https://www .start.umd.edu/gtd/search/IncidentSummary.aspx?gtdid=200905260013; Global Terrorism Database, Incident Summary, Incident ID: 200905260012, https://www.start.umd.edu /gtd/search/IncidentSummary.aspx?gtdid=200905260012.

64. Bill Roggio and Caleb Weiss, "Islamic Jihad Union Details Its Involvement in Taliban's Azm Offensive," *Long War Journal*, July 25, 2015, https://www.longwarjournal.org/archives /2015/07/islamic-jihad-union-details-its-involvement-in-talibans-azm-offensive.php.

65. Kazakhstan has fourteen provinces, or oblasts (Akmola, Aktobe, Almaty, Atyrau, East Kazakhstan, Jambyl, Karaganda, Kostanay, Kyzylorda, Mangystau, North Kazakhstan, Pavlodar, Turkistan, and West Kazakhstan), and the cities of Astana and Almaty; Kyrgyzstan consists of seven oblasts (Batken, Chuy, Jalal-Abad, Naryn, Osh region, Issyk-Kul, Talas) in addition to the cities of Osh and Bishkek. Tajikistan is divided into the Districts of Republican Subordination, Gorno-Badakhstan, Sughd, Khatlon, and the city of Dushanbe. Uzbekistan and Turkmenistan had no province-level data available and, therefore, were not included into the statistical analysis.

66. Paris Pact Initiative, the Afghan Opiate Trade Project of the United Nations Office on Drugs and Crime (UNODC), and the UNODC Regional Office for Central Asia, Drugs Monitoring Platform, http://drugsmonitoring.unodc-roca.org/.

67. Infant mortality rate has been used as a direct measure of community health, but it has also been used more broadly as an indicator of socioeconomic development. Studies have found a high correlation between infant mortality rate and development indicators. See, for example, Mehran Alijanzadeh, Saeed Asezadeh, and Seyed Ali Moosaniyae Zar, "Correlation Between Human Development Index and Infant Mortality Rate Worldwide," *Biotechnology and Health Sciences* 3, no. 1 (2016): 1–5.

68. Agency of Statistics of the Republic of Kazakhstan, http://www.stat.gov.kz; Agency on Statistics under the President of Tajikistan, http://www.stat.tj/ru/; National Statistical Committee of the Kyrgyz Republic, http://www.stat.kg/ru/.

69. Joe Eyerman, "Terrorism and Democratic States: Soft Targets or Accessible Systems," *International Interactions* 24, no. 2 (1998): 151–170; Jeffery Ian Ross, "Structural Causes of Oppositional Political Terrorism: A Causal Model," *Journal of Peace Research* 30, no. 3 (1993): 317–329; James A. Piazza, "The Opium Trade and Patterns of Terrorism in the Provinces of Afghanistan: An Empirical Analysis," *Terrorism and Political Violence* 24, no. 2 (2012): 213–234.

70. As the infant mortality rate increases by 1, the odds ratio of the nexus decreases by a factor of 0.89 (the probability of the nexus goes down by 0.48).

71. In Kazakhstan, for example, the General Prosecutor's Office announced statistics that indicate that 95 percent of those detained under extremism and terrorism were unemployed youth. Serik Beissembayev, "Religious Extremism in Kazakhstan: From Criminal Networks to Jihad," Central Asia Fellowship Papers, no. 15 (Central Asia Program, George Washington University, February 2016), http://centralasiaprogram.org/archives/9484.

72. Kelly M. McMann, *Economic Autonomy and Democracy: Hybrid Regimes in Russia and Kyrgyzstan* (New York: Cambridge University Press, 2006); Johann Engvall, "Why Are Public Offices Sold in Kyrgyzstan?," *Post-Soviet Affairs* 30, no. 1 (2014): 67–85.

73. To test for the robustness of our findings, we reassessed the model using a zero-inflated poisson regression. The results were consistent with the reported findings.

74. Andreas Forø Tollefsen, Håvard Strand, and Halvard Buhaug, "PRIO-GRID: A Unified Spatial Data Structure," *Journal of Peace Research* 49, no. 2 (2012): 363–374.

75. As recommended by Adrian Colin Cameron and Pravin K. Trivedi, *Microeconometrics Using Stata* (College Station, Tex.: Stata Press, 2009).

3. CONVERGENCE AND COEXISTENCE: DIVERGENT PATHS OF TAJIKISTAN AND UZBEKISTAN

1. The phrase "criminalization of the state" comes from Jean-François Bayart, Stephen Ellis, and Béatrice Hibou, *The Criminalization of the State in Africa* (Bloomington: Indiana University Press, 2009).

2. Lawrence P. Markowitz, *State Erosion: Unlootable Resources and Unruly Elites* (Ithaca, N.Y.: Cornell University Press, 2013).

3. Jesse Driscoll, *Warlords and Coalition Politics in Post-Soviet States* (Cambridge: Cambridge University Press, 2015); John Heathershaw, *Post-Conflict Tajikistan: The Politics of Peacebuilding and the Emergence of Legitimate Order* (London: Routledge, 2009); Markowitz, *State Erosion*; Kirill Nourzhanov, "Saviours of the Nation or Robber Barons? Warlord Politics in Tajikistan," *Central Asian Survey* 24, no. 2 (2005): 109–113.

4. John Heathershaw and Sophie Roche, "Islam and Political Violence in Tajikistan: An Ethnographic Perspective on the Causes and Consequences of the 2010 Armed Conflict in the Kamarob Gorge," *Ethnopolitics Papers* 8 (2011): 1–21.

5. Sadullom Izzatullo, "IRPT and ISIL: The Practical Evidence of the Same Teachings, Activities, and Aims of These Two Extremist Organizations," Embassy of the Republic of Tajikistan in Malaysia, last modified November 16, 2017, http://tajemb-my.org/en/embassy/addresses-2/45-irpt-and-isil-the-practical-evidence-of-the-same-teachings-activities-and-aims-of-these-two-extremist-organizations.

6. Letizia Paoli et al., "Tajikistan: The Rise of a Narco-State," *Journal of Drug Issues* 37, no. 4 (1997): 969–971.

7. Interview #21 with senior law enforcement official, Dushanbe, December 2016.

8. Nourzhanov, "Saviours of the Nation or Robber Barons?"; Stina Torjesen and S. Neil McFarlane, "R before D: The Case of Postconflict Reintegration in Tajikistan," *Conflict, Security and Development* 7, no. 2 (2007): 311–332; Stina Torjesen, Christina Wille, and Stephen Neil MacFarlane, *Tajikistan's Road to Stability: Reduction in Small Arms Proliferation and Remaining Challenges* (Geneva: Small Arms Survey, 2005),13.

9. Nourzhanov, "Saviours of the Nation or Robber Barons?"

10. Driscoll, *Warlords and Coalition Politics in Post-Soviet States*.

11. Johan Engvall, "The State under Siege: The Drug Trade and Organised Crime in Tajikistan," *Europe-Asia Studies* 58, no. 6 (2006): 827–854.

12. Torjesen and McFarnlane, "R before D"; Torjesen, Wille, and MacFarlane, *Tajikistan's Road to Stability.*

13. Much of this comes from Svante Cornell, "The Islamic Movement of Uzbekistan," in *Conflict, Crime, and the State in Postcommunist Eurasia,* ed. Svante Cornell and Michael Jonsson (Philadelphia: University of Pennsylvania Press, 2014): 68–82.

14. Michael Fredholm, "Uzbekistan and the Threat from Islamic Extremism," in *Conflict Studies Research Centre Report K39* (Sandhurst, UK: Royal Military Academy, 2003); Maral Madi, "Drug Trade in Kyrgyzstan, Structure, Implications and Countermeasures," *Central Asian Survey* 23, nos. 3–4 (2004): 249–273; Tamara Makarenko, "The Crime-Terror Continuum: Tracing the Interplay between Transnational Organized Crime and Terrorism," *Global Crime* 6, no. 1 (2004): 129–145; Thomas M. Sanderson, Daniel Kimmage, and David A. Gordon, *From Ferghana Valley to South Waziristan: The Evolving Threat of Central Asian Jihadists* (Washington, D.C.: CSIS, 2010), https://csis-prod.s3.amazonaws.com/s3fs-public/legacy_files/files/publication/100324_Sanderson_FerghanaValley_WEB_0.pdf.

15. Suzanne Levi-Sanchez, *The Afghan-Central Asia Borderlands: The State and Local Leaders* (New York: Routledge, 2017).

16. Interview #25 with NGO worker, Dushanbe, December 2016.

17. Cornell, "Islamic Movement of Uzbekistan."

18. These attacks were carried out by the IMU's splinter group, the Islamic Jihad Union (IJU).

19. Vitaly Naumkin, "Militant Islam in Central Asia: The Case of the Islamic Movement of Uzbekistan" (Berkeley Program in Soviet and Post-Soviet Studies Working Paper Series, University of California, Berkeley, 2003).

20. Carlotta Gall, "Tajikistan Puts End to Rogue Warlord," *Moscow Times*, last modified December 3, 1997, http://old.themoscowtimes.com/sitemap/free/1997/12/article/tajikistan-puts-end-to-rogue-warlord/296747.html.

21. Interview #19 with senior law enforcement official, Dushanbe, December 2016.

22. Uzbekistan provided support to some antigovernment forces in Tajikistan during the civil war to destabilize its regime and has been implicated in killings and abductions of perceived enemies of the state by its security agents in Kyrgyzstan. Mariya Y. Omelicheva, *Counterterrorism Policies in Central Asia* (New York: Routledge, 2011). See also Stuart Horsman, "Uzbekistan's Involvement in the Tajik Civil War, 1992–97: Domestic Considerations," *Central Asian Survey* 18, no. 1 (1999): 37–48.

23. Lawrence P. Markowitz, "Beyond Kompromat: Coercion, Corruption and Deterred Defection in Uzbekistan," *Comparative Politics* 50, no. 1 (October 2017): 103–121.

24. Interview with former member of presidential apparatus (who served from December 1992 to 1998), Tashkent, May 2003.

25. Interview #34 with former security services official, Dushanbe, April 2017.

26. George Gavrilis, *The Dynamics of Interstate Boundaries* (Cambridge: Cambridge University Press, 2008); Lawrence Markowitz's database of political elites; Lawrence Markowitz's field notes (from stays in Surkhandarya Province in July 2001 and October 2002).

27. Nick Megoran, *Nationalism in Central Asia: A Biography of the Uzbekistan-Kyrgyzstan Boundary* (Pittsburgh: University of Pittsburgh Press, 2017); Madeleine Reeves, *Border Work: Spatial Lives of the State in Rural Central Asia* (Ithaca, N.Y.: Cornell University Press, 2014); John Schoeberlein, "Security Sector Reform in Uzbekistan," in *Security*

Sector Reform in Central Asia: Exploring Needs and Possibilities, ed. Merijn Hartog (Netherlands: Centre of European Security Studies, 2010), 55–62.

28. UNODC, *Opiate Flows Through Northern Afghanistan and Central Asia: A Threat Assessment* (Vienna: UNODC, 2012), accessed May 4, 2017, https://www.unodc.org/documents /data-and analysis/Studies/Afghanistan_northern_route_2012_web.pdf.

29. Interview with professor of economics and finance, Tashkent, April 2003.

30. Nick Megoran, Gael Raballand, and Jerome Bouyou, "Performance, Representation and the Economics of Border Control in Uzbekistan," *Geopolitics* 10, no. 4 (2005): 712–740.

31. U.S. Department of State, "2015 International Narcotics Control Strategy Report: Uzbekistan," Bureau of International Narcotics and Law Enforcement Affairs, last modified 2015, https://www.state.gov/j/inl/rls/nrcrpt/2015/vol1/239027.htm.

32. Schoeberlein, "Security Sector Reform in Uzbekistan." See also Erica Marat, *The Military and the State in Central Asia: From Red Army to Independence* (London: Routledge, 2009).

33. Seth G. Jones et al., *Security Tyrants or Fostering Reform? U.S. Internal Security Assistance to Repressive and Transitioning Regimes* (Santa Monica, Calif.: RAND Corporation, 2006).

34. Jones et al., *Security Tyrants or Fostering Reform?*

35. Pauline Jones Luong, *Institutional Change and Political Continuity in Post-Soviet Central Asia: Power, Perceptions, and Pacts* (Cambridge: Cambridge University Press, 2002).

36. Local *prokurator*'s manuscript on the history of the Prokuratura in Uzbekistan (author's name withheld); E. S. Ibragimov, *Prokuratura Suverrennogo Uzbekistana* (Tasket: Akademiia Ministerstva vnutrennix del respubliki Uzbekistan, 2000), 70.

37. Markowitz, *State Erosion*.

38. Abdumannob Polat and Nickolai Butkevich, "Unraveling the Mystery of the Tashkent Bombings: Theories and Implications," *Demokratizatsiya* 8, no. 4 (2000): 541–553.

39. Jacob Zenn, "The Indigenization of the Islamic Movement of Uzbekistan," *Terrorism Monitor* 10, no. 2 (2012), https://jamestown.org/program/the-indigenization-of-the-islamic -movement-of-uzbekistan/.

40. Zenn, "Indigenization of the Islamic Movement of Uzbekistan."

41. According to analysts, most of Hizb ut-Tahrir's resources are raised in Europe and the Middle East, with members expected to make small contributions. Operational costs of the organization are, however, low, because most of its members operate out of their homes and are unpaid. American Foreign Policy Council, "Hizb ut-Tahrir," last modified 2017, http://almanac.afpc.org/sites/almanac.afpc.org/files/HuT%202017%20Update.pdf.

42. "Bombings and Shootings Rock Uzbekistan," Eurasianet.org, last modified March 29, 2004, http://www.eurasianet.org/departments/insight/articles/eav032904b.shtml.

43. National Consortium for the Study of Terrorism and Responses to Terrorism (START), Global Terrorism Database, Incident Summary, Incident #200905260013, https://www .start.umd.edu/gtd/search/IncidentSummary.aspx?gtdid=200905260013; Incident Summary, Incident #200905260012, https://www.start.umd.edu/gtd/search/IncidentSummary .aspx?gtdid=200905260012.

44. Murat Laumulin, "Islamic Radicalism in Central Asia," in *Religion and Security in South and Central Asia*, ed. K. Warikoo (Abingdon, UK: Routledge, 2011), 146.

45. Reports of the number of people killed vary widely. According to the Uzbek government, 187 people were killed. International organizations estimate casualties at about 700 or

more. See OSCE, "Preliminary Findings on the Events in Andijan, Uzbekiztan, 13 May 2005," last modified June 20, 2005, www.osce.org/item/15234.html; Human Rights Watch, "'Bullets Were Falling Like Rain': The Andijan Massacre," last modified May 13, 2005, https://www.hrw.org/reports/2005/uzbekistan0605/.

4. EMERGING RELATIONSHIPS WITHIN THE NEXUS: KAZAKHSTAN, KYRGYZSTAN, AND TAJIKISTAN

1. Lawrence P. Markowitz, *State Erosion: Unlootable Resources and Unruly Elites* (Ithaca, N.Y.: Cornell University Press, 2013); Jesse Driscoll, *Warlords and Coalition Politics in Post-Soviet States* (Cambridge: Cambridge University Press, 2015); John Heathershaw, *Post-Conflict Tajikistan: The Politics of Peacebuilding and the Emergence of Legitimate Order* (London: Routledge; 2009); Kirill Nourzhanov, "Saviours of the Nation or Robber Barons? Warlord Politics in Tajikistan," *Central Asian Survey* 24, no. 2 (2005): 109–130.

2. Svante Cornell and Michael Jonsson, eds., *Conflict, Crime, and the State in Postcommunist Eurasia* (Philadelphia: University of Pennsylvania Press; 2014); Filippo De Danieli, "Beyond the Drug-Terror Nexus: Drug Trafficking and State-Crime Relations in Central Asia," *International Journal of Drug Policy* 25, no. 6 (2014): 1235–1240; David Lewis, "High Times on the Silk Road: The Central Asian Paradox," *World Policy Journal* 27, no. 1 (2010): 39–49; Alexander Kupatadze, "Organized Crime before and after the Tulip Revolution: The Changing Dynamics of Upperworld-Underworld Networks," *Central Asian Survey* 27, no. 3 (2008): 279–299; Alisher Latypov, "Understanding Post 9/11 Drug Control Policy and Politics in Central Asia," *International Journal of Drug Policy* 20, no. 5 (2009): 387–391; Johann Engvall, "The State under Siege: The Drug Trade and Organised Crime in Tajikistan," *Europe-Asia Studies* 58, no. 6 (2006): 827–854; Erica Marat, *The State-Crime Nexus in Central Asia: State Weakness, Organized Crime, and Corruption in Kyrgyzstan and Tajikistan* (Washington, D.C.: Central Asia-Caucasus Institute and Silk Road Studies Program, 2006).

3. Dmitry Gorenburg, "External Support for Central Asian Military and Security Forces" (working paper, Stockholm International Peace Research Institute and Open Society Foundations, January 2014).

4. Eric M. McGlinchey, *Chaos, Violence, Dynasty: Politics and Islam in Central Asia* (Pittsburgh: University of Pittsburgh Press, 2011), 80–81.

5. On the massive rents flowing into Akaev's (and later Bakiev's) coffers for American and Russian use of Manas Air Base, see Alexander Cooley, *Base Politics: Democratic Change and the U.S. Military Overseas* (Ithaca, N.Y.: Cornell University Press, 2008).

6. Kupatadze, "Organized Crime before and after the Tulip Revolution."

7. Scott Radnitz, *Weapons of the Wealthy: Predatory Regimes and Elite-Led Protests in Central Asia* (Ithaca, N.Y.: Cornell University Press, 2010).

8. Interview #9 with former senior law enforcement official, Bishkek, June–July 2016.

9. Interview #2 with political analyst and academic, Bishkek, June–July 2016.

10. Alexander Kupatadze, *Organized Crime, Political Transitions and State Formation in Post-Soviet Eurasia* (New York: Macmillan, 2012), 142–114.

11. Regine A. Spector, "Securing Property in Contemporary Kyrgyzstan," *Post-Soviet Affairs* 24, no. 2 (2008): 149–176; Marat, *State-Crime Nexus in Central Asia*.

12. UNODC, *An Assessment of Organized Crime in Central Asia* (New York: UNODC, 2007.) https://www.unodc.org/documents/organized-crime/Central_Asia_Crime_Assessment .pdf.

13. Interview #1 with political analyst and academic, Bishkek, June–July 2016.

14. These include well-known individuals such as the internal affairs minister, Melis Turgenbaev, and the so-called gray cardinal, Kurson Asanov. Interview with political analyst, Bishkek, June–July 2016; Interview #9 with former senior law enforcement official, Bishkek, June–July 2016; Interview #5 with political analyst and former government official, Bishkek, June–July 2016. On the involvement of the customs service, see Bruce Pannier, "Kyrgyzstan: Government Accused of Framing Opposition Leader," Radio Free Europe/Radio Liberty, last modified September 12, 2006, http://www.rferl.org/content/article/1071272.html.

15. Kupatadze, *Organized Crime, Political Transitions*.

16. Marat, *State-Crime Nexus in Central Asia*, 100.

17. Interview #6 with former senior law enforcement official, Bishkek, June–July 2016.

18. Interview #9 with former senior law enforcement official, Bishkek, June–July 2016.

19. Senior officials demand only aggregate data, so lower level officials see little incentive to collect this data. Efforts by international organizations to change these practices are met by suspicion, with security officials believing such reforms are an attempt to access secret information (a mentality some ascribe to their age and their Soviet-era training). Interview #12 with UNODC expert, Bishkek, June–July 2016.

20. Interview #12 with UNODC expert, Bishkek, June–July 2016.

21. Interview #4 with political analyst and academic, Bishkek, June–July 2016. Indeed, the flow of rents to elites for oil delivered to Manas Air Base went uninterrupted during these uprisings, so it stands to reason that rents from the drug trade were similarly unaffected. Interview #2 with political analyst and academic, Bishkek, June–July 2016.

22. Interview #5 with political analyst and former government official, Bishkek, June–July 2016.

23. Anna Matveeva, "Violence in Kyrgyzstan, Vacuum in the Region. The Case for Russia-EU Joint Crisis Management" (working paper, LSE Civil Society and Human Security Research Unit, London, 2011).

24. Erica Marat, "Kyrgyzstan's Fragmented Police and Armed Forces," *Journal of Power Institutions in Post-Soviet Societies* 11 (2010): 4, https://journals.openedition.org/pipss/3803.

25. International Crisis Group, "Kyrgyzstan: A Hollow Regime Collapses," Briefing no. 102, Europe and Central Asia, last modified April 27, 2010, 8, https://www.crisisgroup.org /europe-central-asia/central-asia/kyrgyzstan/kyrgyzstan-hollow-regime-collapses.

26. Interview #3 with political and security analyst, Bishkek, June–July 2016.

27. Kyrgyzstan Inquiry Commission, "Report of the Independent International Commission of Inquiry into the Events in Southern Kyrgyzstan in June 2010," 2011, http://reliefweb.int /sites/reliefweb.int/files/resources/full_Report_490.pdf.

28. Erica Marat, "Reforming Police in Post-Communist Countries: International Efforts, Domestic Heroes," *Comparative Politics* 48, no. 3 (2016): 333–352.

29. Interview #12 with UNODC expert, Bishkek, June–July 2016.

30. Interview #3 with political and security analyst, Bishkek, June–July 2016.

31. Albeit most of these working groups consisted of academics. Interview #4 with political analyst and academic, Bishkek, June–July 2016.

32. Interview #3 with political and security analyst, Bishkek, June–July 2016.

33. Interview #7 with academic, Bishkek, June–July 2016.

34. It was known that at least one top-level law enforcement official could not be reached during the 2010 violence for lack of a satellite phone. Interview #2 with political analyst and academic, Bishkek, June–July 2016.

35. Similarly, a proposal put forward by interim president Roza Otunbaeva to carry out reforms of the MIA was not carried out. Interview #3 with political and security analyst, Bishkek, June–July 2016.

36. Interview #3 with political and security analyst, Bishkek, June–July 2016.

37. Interview #10 with NGO head and expert on religious extremism, Bishkek, June–July 2016; Chris Rickleton, "Kyrgyzstan's Security Agents Intimidating Uzbek Minority, Activists Say," Eurasia.net, last modified April 2, 2015, http://www.eurasianet.org/node /72836.

38. Uzbeks are not recruited because it is feared they will serve the interests of Uzbekistan and not Kyrgyzstan (i.e., that they will somehow share information with Uzbekistan and spy for it). This also reflects a broader sentiment in society that sees Uzbeks as aliens and not as equal citizens in Kyrgyzstan. This is also true of political officers in Osh City, 95 percent of which are Kyrgyz. Interview #3 with political and security analyst, Bishkek, June–July 2016.

39. Human Rights Watch, *"Where Is the Justice?" Interethnic Violence in Southern Kyrgyzstan and Its Aftermath* (New York: Human Rights Watch, 2010), https://www.hrw.org/sites /default/files/reports/kyrgyzstan0810webwcover_1.pdf.

40. U.S. Department of State, "International Religious Freedom Report," last modified 2017, https://www.state.gov/j/drl/rls/irf/.

41. Interview #5 with political analyst and former government official, Bishkek, June –July 2016.

42. UNODC, *Opiate Flows Through Northern Afghanistan and Central Asia: A Threat Assessment* (Vienna: UNODC, 2012), accessed May 4, 2017, https://www.unodc.org/documents /data-and analysis/Studies/Afghanistan_northern_route_2012_web.pdf.

43. See, for example, Chyngyz Kambarov, lieutenant colonel of police in the Kyrgyz Interior Ministry. Chyngyz Kambarov, "Organized Criminal Groups in Kyrgyzstan and the Role of Law Enforcement," *Voices from Central Asia*, no. 20, January 2015, Central Asia Program, George Washington University, http://centralasiaprogram.org/wp-content/uploads /2015/03/Voices-from-CA-20-January-2015.pdf.

44. Interview #4 with political analyst and academic, Bishkek, June–July 2016.

45. Interview #6 with former senior law enforcement official, Bishkek, June–July 2016.

46. Interview #3 with political and security analyst, Bishkek, June–July 2016.

47. Interview #10 with NGO head and expert on religious extremism, Bishkek, June–July 2016; "Kyrgyzstan Silences Popular Imam with Extremism Charges," Eurasianet.org, last modified February 17, 2015, http://www.eurasianet.org/node/72116.

48. The report states: "Law enforcement agencies are actively engaged in arresting radical members and extremists. However, there is an increased fear of arbitrary arrests, especially among members of non-Kyrgyz ethnicities. . . . In this environment, there is a high level of distrust in law enforcement and government authorities regarding matters of the fight against extremism by the population . . . which is seen as unfair by families of arrestees, thus lead[ing] them to join extremist organizations. The extremist organizations, in turn, can take advantage of this situation and start recruiting the relatives of those who were innocently arrested, offering support to their families." Search for Common Ground, "Radicalization of the Population in Osh, Jalal-Abad and Batken Oblasts:

Factors, Types, and Risk Groups," *Internal Report* (2016), 18, https://www.sfcg.org/tag/kyr gyzstan-reports/.

49. Search for Common Ground, "Radicalization of the Population in Osh," 18–19.

50. Interview #10 with NGO head and expert on religious extremism, Bishkek, June–July 2016.

51. Ghoncheh Tazmini, "The Islamic Revival in Central Asia: A Potent Force or a Misconception?," *Central Asian Survey* 20, no. 1 (2001): 63–83; International Crisis Group, *Central Asian Islamist Mobilisation and Regional Security* (Osh, Kyrgyzstan: International Crisis Group, 2001).

52. The clashes of the demonstrators with security forces in April 2010 resulted in more than eighty deaths among the protesters.

53. Jacob Zenn and Kathleen Kuehnast, *Preventing Violent Extremism in Kyrgyzstan* (Washington, D.C.: U.S. Institute of Peace, 2014), 7.

54. Franco Galdini and Zukhra Iakupbaeva, "The Strange Case of Jayash Al-Mahdi and Mr. ISIS: How Kyrgyzstan's Elites Manipulate the Threat of Terrorism for Their Own Benefit," CAP Papers 179, Central Asia Program, CERIA Briefs, last modified October 13, 2016, http://centralasiaprogram.org/archives/10075; Kyrgyz Committee for Human Rights, "The Representatives of Muslims Think State Committee for National Security (SCNK) Is Suppressing the Muslim Community," KCHR, 2011, http://kchr.org/modules.php?name=News&file=article&sid=1953.

55. Similarly, several small-scale incidents in Bishkek had been questionably attributed to Uygur separatists in the early 2000s, but this attribution has been seen as politically motivated. Sean R. Roberts, *Imaginary Terrorism: The Global War on Terror and the Narrative of the Uyghur Terrorist Threat* (Washington, D.C.: Institute for European, Russian, and Eurasian Studies, George Washington University, 2012), 20–21.

56. In 2005, for example, a famous Kyrgyz athlete, lawmaker, and businessman from Osh—Bayaman Erkinbaev—was assassinated. Erkinbaev's main source of income was drug trafficking, and he had extensive linkages with Tajik and Uzbek transnational drug traffickers. Spector, "Securing Property," 169.

   Erkinbaev's rival—Taalaibek Kadiraliev—another criminal boss from the South with a background in boxing, who also became a member of the Kyrgyz Parliament, was assassinated in 2009. See Kupatadze, *Organized Crime, Political Transitions*. In March 2014, an explosive device planted in Ruslan Abasov's vehicle detonated in Tokmok City, Chuy Province, Kyrgyzstan. Abasov, a kickboxing champion, was killed, and his wife was wounded in the blast.

57. The composition of the Kyrgyz criminal underworld is not limited to athletes. It also includes national groups (Chechens and Uyghurs, for example), former convicts, clans, and transnational groups. Tamara Makarenko, "The Crime-Terror Continuum: Tracing the Interplay Between Transnational Organized Crime and Terrorism," *Global Crime* 6, no. 1 (2004): 129–145.

58. Saltanat Berdikeeva, "Organized Crime in Central Asia: A Threat Assessment," *China and Eurasia Forum Quarterly* 7, no. 2 (2009): 75–100.

59. For example, one of those killed in the operation—Kamchybek Kolbayev—was placed on the U.S. list of sanctions for involvement in transnational organized crime. Galdini and Iakupbaeva, "The Strange Case of Jayash Al-Mahdi."

60. "Kyrgyzstan Says It Has Been Hit by 'Wave of Terrorism,'" Eurasianet.org, December 11, 2015, http://www.eurasianet.org/node/76516.

61. UNODC, *Opiate Flows Through Northern Afghanistan and Central Asia*, 75. Certainly, the underlying causes of the 2010 interethnic violence in Kyrgyzstan were more complex and included social stratification of the society and latent interethnic tensions. The 2008 global economic crisis undercut remittance transfers from Russia and forced Kyrgyz laborers working abroad to return home. This exerted additional pressure on a society already facing socioeconomic challenges, elite rivalries, and weak central government.

62. UNODC, *Opiate Flows Through Northern Afghanistan and Central Asia*, 75.

63. Bhavna Dave, *Kazakhstan: Ethnicity, Language and Power* (London: Routledge, 2007); Marlene Laruelle, ed., *Kazakhstan in the Making: Legitimacy, Symbols, and Social Changes* (Lanham, Md.: Lexington Books, 2016); Edward Schatz, *Modern Clan Politics. The Power of "Blood" in Kazakhstan and Beyond* (Seattle: University of Washington Press, 2004).

64. Jeffrey Herbst, *States and Power in Africa: Comparative Lessons in Authority and Control* (Princeton, N.J.: Princeton University Press, 2000).

65. Sergey V. Golunov, "Drug-Trafficking through the Russia-Kazakhstan Border: Challenge and Response," in *Empire, Islam, and Politics in Central Eurasia*, ed. Uyama Tomohiko, 331–350. Sapporo: Slavic Research Center of Hokkaido University, 2007, http://src-home .slav.hokudai.ac.jp/coe21/publish/no14_ses/13_golunov.pdf; Sergey V. Golunov and Roger N. McDermott, "Border Security in Kazakhstan: Threats, Policies and Future Challenges," *Journal of Slavic Military Studies* 18, no. 1 (2005): 31–58.

66. U.S. Energy Information Administration, "Country Analysis Brief: Kazakhstan," last modified May 10, 2017, https://www.eia.gov/beta/international/analysis_includes/coun tries_long/Kazakhstan/kazakhstan.pdf.

67. Rico Isaacs, "Elite Fragmentation and Propresidential Party Consolidation: Understanding Party System Development in Kazakhstan since 2001," *Journal of East European and Asian Studies* 2, no. 1 (2011): 111–136.

68. Prague Open Media Research Institute, *The OMRI Annual Survey of Eastern Europe and the Former Soviet Union: 1995: Building Democracy* (London: Routledge, 1996), 272.

69. Golunov, *Drug-Trafficking Through the Russia-Kazakhstan Border.*

70. Golunov and McDermott, "Border Security in Kazakhstan."

71. "'Nomad—Komitet Natsional'noi Bezopasnosti Kazakhstana: Istoriya, Struktura, Litsa," Centrasia, last modified July 15, 2002, https://www.centrasia.org/newsA.php ?st=1026687180.

72. Jos Boonstra, "Uncharted Waters: Presidential Successions in Kazakhstan and Uzbekistan," *EUCAM Policy Brief*, no. 33 (2014).

73. This follows from the reports of the Procurator General of Kazakhstan as reported in "Narkotorgovlya i Provoohranitel'nye Organy Kazakhstana," *Vremya Vostoka*, last modified June 3, 2013, http://easttime.ru/news/kazakhstan/narkotorgovlya-i-pravookhran itelnye-organy-kazakhstana/4002.

74. George Voloshin, "Kazakhstan's Border Protection Service Rocked by a New Wave of Incidents," *Eurasia Daily Monitor*, February 13, 2013, https://jamestown.org/program/kazakh stans-border-protection-service-rocked-by-a-new-wave-of-incidents/.

75. George Gavrilis, *The Dynamics of Interstate Boundaries* (Cambridge: Cambridge University Press, 2008).

76. President Nazarbayev sought to increase the share of military equipment and weapons produced domestically to 70 percent by 2015. According to UNODC, the quality of military and security equipment produced by national companies compares unfavorably to

Western military equipment. UNODC, *Opiate Flows Through Northern Afghanistan and Central Asia.*

77. A special unit, Arystan, was established from the remains of the regional corps of the Soviet unit Alpha, the famous "A" group that was formed in 1974 for reconnaissance, surveillance, surgical raids, hostage rescue, and other operations. Mariya Y. Omelicheva, *Counterterrorism Policies in Central Asia* (New York: Routledge, 2011). There are also several other special operations groups in Kazakhstan, such as Synkar and Berkyt, overseen by the president himself.

78. Erica Marat, *The Military and the State in Central Asia: From Red Army to Independence* (London: Routledge, 2009).

79. Roger N. McDermott, *Kazakhstan's Defense Policy: An Assessment of the Trends* (Carlisle, Penn.: U.S. Army War College, Strategic Studies Institute, 2009), https://www.globalsecurity.org/military/library/report/2009/ssi_mcdermott.pdf.

80. Erica Marat, *The Politics of Police Reform: Society Against the State in Post-Soviet Countries* (New York: Oxford University Press, 2017).

81. International Crisis Group, "Kazakhstan: Waiting for Change," *Asia Report*, no. 250, September 30, 2013, https://d2071andvipowj.cloudfront.net/kazakhstan-waiting-for-change.pdf.

82. Marat, *Politics of Police Reform.*

83. The deadliest terrorist incidents that took place in Kazakhstan during the period of the study occurred in November 2011. A suspected Islamist identified as Maksat Kariyev committed multiple shootings that killed seven persons before self-detonating in Taraz City, in the southern Jambyl Province of Kazakhstan bordering Kyrgyzstan. The rampage began with the robbery of a gun store, where Kariyev stole two hunting rifles and shot dead a security guard and a visitor. While fleeing in a stolen vehicle, Kariyev shot two police officers and took their service weapons. He was able to return home to pick up a grenade launcher that he later shot at the National Security Committee Department of the Jambyl region. While nobody was hurt in this attack, Kariyev shot and injured two other officers of the equestrian police patrol. When a police officer tried to arrest him, he blew himself up, claiming the life of one more person. Kariyev was a drug user and, according to some sources, committed the rampage under the influence of drugs. While we do not know the nature of the illegal substance used by Kariyev and who gave it to the assailant, his case fits the narrative of radical groups recruiting members with criminal pasts and histories of drug abuse and highlights how the degraded capacity of state security institutions translates into the operational relationship between drug trafficking and terrorism. See Botagoz Rakisheva and Gulden Shalova, "Suicide Acts in the Republic of Kazakhstan: A Chronology of Events Content-Analysis of Mass-Media," in *Contemporary Suicide Terrorism: Origins, Trends and Ways of Tackling It*, ed. Tatyana Dronzina and Rachid El Houdigui (Amsterdam: IOS Press, 2012), 137–143.

84. Rakisheva and Shalova, "Suicide Acts in the Republic of Kazakhstan"; Jacob Zenn, "Network of Jund al-Khilafah in Kazakhstan Wider Than Predicted," *Eurasia Daily Monitor*, last modified January 18, 2012, https://jamestown.org/program/network-of-jund-al-khilafah-in-kazakhstan-wider-than-predicted/.

85. "Kazakh 'Counterterror Operation' Continues after Deadly Attacks in Aqtobe," Radio Free Europe/Radio Liberty, last modified June 6, 2016, https://www.rferl.org/a/kazakhstan-aqtobe-gunmen-attack-military-facility-gun-stores/27781652.html.

86. International Crisis Group, "Kazakhstan: Waiting for Change," 18.

87. Interview #34 with former security services official, Dushanbe, April 2017.

88. Letizia Paoli et al., "Tajikistan: The Rise of a Narco-State," *Journal of Drug Issues* 37, no. 4 (1997): 951–971.

89. On the arrests of senior government officials (or their relatives) for involvement in drug trafficking, see Danieli, "Beyond the Drug-Terror Nexus."

90. Interview #25 with NGO staff, Dushanbe, January 2017.

91. Interview # 17 with academic, Dushanbe, December 2016; Interview #20 with senior law enforcement official, Dushanbe, December 2016; Interview #23 with NGO staff, Dushanbe, January 2017. See also Christian Bleuer and Said Reza Kazemi, "Between Co-operation and Insulation: Afghanistan's Relations with the Central Asian Republics," Afghanistan Analysts Network, June 2014, https://www.afghanistan-analysts.org/wp-content/uploads/2014/06/20140608-Bleuer_Kazemi-Central_Asia.pdf; Lewis, "High Times on the Silk Road."

92. Interview #16 with IO senior staff member, Dushanbe, January 2017.

93. Interview #17 with academic, Dushanbe, December 2016; Interview #23 with NGO staff, Dushanbe, January 2017.

94. Multiple interviews with security experts, Dushanbe, December 2016, January 2017, and April 2017.

95. Interview #33 with UNODC staff, Dushanbe, April 2017.

96. Interview #12 with UNODC expert, Bishkek, June–July 2016; Bleuer and Kazemi, "Between Co-operation and Insulation."

97. However, this has created potential conflict between these officials and local leaders in the province, which appears to have contributed to open clashes among state security actors. Interview #26 with IO staff, Dushanbe, January 2017.

98. Edward Lemon, "From Moscow to Madrid: Governing Security Threats beyond Tajikistan's Borders," in *Tajikistan on the Move: Statebuilding and Societal Transformations*, ed. Marlene Laruelle (London: Rowman & Littlefield, 2018), 63–86.

99. Even the everyday person who speaks against the government will likely be fired from his or her job and face a lawsuit. Interview #28 with NGO staff, Dushanbe, April 2017. On the threat of firing workers as an instrument of repression in the region, see Kelly M. McMann, *Economic Autonomy and Democracy: Hybrid Regimes in Russia and Kyrgyzstan* (Cambridge: Cambridge University Press, 2006).

100. U.S. Department of State, "International Religious Freedom Report," https://www.state.gov/j/drl/rls/irf/.

101. Interview #26 with IO staff, Dushanbe, January 2017.

102. Many felt that repression tends to push religious activity underground; others contended that it undermined effective intelligence collection and recommended closely monitoring groups before arresting them. Multiple interviews, Dushanbe, December 2016, January and April 2017.

103. Interview #35 with senior official from U.S. Embassy, Dushanbe, April 2017

104. Interview #21 with senior law enforcement official, Dushanbe, December 2016.

105. Interview #29 with NGO staff, Dushanbe, April 2017; Interview #34 with former security services official, Dushanbe, April 2017.

106. Farangis Najibullah, "Four Suspected IMU Members Killed in Tajikistan," Radio Free Europe/Radio Liberty, last modified October 19, 2009, http://reliefweb.int/report/kyrgyzstan/four-suspected-imu-members-killed-tajikistan.

107. Thomas Ruttig, a co-director and co-founder of the Afghanistan Analysts Network, delivered an in-depth analysis of the discussed series of incidents blamed on Islamists by the

Tajik authorities. See Thomas Ruttig, "Talibes in Tajikistan? The 'Terrorist Spillover' Hype," Afghanistan Analysts Network, last modified October 10, 2013, https://www.afghanistan-analysts.org/talebs-in-tajikistan-the-terrorist-spill-over-hype/.

108.   Yaacov Ro'i and Alon Wainer, "Muslim Identity and Islamic Practice in Post-Soviet Central Asia," *Central Asian Survey* 28, no. 3 (2009): 303–322.

109.   Igor Rotar, "Islamic Extremist Group Jamaat Ansarullah Overcomes Tajikistan's Inter-Tribal Conflicts," *Eurasia Daily Monitor,* last modified September 25, 2012, http://www.ecoi.net/local_link/230996/339430_en.html.

110.   For a similar assessment, see John Heathershaw and Parviz Mullojonov, "Rebels Without a Cause? Authoritarian Conflict Management in Tajikistan, 2008–2015," in *Tajikistan on the Move: Statebuilding and Societal Transformations*, ed. Marlene Laruelle (London: Rowman & Littlefield, 2018), 33–62.

111.   The following summary is drawn from Markowitz, *State Erosion*; Edward Lemon, "Mediating the Conflict in the Rasht Valley, Tajikistan," *Central Asian Affairs* 1, no. 2 (2014): 247–272; Eric Hamrin and Edward Lemon, "Rasht Revisited: Five Years After the Conflict," *Central Asia Policy Brief* no. 29 (October 2015).

112.   A former member of the Islamist opposition fighting the central government in the civil war, Rahimov refused to lay down arms following the 1997 peace agreement and integrate his units into Tajikistan's Ministry of Defense. Martha Brill Olcott, *Tajikistan's Difficult Development Path* (Washington, D.C.: Carnegie Endowment for International Peace, 2012).

113.   Olcott, *Tajikistan's Difficult Development Path.*

114.   According to local observers, on the day of the "terrorist incident," an inebriated Nazarov was at the Ishkashim border crossing stopping the traffic and demanding bribes for the contraband. When Tolib Ayombekov and his "men" refused to pay a higher "tax" on the smuggled goods, a brawl ensued that led to the knife killing. Mariya Yanovskaya, "Kak Possorilis' General Nazarov i Pogranichnik Ayombekov, i Chem Eto Zakonchilos' dlya Zhitelei Pamira," Fergana News Agency, last modified July 27, 2012, http://www.fergananews.com/articles/7433.

115.   "Tajikistan: Accused Warlord Speaks Out on Gorno-Badakhshan Violence," Eurasianet.org, last modified October 24, 2012, http://www.eurasianet.org/node/66101.

CONCLUSION

1.   Chris Dishman, "Terrorism, Crime, and Transformation," *Studies in Conflict & Terrorism*, 24, no. 1 (2001): 43–58; Peng Wang, "The Crime-Terror Nexus: Transformation, Alliance, Convergence," *Asian Social Science* 6, no. 6 (2010): 11–20, http://www.ccsenet.org/journal/index.php/ass/article/view/6218.

2.   Glenn E. Curtis and Tara Karacan, *The Nexus among Terrorists, Narcotics Traffickers, Weapons Proliferators, and Organized Crime Networks in Western Europe* (Washington, D.C.: Library of Congress, 2002).

3.   Dishman, "Terrorism, Crime, and Transformation."

4.   This distinction has been strengthened in the wake of the 9/11 terrorist attacks, which shaped views of terrorism as a security issue requiring international efforts. Organized crime, on the other hand, has been typically perceived as a domestic problem. Wang, "The Crime-Terror Nexus," 11; Charlie Edwards and Calum Jeffray, "The Growing Nexus Between Terrorism and Organized Crime in the Atlantic Basin," in *Dark Networks in the*

Atlantic Basin: Emerging Trends and Implications for Human Security, ed. Daniel S. Hamilton (Washington, D.C.: Center for Transatlantic Relations, Johns Hopkins University, 2015), 57–74.

5. Edwards and Calum, "Growing Nexus Between Terrorism and Organized Crime"; Wang, "Crime-Terror Nexus," 11.

6. John T. Picarelli, "Osama bin Corleone? Vito the Jackal? Framing Threat Convergence Through an Examination of Transnational Organized Crime and International Terrorism," *Terrorism and Political Violence* 24, no. 2 (2012): 180–198.

7. Tamara Makarenko, "The Crime-Terror Continuum: Tracing the Interplay Between Transnational Organized Crime and Terrorism," *Global Crime* 6, no. 1 (2004): 134.

8. Joel Hernandez, "Terrorism, Drug Trafficking, and the Globalization of Supply," *Perspectives on Terrorism* 7, no. 4 (2013): 49.

9. Edwards and Jeffray, "Growing Nexus Between Terrorism and Organized Crime," 61.

10. Experts and government officials in the Central Asian states often mention the significance of these factors for citizens' radicalization. Serik Beissembayev, "Religious Extremism in Kazakhstan: From Criminal Networks to Jihad" (Central Asia Fellows Papers, no. 15, Central Asia Program, George Washington University, February 2016).

11. UNODC, *Opiate Flows Through Northern Afghanistan and Central Asia: A Threat Assessment* (Vienna: UNODC, 2012), accessed May 4, 2017, https://www.unodc.org/documents/data-and analysis/Studies/Afghanistan_northern_route_2012_web.pdf. Countries in the region have already agreed, in principle, to cooperate on counternarcotics, with the establishment of the Central Asian Regional Information and Coordination Centre (CARICC). While this is a fundamental step, some countries have not taken advantage of available cooperation mechanisms through CARICC; others are still developing their border security policies largely in isolation from other Central Asian republics. The resulting lack of professional trust makes it difficult to create relationships strong enough to support effective cooperation.

12. UNODC, *Opiate Flows Through Northern Afghanistan and Central Asia.*

13. Gerald H. Peiris, "Narcotics: Hanging on to the Tiger's Tail," *The Island*, June 17, 2015, https://thuppahi.wordpress.com/2015/06/17/smuggling-shipping-and-the-narcotics-trade-in-the-history-of-the-ltte-1970s-2015/.

14. Paul Staniland, *Networks of Rebellion: Explaining Insurgent Cohesion and Collapse* (Ithaca, N.Y.: Cornell University Press, 2014), 141–181.

15. Mapping Militant Organizations, "Liberation Tigers of Tamil Elam," Mapping Militants Project, Stanford University, http://web.stanford.edu/group/mappingmilitants/cgi-bin/groups/view/225. See also Jayshree Bajoria, "The Sri Lankan Conflict," Council on Foreign Relations, last modified May 18, 2009, http://www.cfr.org/terrorist-organizations-and-networks/sri-lankan-conflict/p11407; Hellmann-Rajanayagam Dagmar, *The Tamil Tigers: Armed Struggle for Identity* (Stuttgart: Franz Steiner Verlag, 1994); Tullis LaMond, *Unintended Consequences: Illegal Drugs and Drug Policies in Nine Counties* (London: Lynne Rienner, 1995); Peter Chalk, *LTTE's International Organization and Operations: A Preliminary Analysis* (Toronto: Canadian Security Intelligence Service, 1999–2000).

16. Sri Lanka also experienced a wave of left-wing terrorism during the Janatha Vimukthi Peramuna insurrections in 1971 and 1987–1989 and state terror and repression against its ethnic minorities.

17. West Sands Advisory LLP, "Europe's Crime-Terror Nexus: Links Between Terrorist and Organized Crime Groups in the European Union" (European Parliament, Committee on Civil Liberties, Justice, and Home Affairs, Brussels, October 2012).

18. Makarenko, "Crime-Terror Continuum," 132.
19. Makarenko, "Crime-Terror Continuum," 133.
20. Ian Traynor, "Milosevic Allies Linked to Heroin Stash," *Guardian*, March 15, 2001, https://www.theguardian.com/world/2001/mar/16/balkans.internationalcrime.
21. World Almanac of Islamism, "Kosovo," last modified December 14, 2017, http://almanac.afpc.org/kosovo.
22. Allan Hall and Dan Warburton, "ISIS Seizes £4bn Drug Ring from the Mafia to Fund Its Brutal Terror Campaign," *Daily Mirror*, last modified January 17, 2016, http://www.mirror.co.uk/news/uk-news/isis-seizes-4bn-drug-ring-7191800.
23. Alastair Drysdale, "The Syrian Armed Forces in National Politics: The Role of the Geographic and Ethnic Periphery," in *Soldiers, Peasants, and Bureaucrats: Civil-Military Relations in Communist and Modernizing Societies*, ed. Roman Kolkowicz and Andrzej Korbonski (London: George Allen & Unwin, 1982), 52–76.
24. Radwan Ziadeh, *Power and Policy in Syria: Intelligence Services, Foreign Relations, and Democracy in the Modern Middle East* (London: I. B. Tauris, 2011).
25. Volker Perthes, "*Si Vis Stabilitatem, Para Bellum*: State Building, National Security, and War Preparation in Syria," in *War, Institutions, and Social Change in the Middle East*, ed. Steven Heydemann (Berkeley: University of California Press, 2000), 172.
26. Drysdale, "Syrian Armed Forces in National Politics," 70.
27. Nikolaos Van Dam, *The Struggle for Power in Syria: Politics and Society under Asad and the Ba'th Party* (London: I. B. Tauris, 1996), 73.
28. Gary C. Gambill, "Syria after Lebanon: Hooked on Lebanon," *Middle East Quarterly* 12, no. 4 (2005): 35–42.
29. National Consortium for the Study of Terrorism and Responses to Terrorism (START), Global Terrorism Database, "Syria," accessed December 28, 2017, https://www.start.umd.edu/gtd/search/Results.aspx?country=200.
30. Interview, UNODC staff, Dushanbe, April 2017.
31. UNODC, *Opiate Flows Through Northern Afghanistan and Central Asia.*
32. Mariya Y. Omelicheva, "Russia's Foreign Policy in Central Asia," in *Russian Foreign Policy*, ed. Andrei Tsygankov (New York: Routledge, 2018), 325–337.
33. Alexander Cooley, *Great Games, Local Rules: The New Great Power Contest in Central Asia* (New York: Oxford University Press, 2012).

APPENDIX 1. SOCIOECONOMIC PREDICTORS OF THE TRAFFICKING-TERRORISM NEXUS

1. Paul D. Allison, *Fixed Effects Regression Models* (Thousand Oaks, Calif.: SAGE, 2006).
2. P. J. Huber, "The Behavior of Maximum Likelihood Estimates under Non-Standard Conditions," *Proceedings of the Fifth Berkeley Symposium on Mathematical Statistics and Probability* (Berkeley: University of California Press, 1967), 221–233; Jeffrey M. Wooldridge, "Cluster-Sample Methods in Applied Econometrics," *American Economic Review* 93, no. 2 (2003): 133–138.
3. A. Colin Cameron, Jonah B. Gelbach, and Douglas L. Miller. "Robust Inference with Multiway Clustering," *Journal of Business & Economic Statistics* 29, no. 2 (2011): 238–249.

BIBLIOGRAPHY

Adida, Claire, David Laitin, and Marie-Anne Valfort. *Why Muslim Integration Fails in Christian-Heritage Societies.* Cambridge, Mass.: Harvard University Press, 2016.

Agency of Statistics of the Republic of Kazakhstan. http://www.stat.gov.kz.

Agency on Statistics under the President of Tajikistan. http://www.stat.tj/ru/.

Alijanzadeh, Mehran, Saeed Asezadeh, and Seyed Ali Moosaniyae Zare. "Correlation Between Human Development Index and Infant Mortality Rate Worldwide." *Biotechnology and Health Sciences* 3, no. 1 (2016): 1–5.

Allison, Paul D. *Fixed Effects Regression Models.* Thousand Oaks, Calif.: Sage, 2006.

Allum, Felia, and Jennifer Sands. "Explaining Organized Crime in Europe: Are Economists Always Right?" *Crime, Law, and Social Change* 41, no. 2 (2004): 133–160.

American Foreign Policy Council. "Hizb ut-Tahrir." In *The World Almanac of Islamism.* Last modified April 2018. http://almanac.afpc.org/sites/almanac.afpc.org/files/Hizb-ut%20Tahrir%202018%20Website.pdf.

Andreas, Peter. *Border Games: Policing the U.S.-Mexico Divide.* Ithaca, N.Y.: Cornell University Press, 2000.

——. "Transnational Crime and Economic Globalization." In *Transnational Organized Crime and International Security,* ed. Mats Berdal and Mónica Serrano, 37–52. Boulder, Colo.: Lynne Rienner, 2002.

Asal, Victor, H. Brinton Milward, and Eric W. Schoon. "When Terrorists Go Bad: Analyzing Terrorist Organizations' Involvement in Drug Smuggling." *International Studies Quarterly* 59, no. 1 (2015): 112–123.

Bahgat, Karim, and Richard M. Medina "An Overview of Geographical Perspectives and Approaches in Terrorism Research." *Perspectives on Terrorism* 7, no. 1 (2013). http://www.terrorismanalysts.com/pt/index.php/pot/article/view/242.

Bajoria, Jayshree. "The Sri Lankan Conflict." Council on Foreign Relations. Last modified May 18, 2009. http://www.cfr.org/terrorist-organizations-and-networks/sri-lankan-conflict/p11407.

Basra, Rajan, and Peter R. Neumann. "Criminal Pasts, Terrorist Futures: European Jihadists, and the New Crime-Terror Nexus." *Perspectives on Terrorism* 10, no. 6 (2016): 25–40.

Bayart, Jean-François, Stephen Ellis, and Béatrice Hibou. *The Criminalization of the State in Africa.* Bloomington: Indiana University Press, 2009.

Bayrmli, Gokalp. "Uzbekistan Bombing Allegations Raise Tensions with Turkey." Radio Free Europe/Radio Liberty, July 8, 1999. http://www.rferl.org/nca/features/1999/07/F.RU.990708132919.html.

Beissembayev, Serik. "Religious Extremism in Kazakhstan: From Criminal Networks to Jihad." Central Asia Fellowship Papers, no. 15. Central Asia Program, George Washington University, February 2016. http://centralasiaprogram.org/archives/9484.

Berdikeeva, Saltanat. "Organized Crime in Central Asia: A Threat Assessment." *China and Eurasia Forum Quarterly* 7, no. 2 (2009): 75–100.

Bhavna, Dave. *Kazakhstan: Ethnicity, Language and Power.* London: Routledge, 2007.

Biersteker, Thomas J., and Sue E. Eckert. *Countering the Financing of Terrorism.* London: Routledge, 2008.

Bleuer, Christian, and Said Reza Kazemi. "Between Co-operation and Insulation: Afghanistan's Relations with the Central Asian Republics." Afghanistan Analysts Network, June 2014. https://www.afghanistan-analysts.org/wp-content/uploads/2014/06/20140608-Bleuer_Kazemi-Central_Asia.pdf.

"Bombings and Shootings Rock Uzbekistan." Eurasianet.org, March 29, 2004. http://www.eurasianet.org/departments/insight/articles/eav032904b.shtml.

Boone, Catherine. *Merchant Capital and the Roots of State Power in Senegal: 1930–1985.* Cambridge: Cambridge University Press, 1992.

Boonstra, Jos. "Uncharted Waters: Presidential Successions in Kazakhstan and Uzbekistan." *EUCAM Policy Brief,* no. 33 (2014), https://www.files.ethz.ch/isn/178985/Uncharted%20waters_%20Presidential%20successions%20in%20Kazakhstan%20and%20Uzbekista.pdf.

Bravo, Ana Bela Santos, and Carlos Manuel Mendes Dias. "An Empirical Analysis of Terrorism: Deprivation, Islamism and Geopolitical Factors." *Defense and Peace Economics* 17, no. 4 (2006): 329–341.

Burnashev, Rustam. "Terrorist Routes in Central Asia: Trafficking Drugs, Humans, and Weapons." *Connections: The Quarterly Journal* 6, no. 1 (2007): 65–70.

Cameron, A. Colin, Jonah B. Gelbach, and Douglas L. Miller. "Robust Inference with Multiway Clustering." *Journal of Business & Economic Statistics* 29, no. 2 (2011): 238–249.

Cameron, Adrian Colin, and Pravin K. Trivedi. *Microeconometrics Using Stata.* College Station, Tex.: Stata Press, 2009.

Carraico, Helena, Daniella Irrera, and Bill Tupman. *Criminals and Terrorists in Partnership: Unholy Alliance.* Abingdon, UK: Routledge, 2016.

Chalk, Peter. *LTTE's International Organization and Operations: A Preliminary Analysis.* Toronto: Canadian Security Intelligence Service, 1999–2000.

Chayes, Sarah. *Thieves of State: Why Corruption Threatens Global Security.* New York: Norton, 2015.

Cirino, Julie A., Silvana L. Elizondo, and Geoffrey Wawro. "Latin America's Lawless Areas and Failed States." In *Latin American Security Challenges: A Collaborative Inquiry from North and South,* ed. Paul D. Taylor, 7–48. Newport, R.I.: Naval War College, 2004.

Clarke, Ryan, and Lee Stuart. "The PIRA, D-Company, and the Crime-Terror Nexus." *Terrorism and Political Violence* 20, no. 3 (2008): 376–395.

Clawson, Patrick L., and Rensselaer W. Lee III. *The Andean Cocaine Industry.* New York: St. Martin's Press, 1998.

Collins, Kathleen. *Clan Politics and Regime Transition in Central Asia*. New York: Cambridge University Press, 2006.

Cooley, Alexander. *Base Politics: Democratic Change and the U.S. Military Overseas*. Ithaca, N.Y.: Cornell University Press, 2008.

——. *Great Games, Local Rules: The New Great Power Contest in Central Asia*. New York: Oxford University Press, 2012.

——. *Logics of Hierarchy: The Organization of Empires, States, and Military Occupations*. Ithaca, N.Y.: Cornell University Press, 2005.

Cooley, Alexander A., and John Heathershaw. *Dictators Without Borders: Power and Money in Central Asia*. New Haven, Conn.: Yale University Press, 2017.

Cooley, John. *Unholy Wars: Afghanistan, America and International Terrorism*. London: Pluto Press, 1999.

Cornell, Svante. "The Islamic Movement of Uzbekistan." In *Conflict, Crime, and the State in Post-communist Eurasia*, ed. Svante Cornell and Michael Jonsson, 68–81. Philadelphia: University of Pennsylvania Press, 2014.

——. "The Narcotics Threat in Greater Central Asia: From Crime-Terror Nexus to State Infiltration?" *China and Eurasia Forum Quarterly* 4, no. 1 (2006): 37–67.

Cornell, Svante, and Michael Jonsson, eds. *Conflict, Crime, and the State in Postcommunist Eurasia*. Philadelphia: University of Pennsylvania Press, 2014.

——. "The Nexus of Crime and Conflict." In *Conflict, Crime, and the State in Postcommunist Eurasia*, ed. Svante Cornell and Michael Jonsson, 1–22. Philadelphia: University of Pennsylvania Press, 2014.

Cornell, Svante, and Niklas L. P. Swanströmm. "The Eurasian Drug Trade: A Challenge to Regional Security." *Problems of Post-Communism* 53, no. 4 (2006): 10–28.

Corte, Ibáñez L. de la. "To What Extent Do Global Terrorism and Organized Criminality Converge? General Parameters and Critical Scenarios." *Journal of the Spanish Institute of Strategic Studies* 1, no. 1 (2013): 1–28.

Crenshaw, Martha. *Explaining Terrorism: Causes, Processes, Consequences*. London: Routledge, 2011.

Curtis, Glenn E., and Tara Karacan. *The Nexus among Terrorists, Narcotics Traffickers, Weapons Proliferators, and Organized Crime Networks in Western Europe*. Washington, D.C.: Library of Congress, 2002.

Dagmar, Hellmann-Rajanayagam. *The Tamil Tigers: Armed Struggle for Identity*. Stuttgart: Franz Steiner Verlag, 1994.

Daly, Max. "No, Your Drug Use Is Not Funding Terrorism." *Vice*, September 20, 2016. https://www.vice.com/en_us/article/is-the-drug-trade-really-bank-rolling-terrorists.

Dam, Nikolaos Van. *The Struggle for Power in Syria: Politics and Society Under Asad and the Ba'th Party*. London: I. B. Tauris, 1996.

Danieli, Filippo De. "Beyond the Drug-Terror Nexus: Drug Trafficking and State-Crime Relations in Central Asia." *International Journal of Drug Policy* 25, no. 6 (2014): 1235–1240.

——. "Counter-Narcotics Policies in Tajikistan and Their Impact on State Building." *Central Asian Survey* 30, no. 1 (2011): 129–145.

Dishman, Chris. "The Leaderless Nexus: When Crime and Terror Converge." *Studies in Conflict & Terrorism* 28, no. 3 (2005): 237–252.

——. "Terrorism, Crime, and Transformation." *Studies in Conflict & Terrorism* 24, no. 1 (2001): 43–58.

Driscoll, Jesse. *Warlords and Coalition Politics in Post-Soviet States.* Cambridge: Cambridge University Press, 2015.

Drysdale, Alastair. "The Syrian Armed Forces in National Politics: The Role of the Geographic and Ethnic Periphery." In *Soldiers, Peasants, and Bureaucrats: Civil-Military Relations in Communist and Modernizing Societies,* ed. Roman Kolkowicz and Andrzej Korbonski, 52–76. London: George Allen & Unwin, 1982.

Dupont, Alan. "Transnational Crime, Drugs and Security in East Asia." *Asian Survey* 39, no. 3 (1999): 433–455.

Easson, Joseph J., and Alex P. Schmid. "Appendix 2.1: 250-plus Academic, Governmental and Intergovernmental Definitions of Terrorism." In *The Routledge Handbook of Terrorism Research,* ed. Alex P. Schmid, 99–200. London: Routledge, 2011.

Easter, G. M. *Capital, Coercion, and Postcommunist States.* Ithaca, N.Y.: Cornell University Press, 2012.

Edwards, Charlie, and Calum Jeffray. "The Growing Nexus between Terrorism and Organized Crime in the Atlantic Basin." In *Dark Networks in the Atlantic Basin: Emerging Trends and Implications for Human Security,* ed. Daniel S. Hamilton, 57–74. Washington, D.C.: Center for Transatlantic Relations, Johns Hopkins University, 2015.

Ehrlich, Paul R. "Some Roots of Terrorism." *Population and Environment* 24, no. 2 (2002): 183–192.

"Ekzotika v obmen na . . . zhizn.'" Last modified July 27, 2015. http://caricc.org/index.php/ru /media-center-ru/nashi-publikacii.

Engvall, Johann. "The State under Siege: The Drug Trade and Organised Crime in Tajikistan." *Europe-Asia Studies* 58, no. 6 (2006): 827–854.

——. "Why Are Public Offices Sold in Kyrgyzstan?" *Post-Soviet Affairs* 30, no. 1 (2014): 67–85.

Eyerman, Joe. "Terrorism and Democratic States: Soft Targets or Accessible Systems." *International Interactions* 24, no. 2 (1998): 151–170.

Falkenburg, Luke. "Trafficking Terror Through Tajikistan." *Military Review* 93, no. 4 (2013): 7–15. http://usacac.army.mil/CAC2/MilitaryReview/Archives/English/MilitaryReview_20130831 _art005.pdf.

Fanusie, Yaya J., and Alex Entz. *Boko Haram: Financial Assessment.* Center on Sanctions and Illicit Finance, Foundation for Defense of Democracies. May 2017. https://s3.us-east-2 .amazonaws.com/defenddemocracy/uploads/documents/CSIF_Boko_Haram.pdf.

——. *Islamic State: Financial Assessment.* Center on Sanctions and Illicit Finance, Foundation for Defense of Democracies. March 2017. https://s3.us-east-2.amazonaws.com/defenddemoc racy/uploads/documents/CSIF_TFBB_IS_Finance.pdf.

Fearon, James D., and David D. Laitin. "Ethnicity, Insurgency, and Civil War." *American Political Science Review* 97, no. 1 (2003): 75–90.

Fedorenko, Vladimir. "Conflict in Pamir and Identity Politics." *Washington Review,* September 2012. Last modified January 18, 2013. http://www.the washingtonreview.org /articles/conflict -in-pamir-and-identity-politics.html.

Felbab-Brown, Vanda. "Afghanistan: When Counternarcotics Undermine Counterterrorism." *Washington Quarterly* 28, no. 4 (2005): 55–72. https://doi.org/10.1162/0163660054798735.

——. "Blood and Faith in Afghanistan: A June 2016 Update." Brookings Institution. Last modified June 2016. https://www.brookings.edu/wp-content/uploads/2016/06/Felbab-Brown-Paper -BLOOD-AND-FAITH-IN-AFGHANISTAN-May-2016.pdf.

Fisher, Sarah Kenyon. *Dangerous Sanctuaries: Refugee Camps, Civil War, and the Dilemmas of Humanitarian Aid.* Ithaca, N.Y.: Cornell University Press, 2006.

Fitzpatrick, Michael, and Stephen F. Lynch. "Stopping Terror Finance: Securing the U.S. Financial Sector." Task Force to Investigate Terrorism Financing. Committee on Financial Services, U.S. House of Representatives, 114th Congress. Last modified December 20, 2016. https://financialservices.house.gov/uploadedfiles/terror_financing_report_12-20-2016.pdf.

Flanigan, Shawn Teresa. "Terrorists Next Door? A Comparison of Mexican Drug Cartels and Middle Eastern Terrorist Organizations." *Terrorism and Political Violence* 24, no. 2 (2012): 279–294. https://doi.org/10.1080/09546553.2011.648351.

Fredholm, Michael. "Uzbekistan and the Threat from Islamic Extremism." In *Conflict Studies Research Centre Report K39.* Sandhurst, UK: Royal Military Academy, 2003.

Frevtag, Andreas, Jens Krüger, Daniel Meierrieks, and Friedrich Schneider. "The Origins of Terrorism: Cross-Country Estimates of Socio-Economic Determinants of Terrorism." *European Journal of Political Economy* 27 (2011): S5–S16.

Galdini, Franco, and Zukhra Iakupbaeva. "The Strange Case of Jaysh Al-Mahdi and Mr. ISIS: How Kyrgyzstan's Elites Manipulate the Threat of Terrorism for Their Own Benefit." Central Asia Fellows Papers, no. 179. Central Asia Program, George Washington University. Last modified October 2016. http://centralasiaprogram.org/archives/10075.

Gall, Carlotta. "Tajikistan Puts End to Rogue Warlord." *Moscow Times.* Last modified December 3, 1997. http://old.themoscowtimes.com/sitemap/free/1997/12/article/tajikistan-puts-end-to-rogue-warlord/296747.html.

Gambill, Gary C. "Syria after Lebanon: Hooked on Lebanon." *Middle East Quarterly* 12, no. 4 (2005): 35–42.

Gavrilis, George. *The Dynamics of Interstate Boundaries.* Cambridge: Cambridge University Press, 2008.

Gerring, John. "Is There A (Viable) Crucial-Case Method?" *Comparative Political Studies* 40, no. 3 (2007): 231–253.

Gibson, Richard M., and John B. Haseman. "Prospects for Controlling Narcotics Production and Trafficking in Myanmar." *Contemporary Southeast Asia* 25 (2003): 1–19.

Golunov, Sergey V. "Drug-Trafficking Through the Russia-Kazakhstan Border: Challenge and Responses." In *Empire, Islam, and Politics in Central Eurasia,* ed. Uyama Tomohiko, 331–350. Sapporo: Slavic Research Center of Hokkaido University, 2007. http://src-home.slav.hokudai.ac.jp/coe21/publish/no14_ses/13_golunov.pdf.

Golunov, Sergey V., and Roger N. McDermott. "Border Security in Kazakhstan: Threats, Policies and Future Challenges." *Journal of Slavic Military Studies* 18, no. 1 (2005): 31–58.

Gómez, Juan Miguel del Cid. "A Financial Profile of the Terrorism of Al-Qaeda and Its Affiliates." *Perspectives on Terrorism* 4, no. 4 (2010): 3–27. http://www.terrorismanalysts.com/pt/index.php/pot/article/view/113/html.

Goodhand, Jonathan. "From Holy War to Opium War? A Case Study of the Opium Economy in Northeastern Afghanistan." *Central Asian Survey* 19, no. 2 (2000): 265–280. https://doi.org/10.1080/02634930050079354.

Gorenburg, Dmitry. "External Support for Central Asian Military and Security Forces." Working Paper. Stockholm International Peace Research Institute and Open Society Foundations, January 2014.

Graveline, Sarah. "Is ISIS Making Inroads in East Africa?" IDA Africa Watch, September 22, 2016. https://www.ida.org/idamedia/Corporate/Files/Publications/AfricaWatch/africawatch-September-22-2016-vol12.ashx.

Gunaratna, Rohan. "Introduction." In *Handbook of Terrorism in the Asia-Pacific,* ed. Rohan Gunaratna and Stefanie Kam, xiii–xxviii. London: Imperial College Press, 2016.

Gurr, Ted. *Why Men Rebel*. Princeton, N.J.: Princeton University Press, 1970.

Hag, Ikramul. "Pak-Afghan Drug Trade in Historical Perspective." *Asian Survey* 36, no. 10 (1996): 945–963.

Hagopian, Frances. *Traditional Politics and Regime Change in Brazil*. Cambridge: Cambridge University Press, 1996.

Hall, Allan, and Dan Warburton. "ISIS Seizes £4bn Drug Ring from the Mafia to Fund Its Brutal Terror Campaign." *Daily Mirror*, January 17, 2016. http://www.mirror.co.uk/news/uk-news /isis-seizes-4bn-drug-ring-7191800.

Hamrin, Eric, and Edward Lemon. "Rasht Revisited: Five Years after the Conflict." *Central Asia Policy Brief*, no. 29, October 2015, http://centralasiaprogram.org/wp-content/uploads/2014/07 /Policy-Brief-29-October-2015.pdf.

Hansen, Wibke, and Judith Vorrath. "Atlantic Basin Countries and Organized Crime: Paradigms, Policies, Priorities." In *Dark Networks in the Atlantic Basin: Emerging Trends and Implications for Human Security*, ed. Daniel S. Hamilton, 101–120. Washington, D.C.: Center for Transatlantic Relations, 2015.

Heathershaw, John. *Post-Conflict Tajikistan: The Politics of Peacebuilding and the Emergence of Legitimate Order*. London: Routledge, 2009.

Heathershaw, John, and Nick Megoran. "Contesting Danger: A New Agenda for Policy and Scholarship in Central Asia." *International Affairs* 87, no. 3 (2011): 589–612.

Heathershaw, John, and David W. Montgomery. "The Myth of Post-Soviet Muslim Radicalisation in Central Asian Republics." Research paper, Chatham House, London, 2014. Last modified November 11, 2014. https://www.chathamhouse.org/publication/myth-post-soviet -muslim-radicalization-central-asian-republics.

Heathershaw, John, and Parviz Mullojonov. "Rebels Without A Cause? Authoritarian Conflict Management in Tajikistan, 2008–2015." In *Tajikistan on the Move: Statebuilding and Societal Transformations*, ed. Marlene Laruelle, 33–62. London: Rowman & Littlefield, 2018.

Heathershaw, John, and Sophie Roche. "Islam and Political Violence in Tajikistan: An Ethnographic Perspective on the Causes and Consequences of the 2010-Armed Conflict in the Kamarob Gorge." *Ethnopolitics Papers* 8 (2011): 1–21.

Heathershaw, John, and Edward Schatz. "The Logics of State Weakness in Eurasia: An Introduction." In *Paradox of Power: The Logics of State Weakness in Eurasia*, ed. John Heathershaw and Edward Schatz, 3–24. Pittsburgh: University of Pittsburgh Press, 2017.

Hehir, Aidan. "The Myth of the Failed State and the War on Terror: A Challenge to the Conventional Wisdom." *Journal of Intervention and Statebuilding* 1, no. 3 (2007): 307–332.

Herbst, Jeffrey. *States and Power in Africa: Comparative Lessons in Authority and Control*. Princeton, N.J.: Princeton University Press, 2000.

Hernandez, Joel. "Terrorism, Drug Trafficking, and the Globalization of Supply." *Perspectives on Terrorism* 7, no. 4 (2013): 41–61.

Hesterman, Jennifer L. *The Terrorist-Criminal Nexus: An Alliance of International Drug Cartels, Organized Crime, and Terror Groups*. Boca Raton, Fla.: CRC Press, 2013.

——. "Transnational Crime and Terror in the Pan-Atlantic: Understanding and Addressing the Growing Threat." In *Dark Networks in the Atlantic Basin: Emerging Trends and Implications for Human Security*, ed. Daniel S. Hamilton, 35–56. Washington, D.C.: Center for Transatlantic Relations.

Hoffman, Bruce. *Inside Terrorism*. New York: Columbia University Press, 2006.

Horsman, Stuart. "Themes of Official Discourses on Terrorism in Central Asia." *Third World Quarterly* 26, no. 1 (2005): 99–213.

——. "Uzbekistan's Involvement in the Tajik Civil War, 1992–97: Domestic Considerations." *Central Asian Survey* 18, no. 1 (1999): 37–48.

Howard, Russell D., and Colleen Traughber. "The 'New Silk Road' of Terrorism and Organized Crime: The Key to Countering the Terror-Crime Nexus." In *Armed Groups: Studies in National Security, Counterterrorism, and Counterinsurgency,* ed. Jeffrey H. Norwitz, 371–387. Newport, R.I.: U.S. Naval War College, 2008.

Huber, P. J. "The Behavior of Maximum Likelihood Estimates under Non-Standard Conditions." In *Proceedings of the Fifth Berkeley Symposium on Mathematical Statistics and Probability,* 221–233. Berkeley: University of California Press, 1967.

Human Rights Watch. "'Bullets Were Falling Like Rain': The Andijan Massacre." Last modified May 13, 2005. https://www.hrw.org/reports/2005/uzbekistan0605/.

——. "Where Is the Justice?" *Interethnic Violence in Southern Kyrgyzstan and Its Aftermath.* New York: Human Rights Watch, 2010. https://www.hrw.org/sites/default/files/reports/kyrgyz stan0810webwcover_1.pdf.

Hutchinson, Steven, and Pat O'Malley. "A Crime-Terror Nexus? Thinking on Some of the Links Between Terrorism and Criminality." *Studies in Conflict and Terrorism* 30, no. 12 (2007): 1095–1107.

Ibragimov, E. S. *Prokuratura Suverrennogo Uzbekistana.* Taskent: Akademiia Ministerstva vnu- trennix del respubliki Uzbekistan, 2000.

Ibrahim, Azhar, et al. *Afghanistan Interprovincial Opiate Trafficking Dynamics.* Kabul: Islamic Republic of Afghanistan Ministry of Counter Narcotics, 2013.

Institute for War and Peace Reporting Central Asia. "Kazakhstan Cannabis Klondike." Last mod- ified November 20, 2005. https://iwpr.net/global-voices/kazakstans-cannabis-klondike.

International Crisis Group. *Central Asian Islamist Mobilisation and Regional Security.* Osh, Kyr- gyzstan: International Crisis Group, 2001.

——. "Kazakhstan: Waiting for Change." *Asia Report,* no. 250, September 30, 2013. https:// d2071andvipowj.cloudfront.net/kazakhstan-waiting-for-change.pdf.

——. "Kyrgyzstan: A Hollow Regime Collapses." Briefing no. 102, Europe and Central Asia. Last modified April 27, 2010. https://www.crisisgroup.org/europe-central-asia/central-asia/kyr gyzstan/kyrgyzstan-hollow-regime-collapses.

Isaacs, Rico. "Elite Fragmentation and Propresidential Party Consolidation: Understanding Party System Development in Kazakhstan since 2001." *Journal of East European and Asian Studies* 2, no. 1 (2011): 111–136.

Izzatullo, Sadullom. "IRPT and ISIL: The Practical Evidence of the Same Teachings, Activities, and Aims of These Two Extremist Organizations." Embassy of the Republic of Tajikistan in Malaysia. Last modified November 16, 2017. http://tajemb-my.org/en/embassy/addresses-2/45 -irpt-and-isil-the-practical-evidence-of-the-same-teachings-activities-and-aims-of-these -two-extremist-organizations.

Jessop, Bob. "Territory, Politics, Governance and Multispatial Metagovernance." *Territory, Poli- tics, Governance* 4, no. 1 (2016): 8–32.

Jones, Seth G., Olga Oliker, Peter Chalk, C. Christine Fair, Rollie Ral, and James Dobbins. *Secu- rity Tyrants or Fostering Reform? U.S. Internal Security Assistance to Repressive and Transi- tioning Regimes.* Santa Monica, Calif.: RAND Corporation, 2006.

Jordan, David C. *Drug Politics: Dirty Politics and Democracies.* Norman: University of Oklahoma Press, 1999.

Kambarov, Chyngyz. "Organized Criminal Groups in Kyrgyzstan and the Role of Law Enforcement." *Voices from Central Asia,* no. 20, January 2015. Central Asia Program, George

Washington University. http://centralasiaprogram.org/wp-content/uploads/2015/03/Voices -from-CA-20-January-2015.pdf.

Kangaspunta, Kristiina. "Mapping the Inhuman Trade: Preliminary Findings of the Human Trafficking Database." Paper presented at the Consultative Meeting on "Migration and Mobility and How This Movement Affects Women," Malmö, Sweden, December 2–4, 2003.

Karin, Erlan. "Dilemmy Bezopasnosti Tsentral'noi Azii." *Russie.Net.Visions*, no. 98. February 2017. Institut français des relations internationales (Ifri). https://www.ifri.org/sites/default/files /atoms/files/rnv98_erlan_karin_dilemmy_bezopasnosti_centralnoy_azii_rus_2017.pdf.

"Kazakh 'Counterterror Operation' Continues after Deadly Attacks in Aqtobe." Radio Free Europe/Radio Liberty, June 6, 2016. https://www.rferl.org/a/kazakhstan-aqtobe-gunmen -attack-military-facility-gun-stores/27781652.html.

"Kazakh Police Suspect Uighur 'Separatists' of Murdering Two Policemen." BBC Monitoring Central Asia Unit. Last modified September 2000. http://www.start.umd.edu/gtd/search/IncidentSummary.aspx?gtdid=200009240004.

Keefer, Patrick R. "The Geography of Badness: Mapping the Hubs of the Illicit Global Economy." In *Convergence: Illicit Networks and National Security in the Age of Globalization*, ed. Michael Miklaucic and Jacqueline Brewer, 97–110. Washington, D.C.: National Defense University Press, 2013.

Keem, David. *Complex Emergencies*. Cambridge: Polity Press, 2008.

Kendzior, Sarah. "Inventing Akromiya: The Role of Uzbek Propagandists in the Andijon Massacre." *Demokratizatsiya* 14, no. 4 (2006): 545–562.

Kim, MoonSun. "Geographies of Crime." In *Encyclopedia of Theoretical Criminology*, ed. J. Mitchell Miller, 1–4. Hoboken, N.J.: John Wiley and Sons, 2014.

King, Gary, Robert O. Keohane, and Sidney Verba. *Designing Social Inquiry*. Princeton, N.J.: Princeton University Press, 1994.

Kis-Katos, Krisztina, Helge Liebert, and Gunther G. Schulze. "On the Origin of Domestic and International Terrorism." *European Journal of Political Economy* 27 (2011): S17–S36.

Krueger, Alan. *What Makes a Terrorist: Economics and the Roots of Terrorism*. Princeton, N.J.: Princeton University Press, 2008.

Kucera, Joshua. "Violence in Tajikistan." *The Diplomat*. Last modified November 30, 2010. http: //thediplomat.com/2010/11/violence-in-tajikistan/3/.

Kupatadze, Alexander. "Organized Crime before and after the Tulip Revolution: The Changing Dynamics of Upperworld-Underworld Networks." *Central Asian Survey* 27, no. 3 (2008): 279–299.

——. *Organized Crime, Political Transitions and State Formation in Post-Soviet Eurasia*. New York: Macmillan, 2012.

——. "Political Corruption in Eurasia: Understanding Collusion Between States, Organized Crime and Business." *Theoretical Criminology* 19, no. 2 (2015): 198–215.

Kyrgyz Committee for Human Rights. "The Representatives of Muslims Think State Committee for National Security (SCNK) Is Suppressing the Muslim Community." KCHR, 2011. http:// kchr.org/modules.php?name=News&file=article&sid=1953.

"Kyrgyz Court Jails Members of Terrorist Group." Radio Free Europe/Radio Liberty, July 19, 2013. http://www.rferl.org/a/kyrgyzstan-terrorism-sentencing/25051277.html.

Kyrgyzstan Inquiry Commission. "Report of the Independent International Commission of Inquiry into the Events in Southern Kyrgyzstan in June 2010." 2011. http://reliefweb.int/sites /reliefweb.int/files/resources/full_Report_490.pdf.

"Kyrgyzstan Says It Has Been Hit by 'Wave of Terrorism.'" Eurasianet.org, December 11, 2015. http://www.eurasianet.org/node/76516.

"Kyrgyzstan Silences Popular Imam with Extremism Charges." Eurasianet.org. Last modified February 17, 2015. http://www.eurasianet.org/node/72116.

LaFree, Gary, and Laura Dugan. "How Does Studying Terrorism Compare to Studying Crime?" In *Terrorism and Counter-terrorism: Criminological Perspectives*, ed. Mathieu Deflem, 53–74. Amsterdam: Elsevier, 2004.

Lambsdorff, Johann Graf. "Making Corrupt Deals: Contracting in the Shadow of the Law." *Journal of Economic Behavior & Organization* 48, no. 3 (2002): 221–241.

LaMond, Tullis. *Unintended Consequences: Illegal Drugs and Drug Policies in Nine Counties*. London: Lynne Rienner, 1995.

Laruelle, Marlene, ed. *Kazakhstan in the Making: Legitimacy, Symbols, and Social Changes*. Lanham, Md.: Lexington Books, 2016.

Latypov, Alisher. "Drug Dealers, Drug Lords and Drug Warriors-cum-Traffickers: Drug Crime and the Drug Trade in Kyrgyzstan." In *Drug Trafficking, Drug Abuse, Money Laundering, Judicial Corruption in Central Asia. Collection of Brief Summaries*, 23–41. Bishkek: Altyn Print, 2012.

——. "Understanding Post 9/11 Drug Control Policy and Politics in Central Asia." *International Journal of Drug Policy* 20, no. 5 (2009): 387–391.

Laumulin, Murat. "Islamic Radicalism in Central Asia." In *Religion and Security in South and Central Asia*, ed. K. Warikoo, 139–149. Abingdon, UK: Routledge, 2011.

Lemon, Edward. "From Moscow to Madrid: Governing Security Threats Beyond Tajikistan's Borders." In *Tajikistan on the Move: Statebuilding and Societal Transformations*, ed. Marlene Laruelle, 63–86. London: Rowman & Littlefield, 2018.

——. "Mediating the Conflict in the Rasht Valley, Tajikistan." *Central Asian Affairs* 1, no. 2 (2014): 247–272.

Levi-Sanchez, Suzanne. *The Afghan-Central Asia Borderlands: The State and Local Leaders*. New York: Routledge, 2017.

Levitsky, Steven, and Lucan A. Way. *Competitive Authoritarianism: Hybrid Regimes after the Cold War*. Cambridge: Cambridge University Press, 2010.

Levitt, Matthew. "The Political Economy of Middle East Terrorism." *Washington Institute for Near East Policy* 6, no. 4 (2002): 49–65.

Lewis, David. "Crime, Terror and the State in Central Asia." *Global Crime* 15, nos. 3–4 (2014): 337–356.

——. "High Times on the Silk Road: The Central Asian Paradox." *World Policy Journal* 27, no. 1 (2010): 39–49.

Lieberman, Evan S. "Nested Analysis as a Mixed Method Strategy for Comparative Research." *American Political Science Review* 99, no. 3 (2005): 435–452.

Lintner, Bertil. *Burma in Revolt: Opium and Insurgency Since 1948*. Chiang Mai, Thailand: Silkworm Books, 1999.

Lister, Charles. "Cutting Off ISIS' Cash Flow." Brookings Institution, October 24, 2014. https://www.brookings.edu/blog/markaz/2014/10/24/cutting-off-isis-cash-flow/.

Longmire, Sylvia, and John Longmire. "Redefining Terrorism: Why Mexican Drug Trafficking Is More Than Just Organized Crime." *Journal of Strategic Security* 1, no. 1 (2008): 35–51.

Luna, David M. "Trans-Africa Security: Combating Illicit Trafficking and Organized Crime in Africa." Remarks to the Bureau of International Narcotics and Law Enforcement Affairs of the Under Secretary for Civilian Security, Democracy, and Human Rights. May 12, 2017. https://www.state.gov/j/inl/rls/rm/2017/270858.htm.

Luong, Pauline Jones. *Institutional Change and Political Continuity in Post-Soviet Central Asia: Power, Perceptions, and Pacts.* Cambridge: Cambridge University Press, 2002.

Madi, Maral. "Drug Trade in Kyrgyzstan: Structure, Implications and Countermeasures." *Central Asian Survey* 23, nos. 3–4 (2004): 249–273.

Makarenko, Tamara. "Crime, Terror and the Central Asian Drug Trade." *Harvard Asia Quarterly* 6, no. 3 (2002): 28–38.

——. "The Crime-Terror Continuum: Tracing the Interplay Between Transnational Organized Crime and Terrorism." *Global Crime* 6, no. 1 (2004): 129–145.

Malik, Nikita. *Trafficking Terror: How Modern Slavery and Sexual Violence Fund Terrorism.* London: Henry Jackson Society, 2017. http://henryjacksonsociety.org/wp-content/uploads/2017/10/HJS-Trafficking-Terror-Report-web.pdf.

Mapping Militant Organizations. "Liberation Tigers of Tamil Elam." Mapping Militants Project. Stanford University. http://web.stanford.edu/group/mappingmilitants/cgi-bin/groups/view/225.

Marat, Erica. "Impact of Drug Trade and Organized Crime on State Functioning in Kyrgyzstan and Tajikistan." *China and Eurasia Forum Quarterly* 4, no. 1 (2006): 93–111.

——. "Kyrgyzstan's Fragmented Police and Armed Forces." *Journal of Power Institutions in Post-Soviet Societies* 11 (2010). https://journals.openedition.org/pipss/3803.

——. *The Military and the State in Central Asia: From Red Army to Independence.* London: Routledge, 2009.

——. *The Politics of Police Reform: Society Against the State in Post-Soviet Countries.* New York: Oxford University Press, 2017.

——. "Reforming Police in Post-Communist Countries: International Efforts, Domestic Heroes." *Comparative Politics* 48, no. 3 (2016): 333–352.

——. *The State-Crime Nexus in Central Asia: State Weakness, Organized Crime, and Corruption in Kyrgyzstan and Tajikistan.* Washington, D.C.: Central Asia-Caucasus Institute and Silk Road Studies Program, 2006.

Markowitz, Lawrence P. "Beyond Kompromat: Coercion, Corruption and Deterred Defection in Uzbekistan." *Comparative Politics* 50, no. 1 (October 2017): 103–121.

——. *State Erosion: Unlootable Resources and Unruly Elites.* Ithaca, N.Y.: Cornell University Press, 2013.

Matveeva, Anna. "Violence in Kyrgyzstan, Vacuum in the Region. The Case for Russia-EU Joint Crisis Management." Working paper, LSE Civil Society and Human Security Research Unit, London, 2011.

McDermott, Roger N. *Kazakhstan's Defense Policy: An Assessment of the Trends.* Carlisle, Penn.: U.S. Army War College, Strategic Studies Institute, 2009. https://www.globalsecurity.org/military/library/report/2009/ssi_mcdermott.pdf.

McDougall, Alex. "State Power and Its Implications for Civil War in Colombia." *Studies in Conflict and Terrorism* 32, no. 4 (2009): 322–345.

McGlinchey, Eric M. *Chaos, Violence, Dynasty: Politics and Islam in Central Asia.* Pittsburgh: University of Pittsburgh Press, 2011.

McKenzie, O'Brien. "Fluctuations Between Crime and Terror: The Case of Abu Sayyaf's Kidnapping Activities." *Terrorism and Political Violence* 24, no. 2 (2012): 320–336.

McMann, Kelly M. *Economic Autonomy and Democracy: Hybrid Regimes in Russia and Kyrgyzstan.* Cambridge: Cambridge University Press, 2006.

Medel, Mónica. *Narco Violence in Mexico: A Spatial Analysis of Drug-Related Bloodshed.* Austin: University of Texas Press, 2011.

Medina, Richard M., Laura K. Siebeneck, and George F. Hepner. "A Geographic Information Systems (GIS) Analysis of Spatiotemporal Patterns of Terrorist Incidents in Iraq, 2004–2009." *Studies in Conflict and Terrorism* 34, no. 11 (2011): 862–882.

Meehan, Patrick. "Drugs, Insurgency and State-Building in Burma: Why the Drugs Trade Is Central to Burma's Changing Political Order." *Journal of Southeast Asian Studies* 42, no. 3 (2011): 376–404.

Megoran, Nick. "The Critical Geopolitics of Danger in Uzbekistan and Kyrgyzstan." *Environment and Planning D: Society and Space* 23, no. 4 (2004): 555–580.

——. "Framing Andijon, Narrating the Nation: Islam Karimov's Account of the Events of 13 May 2005." *Central Asian Survey* 27, no. 1 (2008): 15–31.

——. *Nationalism in Central Asia: A Biography of the Uzbekistan-Kyrgyzstan Boundary.* Pittsburgh: University of Pittsburgh Press, 2017.

Megoran, Nick, Gael Raballand, and Jerome Bouyou. "Performance, Representation and the Economics of Border Control in Uzbekistan." *Geopolitics* 10, no. 4 (2005): 712–740.

Messner, J. J., ed. "Fragile States Index Annual Report 2016." Fund for Peace. Last modified April 10, 2017. http://fundforpeace.org/fsi/2016/06/27/fragile-states-index-2016-annual-report /fragile-states-index-annual-report-2016-ver-3e/.

Migdal, Joel S. *Strong Societies and Weak States: State-Society Relations and State Capabilities in the Third World.* Princeton, N.J.: Princeton University Press, 1988.

Miklaucic, Michael, and Jacqueline Brewer, eds. *Convergence: Illicit Networks and National Security in the Age of Globalization.* Washington, D.C.: National Defense University Press, 2013.

Mincheva, Lyubov Grigorova, and Ted Robert Gurr, eds. *Crime-Terror Alliances and The State: Ethnonationalist and Islamist Challenges to Regional Security.* New York: Routledge, 2013.

——. "Unholy Alliances? How Trans-state Terrorism and International Crime Make Common Cause." In *Crime-Terror Alliances and The State: Ethnonationalist and Islamist Challenges to Regional Security,* ed. Lyubov Grigorova Mincheva and Ted Robert Gurr, 1–23. New York: Routledge, 2013.

Mittelman, James, and Robert Johnston. "The Globalization of Organized Crime, the Courtesan State, and the Corruption of Civil Society." *Global Governance* 5, no. 2 (1999): 103–126.

Mohapatra, Nalin Kumar. "Political and Security Challenges in Central Asia: The Drug Trafficking Dimension." *International Studies* 44, no. 2 (2007): 157–174.

Moore, Cerwyn. "The Rise and Fall of the Islamic Jihad Union: What Next for Uzbek Terror Networks?" *Terrorism Monitor* 8, no. 14 (2010). https://jamestown.org/program/the-rise-and -fall-of-the-islamic-jihad-union-what-next-for-uzbek-terror-networks/.

Mustafa, Daanish, and Julian R. Shaw. "Geography of Terrorism." In *Oxford Bibliographies.* New York: Oxford University Press, 2013. http://www.oxfordbibliographies.com/view/document /obo-9780199874002/obo-9780199874002-0066.xml.

Najibullah, Farangis. "Four Suspected IMU Members Killed In Tajikistan." Radio Free Europe /Radio Liberty, October 19, 2009. http://reliefweb.int/report/kyrgyzstan/four-suspected-imu -members-killed-tajikistan.

"Narkotorgovlya i Provoohranitel'nye Organy Kazakhstana." *Vremya Vostoka.* Last modified June 3, 2013. http://easttime.ru/news/kazakhstan/narkotorgovlya-i-pravookhranitelnye -organy-kazakhstana/4002.

National Consortium for the Study of Terrorism and Responses to Terrorism (START). Global Terrorism Database. 2018. https://www.start.umd.edu/gtd.

——. Global Terrorism Database. "Syria." Accessed December 28, 2017. https://www.start.umd .edu/gtd/search/Results.aspx?country=200.

——. Global Terrorism Database. Incident Summary. Incident ID 200905260013. https://www .start.umd.edu/gtd/search/IncidentSummary.aspx?gtdid=200905260013.

——. Global Terrorism Database. Incident Summary. Incident ID 200905260012. https://www .start.umd.edu/gtd/search/IncidentSummary.aspx?gtdid=200905260012.National Statistical Committee of the Kyrgyz Republic, http://www.stat.kg/ru/.

Naumkin, Vitaly V. "Militant Islam in Central Asia: The Case of the Islamic Movement of Uzbekistan." Berkeley Program in Soviet and Post-Soviet Studies Working Paper Series, University of California, Berkeley, 2003.

——. *Radical Islam in Central Asia: Between Pen and Rifle*. Lanham, Md.: Rowman & Littlefield, 2005.

Nawa, Fariba. *Opium Nation: Child Brides, Drug Lords, and One Woman's Journey Through Afghanistan*. New York: Harper Perennial, 2011.

Nemeth, Stephen C., Jacob A. Mauslein, and Craig Stapley. "The Primacy of the Local: Identifying Terrorist Hot Spots Using Geographic Information Systems." *Journal of Politics* 76, no. 2 (2014): 304–317.

Newman, Edward. "Weak States, State Failure, and Terrorism." *Terrorism and Political Violence* 19, no. 4 (2007): 463–488.

"'Nomad—Komitet Natsional'noi Bezopasnosti Kazakhstana: Istoriya, Struktura, Litsa." Centrasia. Last modified July 15, 2002. https://www.centrasia.org/newsA.php?st=1026687180.

Nourzhanov, Kirill. "Saviours of the Nation or Robber Barons? Warlord Politics in Tajikistan." *Central Asian Survey* 24, no. 2 (2005): 109–130.

Ntaryike Divine, Jr. "Drug Trafficking Rising in Central Africa, Warns Interpol." Voice of America, September 8, 2012. http://www.voanews.com/content/drug-trafficking-rising-incentral -africa-warns-interpol/1504026.html.

Nurgaliyev, Bakhyt Moldatjaevich, Kanat Sametovich Lakbayev, and Alexey Vladimirovich Boretsky. "Organized Crime in Kazakhstan: The Past, the Present, Development Tendencies and Social Consequences." *Journal of Applied Sciences* 14, no. 24 (2014): 3436–3445.

Olcott, Martha Brill. *Tajikistan's Difficult Development Path*. Washington, D.C.: Carnegie Endowment for International Peace, 2012.

Omelicheva, Mariya Y. *Counterterrorism Policies in Central Asia*. New York: Routledge, 2011.

——. "Islam in Kazakhstan: A Survey of Contemporary Trends and Sources of Securitization." *Central Asian Survey* 30, no. 2 (2011): 243–256.

——. "Kazakhstan." In *World Almanac of Islamism*. American Foreign Policy Council, 2017. http://almanac.afpc.org/Kazakhstan.

——. "The Multiple Faces of Islamic Rebirth in Central Asia." In *New Approaches to Area Studies in the Global Era: Community, Place, Identity*, ed. Edith Clowes and Shelly Bromberg, 143–158. Dekalb: Northern Illinois University Press, 2015.

——. "Russia's Foreign Policy in Central Asia." In *Russian Foreign Policy*, ed. Andrei Tsygankov, 325–337. New York: Routledge, 2018.

Omelicheva, Mariya Y., and Lawrence P. Markowitz. "When the Crime-Terror Nexus Does Not Materialize: Drug Trafficking, Militants and the State in Russia." Presented at the annual security conference *Crime-Terror Nexus and Intelligence-Led Responses*, University of Kansas, Lawrence, April 2018.

Organization for Security and Co-Operation in Europe (OSCE). "Preliminary Findings on the Events in Andijan, Uzbekiztan, 13 May 2005." June 20, 2005. www.osce.org/item/15234.html.

Pannier, Bruce. "Kyrgyzstan: Government Accused of Framing Opposition Leader." Radio Free Europe/Radio Liberty, September 12, 2006. http://www.rferl.org/content/article/1071272.html.

Paoli, Letizia, Irina Rabkov, Victoria A. Greenfield, and Peter Reuter. "Tajikistan: The Rise of a Narco-State." *Journal of Drug Issues* 37, no. 4 (1997): 969–971.

Paris Pact Initiative, the Afghan Opiate Trade Project of the United Nations Office on Drugs and Crime (UNODC), and the UNODC Regional Office for Central Asia. Drugs Monitoring Platform. http://drugsmonitoring.unodc-roca.org/.

Patrick, Stewart. *Weak Links: Fragile States, Global Threats, and International Security.* Oxford: Oxford University Press, 2011.

Peiris, Gerald H. "Narcotics: Hanging on to the Tiger's Tail." *The Island*, June 17, 2015. https://thuppahi.wordpress.com/2015/06/17/smuggling-shipping-and-the-narcotics-trade-in-the-history-of-the-ltte-1970s-2015/.

Perl, Raphael F. "State Crime: The North Korean Drug Trade." *Global Crime* 6, no. 1 (2004): 117–128.

Perthes, Volker. "*Si Vis Stabilitatem, Para Bellum*: State Building, National Security, and War Preparation in Syria." In *War, Institutions, and Social Change in the Middle East*, ed. Steven Heydemann, 149–173. Berkeley: University of California Press, 2000.

Peyrouse, Sébastian. "Drug Trafficking in Central Asia: A Poorly Considered Fight?" PONARS Eurasia Policy Memo, no. 218, September 2012. http://www.ponarseurasia.org/sites/default/files/policy-memos-pdf/pepm_218_Peyrouse_Sept2012.pdf.

——. "Islam in Central Asia: National Specificities and Postsoviet Globalisation." *Religion, State and Society* 35, no. 3 (2007): 245–260.

Piazza, James A. "Does Poverty Serve as a Root Cause of Terrorism? No, Poverty Is a Weak Causal Link." In *Debating Terrorism and Counterterrorism: Conflicting Perspectives on Causes, Contexts and Responses*, ed. Stuart Gottlieb, 38–51. Washington, D.C.: Congressional Quarterly Press, 2009.

——. "The Opium Trade and Patterns of Terrorism in the Provinces of Afghanistan: An Empirical Analysis." *Terrorism and Political Violence* 24, no. 2 (2012): 213–234.

——. "Rooted in Poverty? Terrorism, Poor Economic Development, and Social Cleavages." *Terrorism and Political Violence* 18, no. 1 (2006): 159–177.

Picarelli, John T. "Osama bin Corleone? Vito the Jackal? Framing Threat Convergence Through an Examination of Transnational Organized Crime and International Terrorism." *Terrorism and Political Violence* 24, no. 2 (2012): 180–198.

Polat, Abdumannob, and Nickolai Butkevich. "Unraveling the Mystery of the Tashkent Bombings: Theories and Implications." *Demokratizatsiya* 8, no. 4 (2000): 541–553.

Pontonier, Paolo. "In Italy, Al Qaeda Turns to Organized Crime for Protection." New American Media. October 21, 2005. http://www.freerepublic.com/focus/f-news/1507005/posts.

Popper, Karl. *The Logic of Scientific Discovery.* London: Routledge, 1959.

Prague Open Media Research Institute. *The OMRI Annual Survey of Eastern Europe and the Former Soviet Union: 1995: Building Democracy.* London: Routledge, 1996.

Putz, Catherine. "Kyrgyz and Tajiks Clash along Disputed Border." *The Diplomat*, August 4, 2015. http://thediplomat.com/2015/08/kyrgyz-and-tajiks-clash-along-disputed-border/.

Rabasa, Angel, Christopher M. Schnaubelt, Peter Chalk, Douglas Farah, Gregory Midgette, and Howard J. Shatz. *Counternetwork: Countering the Expansion of Transnational Criminal Networks.* Santa Monica, Calif.: RAND Corporation, 2017.

Radnitz, Scott. *Weapons of the Wealthy: Predatory Regimes and Elite-Led Protests in Central Asia.* Ithaca, N.Y.: Cornell University Press, 2010.

Rakisheva, Botagoz, and Gulden Shalova. "Suicide Acts in the Republic of Kazakhstan: A Chronology of Events Content-Analysis of Mass-Media." In *Contemporary Suicide Terrorism: Origins, Trends and Ways of Tackling It*, ed. Tatyana Dronzina and Rachid El Houdigui, 137–143. Amsterdam: IOS Press, 2012.

Reeves, Madeleine. *Border Work: Spatial Lives of the State in Rural Central Asia*. Ithaca, N.Y.: Cornell University Press, 2014.

Reitano, Tuesday, Colin Clarke, and Laura Adal. *Examining the Nexus Between Organized Crime and Terrorism and Its Implications for EU Programming*. The Hague: International Center for Counter-Terrorism, 2017. https://icct.nl/publication/examining-the-nexus-between-organised-crime-and-terrorism-and-its-implications-for-eu-programming/.

Reyes, Liana Eustacia, and Shlomi Dinar. "The Convergence of Terrorism and Transnational Crime in Central Asia." *Studies in Conflict and Terrorism* 38, no. 5 (2015): 380–393.

Rickleton, Chris. "Kyrgyzstan's Security Agents Intimidating Uzbek Minority, Activists Say." Eurasianet.org, April 2, 2015. http://www.eurasianet.org/node/72836.

Roberts, Sean R. *Imaginary Terrorism: The Global War on Terror and the Narrative of the Uyghur Terrorist Threat*. Washington, D.C.: Institute for European, Russian, and Eurasian Studies, George Washington University, 2012.

Roggio, Bill, and Caleb Weiss. "Islamic Jihad Union Details Its Involvement in Taliban's Azm Offensive." *Long War Journal*, July 25, 2015. https://www.longwarjournal.org/archives/2015/07/islamic-jihad-union-details-its-involvement-in-talibans-azm-offensive.php.

Ro'i, Yaacov, and Alon Wainer. "Muslim Identity and Islamic Practice in Post-Soviet Central Asia." *Central Asian Survey* 28, no. 3 (2009): 303–322.

Rollins, John, and Liana Sun Wyler. "Terrorism and Transnational Crime: Foreign Policy Issues for Congress." Congressional Research Service, June 11, 2013. http://www.fas.org/sgp/crs/terror/R41004.pdf.

Rollins, John, Liana Sun Wyler, and Seth Rosen. "International Terrorism and Transnational Crime: Security Threats, U.S. Policy and Considerations for Congress." Congressional Research Service, January 5, 2010. https://fas.org/sgp/crs/terror/R41004-2010.pdf.

Ross, Jeffery Ian. "Structural Causes of Oppositional Political Terrorism: A Causal Model." *Journal of Peace Research* 30, no. 3 (1993): 317–329.

Rotar, Igor. "Islamic Extremist Group Jamaat Ansarullah Overcomes Tajikistan's Inter-Tribal Conflicts." *Eurasia Daily Monitor*, September 25, 2012. http://www.ecoi.net/local_link/230996/339430_en.html.

Rotberg, Robert I., ed. *Burma: Prospects for a Democratic Future*. Washington, D.C.: Brookings Institution, 1998.

——. *State Failure and State Weakness in a Time of Terror*. Washington, D.C.: Brookings Institution Press, 2003.

——, ed. *When States Fail: Causes and Consequences*. Princeton, N.J.: Princeton University Press, 2003.

Roy, Olivier. *The New Central Asia: Geopolitics and the Creation of Nations*. London: I. B. Tauris, 2007.

Ruttig, Thomas. "Talibes in Tajikistan? The 'Terrorist Spillover' Hype." Afghanistan Analysts Network, October 10, 2013. https://www.afghanistan-analysts.org/talebs-in-tajikistan-the-terrorist-spill-over-hype/.

Sanderson, Thomas M. "Transnational Terror and Organized Crime: Blurring the Lines." *SAIS Review* 24, no. 1 (2004): 49–61.

Sanderson, Thomas M., Daniel Kimmage, and David A. Gordon. *From Ferghana Valley to South Waziristan: The Evolving Threat of Central Asian Jihadists.* Washington, D.C.: CSIS, 2010. https://csis-prod.s3.amazonaws.com/s3fs-public/legacy_files/files/publication/100324_Sand erson_FerghanaValley_WEB_0.pdf.

"Saudi Arabia: Terror Groups Rely on Drugs to Recruit Suicide Bombers." *Arab News*, July 13, 2016. http://www.arabnews.com/node/952996/saudi-arabia.

Schatz, Edward. *Modern Clan Politics: The Power of "Blood" in Kazakhstan and Beyond.* Seattle: University of Washington Press, 2004.

Schoeberlein, John. "Security Sector Reform in Uzbekistan." In *Security Sector Reform in Central Asia: Exploring Needs and Possibilities*, ed. Merijn Hartog, 55–62. Groningen, Netherlands: Centre of European Security Studies, 2010.

Search for Common Ground. "Radicalization of the Population in Osh, Jalal-Abad and Batken Oblasts: Factors, Types, and Risk Groups." *Internal Report* (2016). https://www.sfcg.org/tag /kyrgyzstan-reports.

Shelley, Louise. *Dirty Entanglements: Corruption, Crime, and Terrorism.* Cambridge: Cambridge University Press, 2014.

——. "The Relationship of Drug and Human Trafficking: A Global Perspective." *European Journal on Criminal Policy and Research* 18, no. 3 (2012): 241-53.

Slawomir, Redo. *Organized Crime and Its Control in Central Asia.* Huntsville, Tex.: Office of International Criminal Justice, 2004.

Snyder, Richard. "Does Lootable Wealth Breed Disorder? A Political Economy of Extraction Framework." *Comparative Political Studies* 39, no. 8 (2006): 943–968.

Soufan Group. "Foreign Fighters: An Updated Assessment of the Flow of Foreign Fighters into Syria and Iraq." Last modified December 2015. http://soufangroup.com/wp-content/uploads /2015/12/TSG_ForeignFightersUpdate3.pdf.

Spector, Regine A. "Securing Property in Contemporary Kyrgyzstan." *Post-Soviet Affairs* 24, no. 2 (2008): 149–176.

Staniland, Paul. *Networks of Rebellion: Explaining Insurgent Cohesion and Collapse.* Ithaca, N.Y.: Cornell University Press, 2014.

Stavridis, James G. "Foreword." In *Convergence: Illicit Networks and National Security in the Age of Globalization*, ed. Michael Miklaucic and Jacqueline Brewer, vii–x. Washington, D.C.: National Defense University Press, 2013.

"Tajikistan: Accused Warlord Speaks Out on Gorno-Badakhshan Violence." Eurasianet.org, October 24, 2012. http://www.eurasianet.org/node/66101.

"Tajikistan, Uzbekistan Resume Border Delimitation Talks." Fergana News Agency, November 22, 2016. http://enews.fergananews.com/news.php?id=3181&mode=snews.

Tazmini, Ghoncheh. "The Islamic Revival in Central Asia: A Potent Force or a Misconception?" *Central Asian Survey* 20, no. 1 (2001): 63–83.

Terrorism Research and Analysis Consortium (TRAC). http://www.trackingterrorism.org/groups.

Tilly, Charles. "War Making and State Making as Organized Crime." In *Bringing the State Back In*, ed. Peter Evans, Dietrich Rueschemeyer, and Theda Skocpol, 169–191. Cambridge: Cambridge University Press, 1985.

Tollefsen, Andreas Forø, Håvard Strand , and Halvard Buhaug. "PRIO-GRID: A Unified Spatial Data Structure." *Journal of Peace Research* 49, no. 2 (2012): 363–374.

Torjesen, Stina, and S. Neil MacFarlane. "R before D: The Case of Post Conflict Reintegration in Tajikistan." *Conflict, Security & Development* 7, no. 2 (2007): 311–332.

Torjesen, Stina, Christina Wille, and S. Neil MacFarlane. *Tajikistan's Road to Stability: Reduction in Small Arms Proliferation and Remaining Challenges.* Geneva: Small Arms Survey, 2005.

Traughber, M. "Terror-Crime Nexus? Terrorism and Arms, Drug, and Human Trafficking in Georgia." Master's thesis, Tufts University, 2007.

Traynor, Ian. "Milosevic Allies Linked to Heroin Stash." *Guardian*, March 15, 2001. https://www.theguardian.com/world/2001/mar/16/balkans.internationalcrime.

Trofimov, Yaroslav. "Al Ansari Exchange Finds Itself Embroiled in Terror Investigation." *Wall Street Journal*, November 1, 2001. http://www.wsj.com/articles/SB1004652055539614360.

Tsoy, Darya, V. "Kazahstane nastupaet 'sredneaziatskaya vesna'." *Izvestia*, June 7, 2016. http://izvestia.ru/news/616954#ixzz4CESvidHkhttp://izvestia.ru/news/616954.

Tucker, Noah. *Central Asian Involvement in the Conflict in Syria and Iraq: Drivers and Responses.* Arlington, Va.: Management Systems International, 2015. http://pdf.usaid.gov/pdf_docs/PBAAE879.pdf.

Tuncer-Kilavuz, Idil. "Political and Social Networks in Tajikistan and Uzbekistan: 'Clan', Region, and Beyond." *Central Asian Survey* 28, no. 3 (2009): 323–334.

United Nations Office on Drugs and Crime (UNODC). *Addiction, Crime, Insurgency: The Transnational Threat of Afghan Opium.* Vienna: UNODC, 2009. https://www.unodc.org/unodc/en/data-and-analysis/addiction-crime-and-insurgency.html.

——. *An Assessment of Transnational Organized Crime in Central Asia.* New York: UNODC, 2007. https://www.unodc.org/documents/organized-crime/Central_Asia_Crime_Assessment.pdf.

——. "Drug Trafficking." Accessed April 22, 2017. https://www.unodc.org/unodc/en/drug-trafficking/.

——. *The Global Afghan Opium Trade: A Threat Assessment.* Vienna: UNODC, 2011. http://www.unodc.org/documents/data-and-analysis/Studies/Global_Afghan_Opium_Trade_2011-web.pdf.

——. *Global Illicit Drug Trends 2002.* United Nations Publications, 2002. https://www.unodc.org/pdf/report_2002-06-26_1/report_2002-06-26_1.pdf.

——. *Opiate Flows Through Northern Afghanistan and Central Asia: A Threat Assessment.* Vienna: UNODC, 2012. Accessed May 4, 2017. https://www.unodc.org/documents/data-and-analysis/Studies/Afghanistan_northern_route_2012_web.pdf.

——. *The Opium Economy in Afghanistan: An International Problem.* New York: UNODC, 2003. https://www.unodc.org/documents/afghanistan//Counter_Narcotics/The_Opium_Economy_in_Afghanistan_-_2003.pdf.

——. "Research Report: Estimating Illicit Financial Flows Resulting from Drug Trafficking and Other Transnational Organized Crimes." Accessed May 1, 2017. https://www.unodc.org/documents/dataandanalysis/Studies/Illicit_financial_flows_2011_web.pdf.

——. "The United Nations Convention Against Transnational Organized Crime and the Protocols Thereto." Accessed April 22, 2017. https://www.unodc.org/documents/treaties/UNTOC/Publications/TOC%20Convention/TOCebook-e.pdf.

——. *World Drug Report.* Vol. 1, *Analysis.* Geneva: United Nations Publications, 2006. https://www.unodc.org/unodc/en/data-and-analysis/WDR-2006.html.

UNODC Individual Drug Seizure reports. https://data.unodc.org/

UNODC Regional Office for Central Asia, Paris Pact Initiative. *Illicit Drug Trends in Central Asia.* April 2008. https://www.unodc.org/documents/regional/central-asia/Illicit%20Drug%20Trends_Central%20Asia-final.pdf.

United Nations Security Council. Resolution 2195. December 19, 2014. http://unscr.com/en/res olutions/doc/2195.

U.S. Department of State. "Designated Foreign Terrorist Organizations." Last modified June 1, 2017. https://www.state.gov/j/ct/rls/other/des/123085.htm.

——. "Individuals and Entities Designated by the State Department under E.O. 13224." Bureau of Counterterrorism. Accessed November 15, 2018, https://www.state.gov/j/ct/rls/other/des /143210.htm.

——. *International Narcotics Control Strategy Report*. Washington, D.C.: Bureau of International Narcotics and Law Enforcement Affairs, March 1995. http://dosfan.lib.uic.edu/ERC/law /INC/1995/02.html.

——. "International Religious Freedom Report." Last modified 2017. https://www.state.gov/j/drl /rls/irf/.

——. "Kazakhstan." *International Narcotics Control Strategy Report*. Vol. 1, *Drug and Chemical Control*. Washington, D.C.: Bureau of International Narcotics and Law Enforcement Affairs, 2015. https://www.state.gov/j/inl/rls/nrcrpt/2015/vol1/238985.htm.

——. "2015 International Narcotics Control Strategy Report: Uzbekistan." Bureau of International Narcotics and Law Enforcement Affairs. Last modified 2015. https://www.state.gov/j /inl/rls/nrcrpt/2015/vol1/239027.htm.

U.S. Department of the Treasury. "Treasury Designates New Ansari Money Exchange." Last modified February 18, 2011. https://www.treasury.gov/press-center/press-releases/Pages /tg1071.aspx.

U.S. Energy Information Administration. "Country Analysis Brief: Kazakhstan." Last modified May 10, 2017. https://www.eia.gov/beta/international/analysis_includes/countries_long /Kazakhstan/kazakhstan.pdf.

Van Dam, Nikolaos. *The Struggle for Power in Syria: Politics and Society under Asad and the Ba'th Party*. London: I. B. Tauris, 1996.

Voloshin, George. "Kazakhstan's Border Protection Service Rocked by a New Wave of Incidents." *Eurasia Daily Monitor*, February 13, 2013. https://jamestown.org/program/kazakhstans-border -protection-service-rocked-by-a-new-wave-of-incidents/.

Wang, Peng. "The Crime-Terror Nexus: Transformation, Alliance, Convergence." *Asian Social Science* 6, no. 6 (2010): 11–20. http://www.ccsenet.org/journal/index.php/ass/article/view/6218.

Wechsler, William F., and Gary Barnabo. "The Department of Defense's Role in Combating Transnational Organized Crime." In *Convergence: Illicit Networks and National Security in the Age of Globalization*, ed. Michael Miklaucic and Jacqueline Brewer, 233–242. Washington, D.C.: National Defense University Press, 2013.

West Sands Advisory LLP. "Europe's Crime-Terror Nexus: Links Between Terrorist and Organized Crime Groups in the European Union." European Parliament, Committee on Civil Liberties, Justice, and Home Affairs, Brussels, October 2012.

White House. 2011. "National Strategy to Combat Transnational Organized Crime, Addressing Converging Threats to National Security." Accessed February 1, 2015. http://www.whitehouse .gov/sites/default/files/Strategy_to_Combat_Transnational_Organized_Crime_July_2011 .pdf.

Williams, Phil. "The Terrorism Debate over Mexican Drug Trafficking Violence." *Terrorism and Political Violence* 24, no. 2 (2012): 259–278.

Wooldridge, Jeffrey M. "Cluster-Sample Methods in Applied Econometrics." *American Economic Review* 93, no. 2 (2003): 133–138.

World Almanac of Islamism. "Kosovo." Accessed December 14, 2017. http://almanac.afpc.org/kosovo.

Yanovskaya, Mariya. "Kak Possorilis' General Nazarov I Pogranichnik Ayombekov i Chem Eto Zakonchilos' dlya Zhitelei Pamira." Fergana News Agency, July 27, 2012. http://www.fergananews.com/articles/7433.

Young, Crawford. "Deciphering Disorder in Africa: Is Identity the Key?" World Politics 54, no. 4 (2002): 532–557.

Zackrison, James L. "La Violencia in Colombia: An Anomaly in Terrorism." Journal of Conflict Studies 9, no. 4 (1989): 5–18.

Zenn, Jacob. "The Indigenization of the Islamic Movement of Uzbekistan." Terrorism Monitor 10, no. 2 (2012). https://jamestown.org/program/the-indigenization-of-the-islamic-movement-of-uzbekistan/.

——. "Network of Jund al-Khilafah in Kazakhstan Wider Than Predicted." Eurasia Daily Monitor, January 18, 2012. https://jamestown.org/program/network-of-jund-al-khilafah-in-kazakhstan-wider-than-predicted/.

Zenn, Jacob, and Kathleen Kuehnast. Preventing Violent Extremism in Kyrgyzstan. Washington, D.C.: U.S. Institute of Peace, 2014.

Ziadeh, Radwan. Power and Policy in Syria: Intelligence Services, Foreign Relations, and Democracy in the Modern Middle East. London: I. B. Tauris, 2011.

INDEX

Page numbers in italics indicate tables or figures.